The
HIDDEN
SCREEN

T0347332

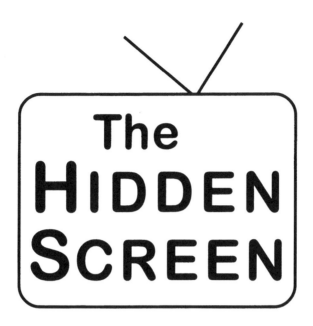

Low-Power Television
in America

Robert L. Hilliard and Michael C. Keith

Routledge
Taylor & Francis Group

LONDON AND NEW YORK

First published 1999 by M.E. Sharpe

Published 2015 by Routledge
2 Park Square, Milton Park, Abingdon, Oxon OX14 4RN
711 Third Avenue, New York, NY 10017, USA

Routledge is an imprint of the Taylor & Francis Group, an informa business

Library of Congress Cataloging-in-Publication Data

Hilliard, Robert L.
The Hidden Screen: low-power television in America / Robert L. Hilliard
and Michael C. Keith
p. cm.
Includes bibliographical references and index.
ISBN 0-7656-0419-1 (hardcover : alk. paper). — ISBN 0-7656-0420-5 (pbk : alk. paper)
1. Low power television--United States. I. Keith, Michael C. II. Title.
HE8700.72.U6H55   1999
384.55´4—dc21   98-44069
CIP

ISBN 13: 9780765604200 (pbk)
ISBN 13: 9780765604194 (hbk)

Contents

List of Figures

Preface

Over the years, as we tracked the count of broadcast media around the country for our various studies, we grew increasingly curious about a category of stations called LPTV. In *Broadcasting and Cable* magazine's weekly tally of radio, television, and cable outlets, these rather cryptic initials (very few of those we queried knew what they represented or—even if they did—where and what these stations broadcast) were always accompanied by a steadily rising figure—600 . . . 800 . . . 1,300 . . . 1,800 . . .

The questions in our minds about this new medium grew as the numbers climbed. How could 2,000 television signals (the FCC has actually issued more low-power than full-power licenses), even if driven by minuscule wattage, escape the notice of those of us devoted to Fifth Estate research? There was very little scholarship published on LPTV, especially concerning its role as an electronic purveyor of information and entertainment. All in all it seemed to us that we were dealing with something almost clandestine or underground in nature—something LPTVer Dave Pierce affectionately calls "guerilla television" in chapter five. This broadcast phenomenon we came to term the "hidden screen," not because it was designed or intended to serve a surreptitious purpose but because of its stealthy, if not enigmatic, presence in the broadcast firmament.

As we began our inquiry into low-power television, it quickly became evident that this was a medium very much above ground and of this world. It was out there for all, or almost all, to see, and it could be found in nearly every part of the country—often in places other mass media had ignored or forsaken. LPTVs also existed in signal-laden metropolitan areas. Our research uncovered many things, but foremost it revealed a determined and diverse group of stalwart broadcasters, whose goal it was (and is) to provide locally and demographically relevant television to viewers. This formidable objective was almost always attempted on a shoestring budget and often in conditions that were less than Spartan, to say the least.

The programming LPTV stations offer is, if anything, eclectic and often homespun—qualities quite rare in mainstream, big-dollar television. Not all LPTV operations devote themselves to diverse, locally oriented shows, however. Many are content to transmit a potpourri of recycled and calcified reruns and aging B-movies for the sake of generating income, but happily this is not a dominant approach. Meanwhile, some vested-interest groups representing right- and left-wing political factions, religious organizations, and community groups employ LPTV signals to help realize their specific agendas.

Ultimately most low-power television broadcasters see themselves as providing a vital primary service for viewers despite their secondary categorization, which they hope will change with status upgrading by the Federal Communications Commission. Should the medium achieve its much-sought-after Class A standing, its broadcasters believe they will be in an enhanced position to fulfill its mandate and continue in the role of providing audiences with a valuable viewing option. *(As this manuscript entered the final stage of its production in March 1999, the FCC appeared about to propose that low-power television stations be granted primary status.)*

Time will tell whether the climate for LPTV broadcasters will improve or if they will lose their much-cherished frequencies in the metamorphosis to digital by the so-called "big-guys"—the full-power television operators. In the meantime, LPTV practitioners will continue to bring their unique vision to a medium that sometimes can be very myopic.

Many individuals contributed to this study and for this deserve appropriate recognition. Therefore we wish to thank, among others, Ken Carter (who gave one of your authors his first broadcast job), Mark Banks and Michael Havice (communications scholars and colleagues), Dave Pierce (ground-breaking bayou broadcaster), Frank Tyro (teacher of Native American future mass media practitioners), Robert Perry (lawyer and champion of First Amendment causes), Ed Shane (sage of the airwaves), and Sherwin Grossman and John Kompas (tireless advocates of the LPTV medium).

For their admirable efforts to enrich the airwaves, we salute LPTV broadcasters and dedicate this humble volume to the communicators who make it possible.

The
HIDDEN
SCREEN

—1—

A New Medium

The Nature and Purpose
of Low-Power Television

LPTV Characteristics

*Low-power television stations are regular broadcast stations
that operate with greatly reduced power compared to that of
full-power traditional television stations and that, consequently, reach a much smaller geographical area and a
smaller number of viewers.*

Low-power television stations or, as they are called, LPTV stations,
were designed to provide additional television channels in communities
that had available frequencies, but which were too close to other cities
with co-frequencies (that is, the same frequency assignments) or adjacent
frequencies, so that the addition of any more full-power television stations
would interfere with other stations' signals. Low-power stations in those
communities, reaching perhaps from 5 to about 15 miles compared to 40 or
50 miles for full-power stations, are not as likely to create interference. This
enables willing entrepreneurs to apply for permits to construct and operate
stations where otherwise no additional TV services could be accommodated. Essentially, therefore, serving a limited geographical area, these
LPTV stations orient their programming and advertising to a specialized,
local audience.

LPTV stations use the same frequencies as full-power stations. To protect stations from interference by other stations, the United States Federal Communications Commission (FCC) has allocated television channels throughout the country on a "domino theory" basis. That is, there must be specified spacing—mileage separation, or distance—between VHF stations on the same frequency and between UHF stations on the same frequency. VHF stations cover a larger geographical area than do UHF stations with the same power. Electronically, the lower the frequency, the further the signal carries through the air. VHF channels are 1 through 13. (Channel 1 was appropriated for federal government use many years ago and is not found on domestic television sets.) UHF channels are from 14 to 83. The channels beyond 83 that some 70 percent of television homes find or will soon find on their sets are not broadcast frequencies but are numbers assigned to cable or satellite channels received through a cable wire, satellite dish, or other non-broadcast means. In some cases a broadcast TV station may be assigned the same channel number it has for its over-the-air signal.

Where two or more cities are closer than the distances specified by the FCC, the same frequency cannot be used in both those cities. In many parts of the country, especially in high-population urban areas, the demand for television stations exceeds the frequency capacity, given the interference restrictions. LPTV solves the problem to a certain extent. By authorizing a low-power station in one or more of those too-close communities, the FCC enables the community to add a station and, because the LPTV range is short, to avoid interference with the signals from co-frequency stations in other communities. LPTV stations are authorized to operate on a "secondary" basis only. If by any chance they do interfere with full-power station signals, the LPTV station must either reduce power to avoid such interference or, if necessary, go off the air. In this respect they are similar to most AM radio stations, which must take measures after sunset to avoid interfering with the signals of stations with broader and more powerful operating parameters. Other comparisons to radio are equally valid and are discussed later.

Service Areas

LPTV stations principally serve urban areas with populations substantial enough to provide enough viewers and potential customers to make advertising worthwhile for businesses wanting to sell products or services in that area. However, LPTV stations also serve rural areas (their original target audience) where there is not a sufficient population to warrant regular-power, full-service television stations, which are expensive to build and operate. These geographical areas, therefore, receive little direct broadcast television service. They are dependent on cable companies, which are reluctant to invest large capital amounts in limited potential subscription, low-population areas, and on satellite reception, which, at this writing, is still relatively expensive for the average household and quite expensive for the generally low-income, isolated rural areas. In some of these areas, however, there may be a sufficient population base to support a smaller, relatively inexpensive LPTV station (Figure 1.1).

In some instances LPTV stations serve distinct communities and fill specialized community needs not served by full-power television stations or cable systems, which must serve broad-based audiences to obtain high enough viewer numbers—that is, ratings—to attract advertisers that will pay profit-making commercial fees. Some of these LPTV stations provide non-commercial educational programming in college and university towns, while at the same time providing a practical broadcasting experience for the college or university media students. Some areas simply do not require full-power stations. A 50,000-watt station in a sizable community in certain geographic areas of the country might cover that community very well, but the remainder of its signal might reach only empty plains or uninhabited mountains or large bodies of water. In such cases, the limited signal of an LPTV station could technically serve the intended audience just as well. The drawback for LPTV is in programming; national networks prefer to affiliate only with full-power stations, although the fledgling WB and UPI networks in the early 1990s were happy to find LPTV affiliates in areas where the four major TV networks had already signed up all the existing full-power stations. One of the big four, FOX, did seek out LPTV affiliates when it first began its network operations and tried to break the hold of the big three, ABC, CBS, and NBC. More on the programming aspects of LPTV appears in chapter 4.

The Head Count

According to *Broadcasting and Cable,* at the end of 1998 there were over 2,000 LPTV stations on the air, over 1,200 of them in the UHF range. This compares with only about 1,560 full-power TV stations—about 690 VHF and about 870 UHF. Although the UHF band, in which the vast majority of LPTV stations operate, comprises channels 14 to 83, the lower frequency UHF channels tend to be utilized whenever possible by the full-power stations because of their stronger signals. Therefore, most of the LPTV UHFs generally are in the 70-to-83 range. The figures reported by the magazine are obtained from the FCC, which LPTV scholar Professor Mark Banks says are unreliable. "In actuality there are far fewer low-power stations operating. Perhaps half the number cited above would be optimistic.

Figure 1.1 Control of a Multiple LPTV Operation in Louisiana. Courtesy KLAF.

The commission doesn't keep track of the number of LPTVs really on the air at any given time."[1]

In Translation

LPTV stations emerged from what are called "translators." Translators, which have been around since the 1940s, were originally used to repeat the signal from a full-power TV station in areas that the original signal did not reach. By repeating, or "translating," the signal from the original frequency to one that did not cause interference to other signals in an area, the translator extended a station's reach to small towns and rural areas that otherwise were out of the range of the signals that originated in distant, larger cities and towns. To further avoid interference, the translators were limited in power and, therefore, distance. Some full-power signals were repeated or translated more than once in order to extend the signals to additional communities. Eventually, in order to serve local needs, some of these translators began to include their own programming, oriented to the targeted audiences. Today, such audiences are able to receive not only broadcast stations, but also cable networks and satellite transmissions. When translators and the subsequent low-power television stations began to develop, however, cable had not yet expanded to most communities and did not have as large a channel capacity as today, and direct broadcast satellite transmission and reception were not yet easily available.

Translators developed quickly in their early days, and by the mid-1950s more than 1,000 were in operation, mostly in rural areas. In addition to their use in the authorized retransmission of signals, many translators began to be used by local groups, such as fraternal and community service organizations, local government offices, and others that wished to provide special material to the people in the area, information that could not be disseminated as quickly or as effectively in any other way.

The translators that operated in this way, programming original material rather than solely retransmitting a distant signal, were not yet authorized by the FCC to do so. Although the FCC licensed translators and established rules governing their operation, no provision had been made for low-power station programming. The FCC, however, was not assiduous in taking action against the translators as long as they caused no interference to licensed stations. On a number of occasions, though, the FCC did object to translators originating programming unless they had specific FCC permission to do so. As might be expected, the full-power TV stations, in many instances acting through their state broadcaster associations, and represented in Washington, D.C., by their lobbying group, the National Association of

Broadcasters (NAB), took exception to any given instance of program origination by translators (the Corporation for Public Broadcasting took umbrage to the idea on much the same grounds). They feared—and time later proved them right—that given programming permission, the translators might develop into direct competitors for the available advertising and underwriting dollars in their service areas. LPTV approval needed strong backing at the FCC. Robert E. Lee, at that time acting chair of the commission, acknowledged that the broadcast industry would be unhappy if a new, potentially competitive service, LPTV, were established. In supporting LPTV, however, he stated:

> When cable first came along, broadcast people didn't like it and looked on it as a predator of programming. They did their best to stifle it over the years. But when it became obvious to all that it was here to stay, the broadcasters got into it with both feet.[2]

Authorization of programming on translator frequencies—in essence, the development of low-power broadcast stations—was at first given principally for noncommercial educational uses. In 1966 an educational organization in New York State, BOCES (Board of Cooperative Educational Services), obtained FCC permission to broadcast on their translator systems serving schools in upstate New York, materials from TV station programs and from other sources that they had put together into educational formats. In 1973 the Alaska Educational Broadcasting Commission (AEBC) asked the FCC for permission to develop low-power stations to broadcast programming to the many isolated villages that make up much of Alaska. This system later developed into an extensive network of LPTV stations (several hundred) providing Alaskan communities and individuals with informational and educational materials they otherwise would not have received. Today, however, this use of LPTV in Alaska is no longer necessary for broad dissemination, although it still has value for community station local programming. Almost every village, no matter how small or isolated, has a satellite-receive dish serving all the dwellings in the community. (See chapter 8.)

A Metamorphosis

The increasing demand for permission to use translators to originate programming prompted the FCC to propose, in September 1980, the creation of a special category of low-power television stations, LPTV. These stations would be limited in power and in the mileage area they would be permitted to cover. Technically, they were like translators, operating on the ultra-high microwave frequencies. They would not, however, be limited solely to retransmitting the signals of full-power stations, as were translators, but would be permitted to originate their own programming, like full-power stations. Because of their limited range and because the FCC wanted to facilitate the development of this new service that ostensibly would serve the special needs of communities not provided for by the already existing television systems, the FCC imposed considerably fewer regulations on LPTV than on the full-power TV stations.

In 1981 the FCC began accepting applications for the construction and subsequent licensing of LPTV stations. The first LPTV station was put on the air by John Bolar, an experienced broadcaster, in December, in Bemidji, Minnesota. In April 1982, the FCC published rules governing LPTV and issued the first LPTV station licenses. Any translator station that wanted to convert to LPTV status was permitted to do so simply by informing the FCC of its changeover. By the end of the year almost 400 translators had been licensed to operate as LPTV stations, most of them in rural areas, and more than 200 of them were already on the air. The most significant portents of things to come, though, were the almost 8,000 applications for construction permits for LPTV stations that had been filed with the FCC.

"Low power" is synonymous with "local." LPTV was not designed to compete with full-power TV stations or with cable systems, although in some fairly rare instances its growth has had that result. Stations were supposed to service, principally, underserved markets. That meant, generally, rural areas. However, it turned out that many urban areas felt that they, too, were underserved—not because there were not enough full-power TV stations in the given market area, but because those stations did not serve the needs of specified groups in those areas; thus, there were applications from urban as well rural areas for LPTV licenses.

Some early definitions of low-power television compared it to cable, insofar as both provided a service to the local community, cable through its mandated access and local origination channels. However, LPTV advocates, while decrying cable's multiple channel advantage, contend that because LPTV stations' dedication is local, the latter more effectively reflect and serve their individual neighborhoods and communities. (See this chapter's appendix for FCC rules and regulations on LPTV.)

Diversity and Democratization

Behind the FCC's authorization of the first new broadcast service in twenty years was the notion of enhanced service to the viewing public. LPTV was perceived by many as a means of filling a gap in terms of availability of service in many communities and in terms of alternative content. The FCC acknowledged LPTV's potential to provide both access to and programming for both urban minorities and relatively isolated rural inhabitants. It was touted as the first genuine attempt to "democratize" the airwaves—that is, as a method and system designed to provide access to the precious broadcast spectrum for those without the deep corporate pockets and huge bank accounts typically required in order to join the ownership ranks of mainstream television. In fact, the idea of low-power television predated its actual implementation by more than a decade and had its origin in a prominent cultural movement, contends writer Mark Pinsky:

> The concept emerged out of the counterculture in the early 1970s, when technically oriented young people began to use cheap new technologies in rural areas that, for topographical reasons, couldn't receive traditional television signals. One place this happened was in Lanesville, New York, in a small valley near Woodstock. A group of people who called themselves the Video-freex set up a low-power station, without troubling the Federal Communications Commission for a license. . . . These populist pioneers, using the slogan "low power to the people," managed to convince the FCC that, in addition to serving the rural people "off the net" of existing television broadcasting, low-power technology could aim for the fringe, providing programming diversity and encouraging minority ownership.[3]

One of the principal arguments for the creation of an alternative television service echoed a position that resulted in the extension of the AM broadcast band to 1705 KHz (from 1605 KHz) in the late 1970s. Racial minorities and women had been essentially blocked from participation in the broadcast industry, due to mainstream economics, if not attitudes. LPTV was perceived as a way to help rectify this disparity. However, not everyone supported the plan to give preference to minority applications, including FCC Chairman Mark Fowler, who expressed concern with this approach to the issuance of licenses on constitutional grounds. "Those who discriminate on the basis of race should be punished under the law, Fowler said, but granting preferences on the basis of race only succeeds in fostering 'further racial polarization.' "[4]

Despite some dissent the commission unanimously voted to establish minority preferences in the awarding of LPTV licenses. Perhaps Commissioner Fogarty best expressed the sentiments of his colleagues when he observed that for too long broadcast ownership had been a "white man's paradise." For many who had long felt excluded from participation in the airwaves, LPTV represented a "great low hope," as Pluria Marshall, CEO of the National Black Media Coalition, called it.

A Note on Diversity
Myoung Hwa Bae
President, KM Communications, Inc.

I am the president, director, and 100 percent shareholder of KM Communications, which makes the company totally female and minority-owned (the latter by virtue of my Asian heritage). KM is the licensee of four LPTV stations in three major television markets (Chicago, Milwaukee, and Atlanta), and we currently provide foreign language programming targeted at local ethnic and minority communities in these markets. For example, our LPTV in Chicago, WOCH 28, provides fifty minutes of locally produced foreign language news daily, a locally produced thirty-minute special each week that features community leaders and prominent foreign dignitaries, and twelve hours of other foreign language programming (Korean, Russian, and Spanish) seven days a week. It should be obvious from this that our mission is to provide foreign language programming for local ethnic and minority communities. It is in diversity that democracy exists.

The Great *Low* Hope

Despite its relatively slow start, the mood was generally optimistic for the future of the newest television medium, and predictions clearly reflected this. This perspective was inspired by the actions of the FCC, which began to issue LPTV licenses in significant numbers in 1984, prompting the president of the newly formed American Low Power Television Association, Richard Hutcheson III, to proclaim "Low-Power Television is going to serve 25 million Americans in the next five years."[5]

The director of the National Association of Low-Power Television, John Reilly, shared Hutcheson's positive mood, saying, "I think it's going to happen. . . I really do. . . All the pieces are in place."

At the onset of LPTV's implementation the FCC projected the creation of several hundred "little TV stations" and later upped its estimates to a few thousand, based on the overwhelming demand for licenses. Ten years later, however, these figures remained unrealized, although the new medium was making its presence known around the country. In 1990, with nearly 900 LPTV stations beaming their signals into the ether, the *New York Times* observed:

Though it rarely registers more than an asterisk in the Nielsen and Arbitron ratings, low-power television has finally begun to live up to the enthusiasm that greeted its inception a decade ago. Bolstered by a proliferation of stations and affordable programming, low-power television has been shedding its image as the neglected stepchild of broadcasting. In just three years, the number of low-power stations on the air has nearly doubled ... and the Federal Communications Commission, which has granted permits for 1,237, expects as many as 4,000 by the end of the decade.[6]

Although the medium was certainly off and running, it had more than its share of Doubting Thomases. For every LPTV proponent and advocate there seemed to be a naysayer—someone predicting its failure—and there was some evidence supporting this position. For some, corroborating this view early on was the National Institute of Low Power Television's failure to attract delegates to its annual gatherings. Reported *Broadcasting* in 1984:

The organization held its second annual meeting and exhibition last Tuesday and Wednesday (March 27–28) at the Disneyland hotel in Anaheim, California. [John] Reilly estimated final attendance would be in the 400–500 range, but a separate estimate, "about 300," made by a registration official, appeared to be more accurate. Only about 130 attendees were counted at keynote sessions on Tuesday. In any case, the total was down substantially from the 600 that NALPTV had predicted and the 800 who registered at the convention 14 months ago.[7]

In another issue during the same year, *Broadcasting* proffered the view that except "for those directly involved in the medium, few are optimistic about LPTV's making a significant impact on the fifth estate."[8] In spite of the gloomy outlook held by a prominent segment of the media community, the "great low hope" of LPTV continued to fan the enthusiasm of its proponents, who would remain steadfast in the face of a growing logjam in the application process at the FCC.

The Rush for Gold

When the idea of low-power television became a reality in the early 1980s many saw it as a potential cash cow, despite its designation as a secondary video service. For many eager entrepreneurs—those who had long dreamed of getting in on the television bonanza but who lacked the opportunity because of a shortage of resources or because of an absence of available frequencies—LPTV seemed the proverbial "crack in the door." However, it was a rush for fool's gold in the eyes of FCC Commissioner Robert E. Lee, who told the industry trades, "I don't want anyone to misunderstand what this low-power proposal really means. It certainly isn't going to be a license to print money."[9] His admonition would go unheeded, as the invitation by the Commission for those interested in LPTV licenses would set off "a scramble for channels unprecedented in broadcasting history," reported *Broadcasting*, which further observed that "eager to become LPTV broadcasters (or, in some cases, entire networks) and cash in on the new medium, hundreds of companies and individuals applied for thousands of the channels, creating a logjam of paper the FCC is still trying to break."[10]

To accommodate this demand, the FCC imposed a freeze on new applications. Ron Merrell, writing for *LPTV* magazine at the time, observed, "There needed to be a halt to new applications so the existing ones could be handled. . . . The freeze is the best thing to have happened."[11] The FCC also initiated a lottery system and established a timetable for the processing of existing applications (some 12,000), which included an expedited processing strategy employing a semiautomated computer-based system expected to handle up to 300 applications monthly. This plan was inspired by the considerable frustration of LPTV applicants with the commission's sluggish manual processing system, which simply was not up to the extraordinary work load. Nonetheless, in 1983 the logjam continued as frustrations mounted on both sides of the application process. Noted *Broadcasting:* "Applicants for low-power outlets say that the FCC is not doing enough to expedite applications, [and] as far as the FCC is concerned, low-power television is an administrative headache that just won't go away."[12]

To its credit, the commission acknowledged its culpability in the melee, citing inadequate planning for the application process itself. Noted the commission's Video Services Division chief, Roy Stewart, "If we made one mistake in LPTV proceedings it was inviting applications before we had a set of rules."[13] This mistake, observed Stewart, came from the Commission's desire to swiftly launch the new television service and its not anticipating the deluge of applications that would ensue. Multiple filers, those submitting hundreds of applications, compounded the processing problem as well, added Stewart.

In an attempt to further streamline the process, in a notice of proposed rule making, the Commission recommended changing the manner in which applicants filed for new LPTV slots. Under the existing rules in 1983, the FCC had established lists of "acceptable" applicants—those for primary consideration by the public (should there be competing applications). However, under the commission proposal,

> applications for all new LPTV's would be accepted only during a specified, preordained number of days. No more would be accepted after this window

was closed. The familiar cut-off list would be eliminated and there would be no opportunity to file competing applications. Under the game plan, more windows would be opened only for applications for channels that had not been claimed in earlier rounds.[14]

In a concerted effort to simplify the LPTV application process, the Commission also proposed the elimination of information attesting to an applicant's financial qualifications to operate a mini-television station. Its many efforts ultimately did ease the gridlock, and by the late 1980s hundreds of licenses had been awarded. Meanwhile, for all but a handful of new low-power television operators, the pot of gold originally anticipated remained beyond their grasp at the other end of the rainbow.[15]

As this book reached production in late 1998, Congress defeated a bill to put LPTV stations on an equal footing with full-power TV stations. The bill was expected to be reintroduced in 1999.

Appendix 1A: FCC Rules and Regulations Pertaining to LPTV

Subpart G—Low Power TV, TV Translator, and TV Booster Stations

§74.701 Definitions.

(a) *Television broadcast translator station.* A station in the broadcast service operated for the purpose of retransmitting the programs and signals of a television broadcast station, without significantly altering any characteristic of the original signal other than its frequency and amplitude, for the purpose of providing television reception to the general public.

(b) *Primary station.* The television broadcast station which provides the programs and signals being retransmitted by a television broadcast translator station.

(c) *VHF translator.* A television broadcast translator station operating on a VHF television broadcast channel.

(d) *UHF translator.* A television broadcast translator station operating on a UHF television broadcast channel.

(e) *UHF translator signal booster.* A station in the broadcasting service operated for the sole purpose of retransmitting the signals of the UHF translator station by amplifying and reradiating such signals which have been received directly through space, without significantly altering any characteristic of the incoming signal other than its amplitude.

(f) *Low power TV station.* A station authorized under the provisions of this subpart that may retransmit the programs and signals of a TV broadcast station and that may originate programming in any amount greater than 30 seconds per hour and/or operates a subscription service. (See §73.641 of part 73 of this chapter.)

(g) *Program origination.* For purposes of this part, program origination shall be any transmissions other than the simultaneous retransmission of the programs and signals of a TV broadcast station. Origination shall include locally generated television program signals and program signals obtained via video recordings (tapes and discs), microwave, common carrier circuits, or other sources.

(h) *Local origination.* Program origination if the parameters of the program source signal, as it reaches the transmitter site, are under the control of the low power TV station licensee. Transmission of TV program signals generated at the transmitter site constitutes local origination. Local origination also includes transmission of programs reaching the transmitter site via TV STL stations, but does not include transmission of signals obtained from either terrestrial or satellite microwave feeds or low power TV stations.

(i) *Television broadcast booster station.* A station in the broadcast service operated by the licensee or permittee of a full service television broadcast station for the purpose of retransmitting the programs and signals of such primary station without significantly altering any characteristic of the original signal other than its amplitude. A television broadcast booster station may only be located such that its entire service area is located within the protected contour of the primary station it retransmits. For purposes of this paragraph, the service area of the booster and the protected contour of the primary station will be determined by the methods prescribed in §74.705(c).

[28 FR 13722, Dec. 14, 1963, as amended at 43 FR 1951, Jan. 13, 1978; 47 FR 21497, May 18, 1982; 48 FR 21486, May 12, 1983; 52 FR 7422, Mar. 11, 1987; 52 FR 31403, Aug. 20, 1987]

§74.702 Channel assignments.

(a) An applicant for a new low power TV or TV translator station or for changes in the facilities of an authorized station shall endeavor to select a channel on which its operation is not likely to cause interference. The applications must be specific with regard to the channel requested. Only one channel will be assigned to each station.

(1) Any one of the 12 standard VHF Channels (2 to 13 inclusive) may be assigned to a VHF low power TV or TV translator station. Channels 5 and 6 assigned in Alaska shall not cause harmful interference to and must accept interference from non-Government fixed

operation authorized prior to January 1, 1982.

(2) Any one of the UHF Channels from 14 to 69, inclusive, may be assigned to a UHF low power TV or TV translator station. In accordance with §73.603(c) of part 73, Channel 37 will not be assigned to such stations.

(3) Application for new low power TV or TV translator stations or for changes in existing stations, specifying operation above 806 MHz will not be accepted for filing. License renewals for existing TV translator stations operating on channels 70 (806–812 MHz) through 83 (884–890 MHz) will be granted only on a secondary basis to land mobile radio operations.

(b) Changes in the TV Table of Allotments (§73.606(b) of Part 73 of this chapter), authorizations to construct new TV broadcast stations or to change facilities of existing ones, may be made without regard to existing or proposed low power TV or TV translator stations. Where such a change results in a low power TV or TV translator station causing actual interference to reception of the TV broadcast station, the licensee or permittee of the low power TV or TV translator station shall eliminate the interference or file an application for a change in channel assignment pursuant to §73.3572 of part 73 of this chapter.

(c) A television broadcast booster station will be authorized on the channel assigned to its primary station.

[47 FR 21497, May 18, 1982, as amended at 47 FR 30068, July 12, 1982; 47 FR 35590, Aug. 18, 1982; 52 FR 7423, Mar. 11, 1987; 52 FR 31403, Aug. 20, 1987]

§74.703   Interference.

(a) An application for a new low power TV, TV translator, or TV booster station or for a change in the facilities of such an authorized station will not be granted when it is apparent that interference will be caused. The licensee of a new low power TV, TV translator, or TV booster shall protect existing low power TV and TV translator stations from interference within the protected contour defined in §74.707.

(b) It shall be the responsibility of the licensee of a low power TV, TV translator, or TV booster station to correct at its expense any condition of interference to the direct reception of the signal of any other TV broadcast station operating on the same channel as that used by the low power TV, TV translator, or TV booster station or an adjacent channel which occurs as a result of the operation of the low power TV, TV translator, or TV booster station. Interference will be considered to occur whenever reception of a regularly used signal is impaired by the signals radiated by the low power TV, TV translator, or TV booster station, regardless of the quality of the reception or the strength of the signal so used. If the interference cannot be promptly eliminated by the application of suitable techniques, operation of the offending low power TV, TV translator, or TV booster station shall be suspended and shall not be resumed until the interference has been eliminated. If the complainant refuses to permit the low Power TV, TV translator, or TV booster station to apply remedial techniques that demonstrably will eliminate the interference without impairment of the original reception, the licensee of the low power TV, TV translator, or TV booster station is absolved of further responsibility. TV booster stations will be exempt from the provisions of this paragraph to the extent that they may cause limited interference to their primary stations' signal subject to the conditions of paragraph (g) of this section.

(c) It shall be the responsibility of the licensee of a low power TV, TV translator, or TV booster station to correct any condition of interference which results from the radiation of radio frequency energy outside its assigned channel. Upon notice by the FCC to the station licensee or operator that such interference is caused by spurious omissions of the station, operation of the station shall be immediately suspended and not resumed until the interference has been eliminated. However, short test transmissions may be made during the period of suspended operation to check the efficacy of remedial measures.

(d) When a low power TV or TV translator station causes interference to a CATV system by radiations within its assigned channel at the cable headend or on the output channel of any system converter located at a receiver, the earlier user, whether cable system or low power TV or TV translator station, will be given priority on the channel, and the later user will be responsible for correction of the interference. When a low power TV or TV translator station causes interference to an MDS of ITFS system by radiations within its assigned channel on the output channel of any system converter located at a receiver, the earlier user, whether MDS system or low power TV or TV translator station, will be given priority on the channel, and the later user will be responsible for correction of the interference.

(e) Low power TV and TV translator stations are being authorized on a secondary basis to existing land mobile uses and must correct whatever interference they cause to land mobile stations or cease operation.

(f) In each instance where suspension of operation is required, the licensee shall submit a full report to the FCC in Washington, DC, after operation is resumed, containing details of the nature of the interference, the source of the interfering signals, and the remedial steps taken to eliminate the interference.

(g) A TV booster station may not disrupt the existing service of its primary station nor may it cause interference to the signal provided by the primary station within the principal community to be served.

[47 FR 21497, May 18, 1982, as amended at 48 FR 21487, May 12, 1983; 52 FR 31403, Aug. 20, 1987; 53 FR 4169, Feb. 12, 1988]

§ 74.705 TV broadcast station protection.

(a) The TV broadcast station protected contour will be its Grade B contour signal level as defined in § 73.683 and calculated from the authorized maximum radiated power (without depression angle correction), the horizontal radiation pattern, height above average terrain in the pertinent direction, and the appropriate chart from § 73.699.

(b)(1) An application to construct a new low power TV or TV translator station or change the facilities of an existing station will not be accepted if

it specifies a site which is within the protected contour of a co-channel or first adjacent channel TV broadast station.

(2) Due to the frequency spacing which exists between TV Channels 4 and 5, between Channels 6 and 7, and between Channels 13 and 14, adjacent channel protection standards shall not be applicable to these pairs of channels. (See § 73.603(a) of part 73 of this chapter.)

(3) A UHF low power TV or TV translator construction permit application will not be accepted if it specifies a site within the UHF TV broadcast station's protected contour and proposes operation on a channel either 14 or 15 channels above the channel in use by the TV broadcast station.

(4) A UHF low power TV or TV translator construction permit application will not be accepted if it specifies a site less than 100 kilometers from the transmitter site of a UHF TV broadcast station operating on a channel which is the seventh channel above the requested channel.

(5) A UHF low power TV or TV translator construction permit application will not be accepted if it specifies a site less than 32 kilometers from the transmitter site of a UHF TV broadcast station operating on a channel which is the second, third, fourth, or fifth channel above or below the requested channel.

(c) The low power TV, TV translator, or TV booster station field strength is calculated from the proposed effective radiated power (ERP) and the antenna height above average terrain (HAAT) in pertinent directions.

(1) For co-channel protection, the field strength is calculated using Figure 9a, 10a, or 10c of § 73.699 (F(50,10) charts) of Part 73 of this chapter.

(2) For low power TV, TV translator, and TV boosters that do not specify the same channel as the TV broadcast station to be protected, the field strength is calculated using Figure 9, 10, or 10b of § 73.699 (F(50,50) charts) of Part 73 of this chapter.

(d) A low power TV, TV translator, or TV booster station application will not be accepted if the ratio in dB of its field strength to that of the TV broadcast station at the protected contour fails to meet the following:

(1) −45 dB for co-channel operations without offset carrier frequency operation or −28 dB for offset carrier frequency operation. An application requesting offset carrier frequency operation must include the following:

(i) A requested offset designation (zero, plus, or minus) identifying the proposed direction of the 10 kHz offset from the standard carrier frequencies of the requested channel. If the offset designation is not different from that of the station being protected, the −45 dB ratio must be used.

(ii) A description of the means by which the low power TV, TV translator, or TV booster station will be maintained within the tolerances specified in §74.761 for offset operation.

(2) 6 dB when the protected TV broadcast station operates on a VHF channel that is one channel above the requested channel.

(3) 12 dB when the protected TV broadcast station operates on a VHF channel that is one channel below the requested channel.

(4) 15 dB when the protected TV broadcast station operates on a UHF channel that is one channel above or below the requested channel.

(5) 23 dB when the protected TV broadcast station operates on a UHF channel that is fourteen channels below the requested channel.

(6) 6 dB when the protected TV broadcast station operates a UHF channel that is fifteen channels below the requested channel.

[47 FR 21497, May 18, 1982, as amended at 48 FR 21487, May 12, 1983; 52 FR 31403, Aug. 20, 1987]

§74.707 Low power TV and TV translator station protection.

(a)(1) A low power TV or TV translator will be protected from interference from other low power TV or TV translator stations, or TV booster stations within the following predicted contours:

(i) 62 dBu for stations on Channels 2 through 6;

(ii) 68 dBu for stations on Channels 7 through 13; and

(iii) 74 dBu for stations on Channels 14 through 69.

Existing licensees and permittees that did not furnish sufficient data required to calculate the above contours by April 15, 1983 are assigned protected contours having the following radii:

Up to 0.001 kW VHF/UHF—1 mile (1.6 km) from transmitter site

Up to 0.01 kW VHF; up to 0.1 k/W UHF—2 miles (3.2 km) from transmitter site

Up to 0.1 kW VHF; up to 1 kW UHF—4 miles (6.4 km) from transmitter site

New applicants must submit the required information; they cannot rely on this table.

(2) The low power TV or TV translator station protected contour is calculated from the authorized effective radiated power and antenna height above average terrain, using Figure 9, 10, or 10b of §73.699 (F(50,50) charts) of Part 73 of this chapter.

(b)(1) An application to construct a new low power TV, TV translator, or TV booster station or change the facilities of an existing station will not be accepted if it specifies a site which is within the protected contour of a co-channel or first adjacent channel low power TV, TV translator, or TV booster station, except that a TV booster station may be located within the protected contour of its co-channel primary station.

(2) Due to the frequency spacing which exists between TV Channels 4 and 5, between Channels 6 and 7, and between Channels 13 and 14, adjacent channel protection standards shall not be applicable to these pairs of channels. (See §73.603(a) of Part 73 of this chapter.)

(3) A UHF low power TV, TV translator, or TV booster construction permit application will not be accepted if it specifies a site within the UHF low power TV, TV translator, or TV booster station's protected contour and proposes operation on a channel either 7 channels below or 14 or 15 channels above the channel in use by the low power TV, TV translator, or TV booster station.

(c) The low power TV, TV translator, or TV booster construction permit application field strength is calculated from the proposed effective radiated power (ERP) and the antenna above average terrain (HAAT) in pertinent directions.

(1) For co-channel protection, the field strength is calculated using Figure 9a, 10a, or 10c of §73.699 (F(50,10) charts) of Part 73 of this chapter.

(2) For low power TV, TV translator, or TV booster applications that do not specify the same channel as the low power TV, TV translator, or TV booster station to be protected, the field strength is calculated using Figure 9, 10, or 10b of §73.699 (F(50,50) charts) of Part 73 of this chapter.

(d) A low power TV, TV translator, or TV booster station application will not be accepted if the ratio in dB of its field strength to that of the authorized low power TV, TV translator, or TV booster station at its protected contour fails to meet the following:

(1) −45 dB for co-channel operations without offset carrier frequency operation or −28 dB for offset carrier frequency operation. An application requesting offset carrier frequency operation must include the following:

(i) A requested offset designation (zero, plus, or minus) identifying the proposed direction of the 10 kHz offset from the standard carrier frequencies of the requested channel. If the offset designation is not different from that of the station being protected, or if the station being protected is not maintaining its frequencies within the tolerance specified in §74.761 for offset operation, the −45 dB ratio must be used.

(ii) A description of the means by which the low power TV, TV translator, or TV booster station's frequencies will be maintained within the tolerances specified in §74.761 for offset operation.

(2) 6 dB when the protected low power TV or TV translator station operates on a VHF channel that is one channel above the requested channel.

(3) 12 dB when the protected low power TV or TV translator station operates on a VHF channel that is one channel below the requested channel.

(4) 15 dB when the protected low power TV or TV translator station operates on a UHF channel that is one channel above or below the requested channel.

(5) 0 dB when the protected low power TV or TV translator station operates on a UHF channel that is seven channels above the requested channel.

(6) 23 dB when the protected low power TV or TV translator station operates on a UHF channel that is fourteen channels below the requested channel.

(7) 6 dB when the protected low power TV or TV translator station operates on a UHF channel that is fifteen channels below the requested channel.

[47 FR 21498, May 18, 1982, as amended at 47 FR 35990, Aug. 18, 1982; 48 FR 21487, May 12, 1983; 52 FR 31403, Aug. 20, 1987]

§74.709 Land mobile station protection.

(a) Stations in the Land Mobile Radio Service, using the following channels in the indicated cities will be protected from interference caused by low power TV or TV translator stations, and low power TV and TV translator stations must accept any interference from stations in the land mobile service operating on the following channels:

City	Chan- nels	Coordinates	
		Latitude	Longitude
Boston, MA	14, 16	42°21′24″	071°03′24″
Chicago, IL	14, 15	41°52′28″	087°38′22″
Cleveland, OH	14, 15	41°29′51″	081°41′50″
Dallas, TX	16	32°47′09″	096°47′37″
Detroit, MI	15, 16	42°19′48″	083°02′57″
Houston, TX	17	29°45′26″	095°21′37″
Los Angeles, CA	14, 20	34°03′15″	118°14′28″
Miami, FL	14	25°46′37″	080°11′32″
New York, NY	14, 15	40°45′06″	073°59′39″
Philadelphia, PA	19, 20	39°56′58″	075°09′21″
Pittsburgh, PA	14, 18	40°26′19″	080°00′00″
San Francisco, CA	16, 17	37°46′39″	122°24′40″
Washington, DC	17, 18	38°53′51″	077°00′33″

(b) The protected contours for the land mobile radio service are 130 kilometers from the above coordinates, except where limited by the following:

(1) If the land mobile channel is the same as the channel in the following list, the land mobile protected contour excludes the area within 145 kilometers of the corresponding coordinates from list below. Except if the land mobile channel is 15 in New York or Cleveland or 16 in Detroit, the land mobile pro-

tected contour excludes the area within 95 kilometers of the corresponding coordinates from the list below.

(2) If the land mobile channel is one channel above or below the channel in the following list, the land mobile protected contour excludes the area within 95 kilometers of the corresponding coordinates from the list below.

City	Chan- nel	Coordinates	
		Latitude	Longitude
San Diego, CA	15	32°41′48″	116°56′10″
Waterbury, CT	20	41°31′02″	073°01′00″
Washington, DC	14	38°57′17″	077°00′17″
Washington, DC	20	38°57′49″	077°08′18″
Champaign, IL	15	40°04′11″	087°54′45″
Jacksonville, IL	14	39°45′52″	090°30′29″
Ft. Wayne, IN	15	41°05′35″	085°10′42″
South Bend, IN	16	41°36′20″	086°12′44″
Salisbury, MD	16	38°24′15″	075°34′45″
Mt. Pleasant, MI	14	43°34′24″	084°46′21″
Hanover, NH	15	43°42′30″	072°09′16″
Canton, OH	17	40°51′04″	081°18′37″
Cleveland, OH	19	41°21′19″	081°44′24″
Oxford, OH	14	39°30′26″	084°44′09″
Zanesville, OH	18	39°55′42″	081°59′06″
Elmira-Corning, NY	18	42°06′20″	076°52′17″
Harrisburg, PA	21	40°20′44″	076°52′09″
Johnstown, PA	19	40°19′47″	078°53′45″
Lancaster, PA	15	40°15′45″	076°27′49″
Philadelphia, PA	17	40°02′30″	075°14′24″
Pittsburgh, PA	16	40°26′46″	079°57′51″
Scranton, PA	16	41°10′56″	075°52′21″
Parkersburg, WV	15	39°20′50″	081°33′56″
Madison, WI	15	43°03′01″	089°29′15″

(c) A low power TV or TV translator station application will not be accepted if it specifies a site that is within the protected contour of a co-channel or first adjacent channel land mobile assignment.

(d) The low power TV or TV translator station field strength is calculated from the proposed effective radiated power (ERP) and the antenna height above average terrain (HAAT) in pertinent directions.

(1) The field strength is calculated using Figure 10c of § 73.699 (F(50, 10) charts) of Part 73 of this chapter.

(2) A low power TV or TV translator station application will not be accepted if it specifies the same channel as one of the land mobile assignments and its field strength at the land mobile protected contour exceeds 52 dBu.

(3) A low power TV or TV translator station application will not be accepted if it specifies a channel that is one channel above or below one of the land mobile assignments and its field

strength at the land mobile protected contour exceeds 76 dBu.

(e) To protect stations in the Offshore Radio Service, a low power TV or TV translator station construction permit application will not be accepted if it specifies operation on channels 15, 16, 17 or 18 in the following areas. West Longitude and North Latitude are abbreviated as W.L. and N.L. respectively.

(1) On Channel 15: west of 92°00′ W.L.; east of 98°30′ W.L.; and south of a line extending due west from 30°30′ N.L., 92°00′ W.L. to 30°30′ N.L., 96°00′ W.L.; and then due southwest to 28°00′ N.L., 98°30′ W.L.

(2) On Channel 16: west of 86°40′ W.L.; east of 96°30′ W.L.; and south of a line extending due west from 31°00′ N.L., 86°40′ W.L. to 31°00′ N.L., 95°00′ W.L. and then due southwest to 29°30′ N.L., 96°30′ W.L.

(3) On Channel 17: west of 86°30′ W.L.; east of 96°00′ W.L.; and south of a line extending due west from 31°00′ N.L., 86°30′ W.L. to 31°30′ N.L., 94°00′ W.L. and then due southwest to 29°30′ N.L., 96°00′ W.L.

(4) On Channel 18: west of 87°00′ W.L.; east of 95°00′ W.L.; and south of 31°00′ N.L.

[47 FR 21499, May 18, 1982, as amended at 50 FR 12027, Mar. 27, 1985; 50 FR 33942, Aug. 22, 1985]

§ 74.731　Purpose and permissible service.

(a) Television broadcast translator stations and television broadcast booster stations provide a means whereby the signals of television broadcast stations may be retransmitted to areas in which direct reception of such television broadcast stations is unsatisfactory due to distance or intervening terrain barriers.

(b) Except as provided in paragraph (f) of this section, a television broadcast translator station or television broadcast booster station may be used only to receive the signals of a television broadcast station, another television broadcast translator station, a television translator relay station, a television intercity relay station, a television STL station, or other suitable source such as a CARS or common carrier microwave station, for the simultaneous retransmission of the programs and signals of a television broadcast station. Such retransmissions may be accomplished by either:

(1) Reception of the television programs and signals of a television broadcast station directly through space, conversion to a different channel by simple heterodyne frequency conversion and suitable amplification; or,

(2) Modulation and amplification of a video and audio feed, in which case modulating equipment meeting the requirements of § 74.750(d) shall be used.

(c) The transmissions of each television broadcast translator station shall be intended for direct reception by the general public and any other use shall be incidental thereto. A television broadcast translator station shall not be operated solely for the purpose of relaying signals to one or more fixed receiving points for retransmission, distribution, or further relaying.

(d) The technical characteristics of the retransmitted signals shall not be deliberately altered so as to hinder reception on conventional television broadcast receivers.

(e) A television broadcast translator station shall not deliberately retransmit the signals of any station other than the station it is authorized by license to retransmit. Precautions shall be taken to avoid unintentional retransmission of such other signals.

(f) A locally generated radio frequency signal similar to that of a TV broadcast station and modulated with visual and aural information may be connected to the input terminals of a television broadcast translator or low power station for the purposes of transmitting still photographs, slides and voice announcements. The radio frequency signals shall be on the same channel as the normally used off-the-air signal being rebroadcast. When transmitting originations concerning financial support or public service announcements, connection of the locally generated signals shall be made automatically either by means of a time switch or upon receipt of a control signal from the TV station being rebroadcast designed to actuate the switching circuit. The switching circuit will be so designed that the input circuit will be

returned to the off-the-air signal within 30 seconds. The connection for emergency transmissions may be made manually. The apparatus used to generate the local signal which is used to modulate the translator or low power station must be capable of producing a visual or aural signal or both which will provide acceptable operation on television receivers defined for the transmission standards employed by TV broadcast stations. The visual and aural materials so transmitted shall be limited to emergency warnings of imminent danger, to local public service announcements and to seeking or acknowledging financial support deemed necessary to the continued operation of the station. Accordingly, the originations concerning financial support and PSAs are limited to 30 seconds each, no more than once per hour. Acknowledgements of financial support may include identification of the contributors, the size and nature of the contribution and advertising messages of contributors. Emergency transmissions shall be no longer or more frequent than necessary to protect life and property.

(g) Low power TV stations may operate under the following modes of service:

(1) As a TV translator station, subject to the requirements of this part;

(2) For origination of programming and commercial matter as defined in § 74.701(f);

(3) For the transmission of subscription television broadcast (STV) programs, intended to be received in intelligible form by members of the public for a fee or charge subject to the provisions of §§ 73.642(e) and 73.644.

(h) A low power TV station may not be operated solely for the purpose of relaying signals to one or more fixed receiving points for retransmission, distribution or relaying.

(i) Low power TV stations are subject to no minimum required hours of operation and may operate in any of the 3 modes described in paragraph (g) of this section for any number of hours.

(j) Television broadcast booster stations provide a means whereby the licensee of a television broadcast station may provide service to areas of low signal strength in any region within the primary station's Grade B contour. The booster station may not be located outside the predicted Grade B of its primary station nor may the predicted Grade B signal of the television booster station extend beyond the predicted Grade B contour of the primary station. A television broadcast booster station is authorized to retransmit only the signals of its primary station; it shall not retransmit the signals of any other stations nor make independent transmissions. However, locally generated signals may be used to excite the booster apparatus for the purpose of conducting tests and measurements essential to the proper installation and maintenance of the apparatus.

(k) The transmissions of a television broadcast booster station shall be intended for direct reception by the general public. Such stations will not be permitted to establish a point-to-point television relay system.

[28 FR 13722, Dec. 14, 1963, as amended at 43 FR 1951, Jan. 13, 1978; 47 FR 21499, May 18, 1982; 47 FR 40172, Sept. 13, 1982; 48 FR 21487, May 12, 1983; 52 FR 31404, Aug. 20, 1987]

§74.732 Eligibility and licensing requirements.

(a) A license for a low power TV or TV translator station may be issued to any qualified individual, organized group of individuals, broadcast station licensee, or local civil governmental body.

(b) More than one low power TV or TV translator station may be licensed to the same applicant whether or not such stations serve substantially the same area. Low power TV and TV translator stations are not counted for purposes of §73.3555, concerning multiple ownership.

(c) Only one channel will be assigned to each low power TV or TV translator station. Additional low power or translator stations may be authorized to provide additional reception. A separate application is required for each station and each application must be complete in all respects.

(d) The FCC will not act on applications for new low power TV or TV translator stations, for changes in facilities of existing stations, or for changes in output channel tendered by displaced stations pursuant to

§73.3572(a)(1), when such changes will result in a major change until the applicable time for filing a petition to deny has passed pursuant to §73.3584(c).

(e) A proposal to change the primary TV station being retransmitted or an application of a licensed translator station to include low power TV station operation, i.e., program origination or subscription service will be subject only to a notification requirement.

(f) Applications for transfer of ownership or control of a low power TV or TV translator station will be subject to petitions to deny.

(g) A television broadcast booster station will be authorized only to the licensee or permittee of the television station whose signals the booster will rebroadcast, to areas within the Grade B contour of the primary station.

(h) No numerical limit is placed on the number of booster stations that may be licensed to a single licensee. A separate license is required for each television broadcast booster station.

[47 FR 21499, May 18, 1982, as amended at 48 FR 21487, May 12, 1983; 49 FR 20504, May 15, 1984; 52 FR 7423, Mar. 11, 1987; 52 FR 10571, Apr. 2, 1987; 52 FR 31404, Aug. 20, 1987]

§74.733 UHF translator signal boosters.

(a) The licensee of a UHF television broadcast translator station may be authorized to operate one or more signal boosters for the purpose of providing reception to small shadowed areas within the area intended to be served by the translator.

(b) The transmitting apparatus shall consist of a simple linear radio frequency amplifier, with one or more amplifying stages, which is capable of receiving, amplifying, and retransmitting the signals of the parent translator without significantly altering any electrical characteristic of the received signal other than its amplitude. The maximum power input to the plate of the final radio frequency amplifier shall not exceed 5 watts.

(c) The amplifier shall be equipped with suitable circuits which will automatically cause it to cease radiating if no signal is being received from the parent translator station. Care shall be taken in the design of the apparatus to insure that out-of-band radiation is not excessive and that adequate isolation is maintained between the input and output circuits to prevent unstable operation.

(d) The installation of the apparatus and its associated receiving and transmitting antennas shall be in accordance with accepted principles of good engineering practice. Either horizontal, vertical, or circular polarization of the electric field of the radiated signal may be employed. If the isolation between the input and output circuits depends in part upon the polarization or directive properties of the transmitting and receiving antennas, the installation shall be sufficiently rugged to withstand the normal hazards of the environment.

(e) The operation of a UHF translator signal booster is subject to the condition that no harmful interference is caused to the reception of any station, broadcast or non-broadcast, other than the parent translator. The licensee of the UHF translator signal booster is expected to use reasonable diligence to minimize interference to the direct reception of the parent translator station.

(f) UHF translator signal boosters may be operated unattended. Repairs and adjustments shall be made by a qualified person. The required qualifications are set forth in §74.750 (g) and (h).

(g) An individual call sign will not be assigned to a UHF translator booster station. The retransmission of the call sign of the parent translator will serve as station identification.

(h) Applications for authority to construct and operate a UHF translator signal booster shall be submitted on FCC Form 346A. No construction of facilities or installation of apparatus at the proposed transmitter site shall be made until a construction permit therefor has been issued by the Commission.

(i) The provisions of §74.765 concerning posting of station license shall apply to a UHF translator signal booster except that the parent UHF translator call sign, followed by the word "Booster", shall be displayed at the signal booster site.

(j) The provisions of §§74.767 and 74.781 concerning marking and lighting

of antenna structures and station records, respectively, apply to UHF translator signal boosters.

NOTE: Effective July 11, 1975, no new UHF signal boosters will be authorized. Licensees of such existing boosters may make application for renewal of license or change in facilities on the applicable FCC forms for Television Broadcast Translator Stations (Form 346, for construction permits; 347, for license to cover construction permit; and 348, for renewal of license). Report and Order, Docket No. 20372. May 28, 1975.

[28 FR 13722, Dec. 14, 1963, as amended at 40 FR 25022, June 12, 1975]

§ 74.734 Attended and unattended operation.

(a) In all circumstances other than during local origination (see § 74.701(h)), during which the operator must be in continuous attendance at the transmitter site, at a remote control point or at the program source, low power TV and TV translator stations may be operated without a licensed radio operator in attendance if the following requirements are met:

(1) If the transmitter site cannot be promptly reached at all hours and in all seasons, means shall be provided so that the transmitting apparatus can be turned on and off at will from a point that readily is accessible at all hours and in all seasons.

(2) The transmitter also shall be equipped with suitable automatic circuits that will place it in a nonradiating condition in the absence of a signal on the input channel or circuit.

(3) The transmitting and the ON/OFF control, if at a location other than the transmitter site, shall be adequately protected against tampering by unauthorized persons.

(4) The FCC shall be supplied with the name, address, and telephone number of a person or persons who may be called to secure suspension of operation of the transmitter promptly should such action be deemed necessary by the FCC. Such information shall be kept current by the licensee.

(5) In cases where the antenna and supporting structure are considered to be a hazard to air navigation and are required to be painted and lighted under the provisions of part 17 of the Rules, the licensee shall make suitable

arrangements for the daily observations, when required, and lighting equipment inspections required by §§ 17.37 and 17.38 of the FCC rules.

(6) In the case of a low power TV or TV translator station using modulating equipment, observation of the transmitted program signal on a suitable receiver shall be made for at least 10 continuous minutes each day by a person designated by the licensee, who shall institute measures sufficient to assure prompt correction of any condition of improper operation that is observed.

(b) An application for authority to construct a new low power TV station (when rebroadcasting the programs of another station) or TV translator station or to make changes in the facilities of an authorized station, and that proposes unattended operation, shall include an adequate showing as to the manner of compliance with this section.

[47 FR 21500, May 18, 1982, as amended at 48 FR 21487, May 12, 1983]

§ 74.735 Power limitation.

(a) The power output of the final radio frequency amplifier of a VHF low power TV, TV translator, or TV booster station, except as provided for in paragraphs (d) and (f) of this section, shall not exceed 0.01 kW visual power. A UHF station shall be limited to a maximum of 1 kW peak visual power except as provided for in paragraph (f) of this section. In no event shall the transmitting apparatus be operated with a power output in excess of the manufacturer's rating.

(b) In individual cases, the FCC may authorize the use of more than one final radio frequency amplifier at a single VHF or UHF station under the following conditions:

(1) Each such amplifier shall be used to serve a different community or area More than one final radiofrequency amplifier will not be authorized to provide service to all or a part of the same community or area.

(2) Each final radiofrequency amplifier shall feed a separate transmitting antenna or antenna array. The transmitting antennas or antenna arrays shall be so designed and installed that the outputs of the separate radio-frequency amplifiers will not combine to reinforce the signals radiated by the separate antennas or otherwise achieve the effect of radiated power in any direction in excess of that which could be obtained with a single antenna of the same design fed by a radiofrequency amplifier with power output no greater than that authorized pursuant to paragraph (a) of this section.

(3) A translator employing multiple final radiofrequency amplifiers will be licensed as a single station. The separate final radiofrequency amplifiers will not be licensed to different licensees.

(c) No limit is placed upon the effective radiated power that may be obtained by the use of horizontally or vertically polarized directive transmitting antennas, providing the provisions of §§ 74.705, 74.707 and 74.709 are met. Applications proposing the use of directional antenna systems must be accompanied by the following:

(1) Complete description of the proposed antenna system, including the manufacturer and model number of the proposed directional antenna. It is not acceptable to label the antenna with only a generic term such as "Yagi" or "Dipole". A specific model number must be provided. In the case of individually designed antennas with no model number, or in the case of a composite antenna composed of two or more individual antennas, the antenna should be described as a "custom" or "composite" antenna, as appropriate. A full description of the design of the antenna should also be submitted.

(2) Relative field horizontal plane pattern (horizontal polarization only) of the proposed directional antenna. A value of 1.0 should be used for the maximum radiation. The plot of the pattern should be oriented so that 0° corresponds to the maximum radiation of the directional antenna or, alternatively in the case of a symmetrical pattern, to the line of symmetry. The 0° on the plot should be referenced to the actual azimuth with respect to true North.

(3) A tabulation of the relative field pattern required in paragraph (c)(2), of this section. The tabulation should use the same zero degree reference as the plotted pattern, and be tabulated at

least every 10°. In addition, tabulated values of all maximas and minimas, with their corresponding azimuths, should be submitted.

(4) All horizontal plane patterns must be plotted to the largest scale possible on unglazed letter-size polar coordinate paper (main engraving approximately 18 cm x 25 cm (7 inches x 10 inches)) using only scale divisions and subdivisions of 1, 2, 2.5 or 5 times 10-nth. Values of field strength on any pattern less than 10% of the maximum field strength plotted on that pattern must be shown on an enlarged scale.

(5) The horizontal plane patterns that are required are the patterns for the complete directional antenna system. In the case of a composite antenna composed of two or more individual antennas, this means that the patterns for the composite antenna composed of two or more individual antennas, not the patterns for each of the individual antennas, must be submitted.

(d) VHF low power TV, TV translator, and TV booster stations authorized on channels listed in the TV table of allocations (see § 73.606(b) of Part 73 of this chapter) will be authorized a maximum output power of the radio frequency amplifier of 0.1 kW peak visual power.

(e) The power output of the final radio amplifier of a VHF or UHF transmitter may be fed into a single transmitting antenna, or may be divided between two or more transmitting antennas or antenna arrays in any manner found useful or desirable by the licensee.

(f) A station proposing to use antenna(s) designed for circularly polarized radiation may be authorized to use a type accepted transmitter or parallel connected of two type accepted translator amplifiers to operate at peak visual output power of twice that specified under the maximum transmitter power limitations given above in this section.

[30 FR 8847, July 14, 1965, as amended at 41 FR 28287, July 9, 1976; 47 FR 21500, May 18, 1982; 48 FR 21487, May 12, 1983; 52 FR 7423, Mar. 11, 1987; 52 FR 31404, Aug. 20, 1987; 58 FR 44951, Aug. 25, 1993]

§ 74.736 Emissions and bandwidth.

(a) The license of a low power TV, TV translator, or TV booster station authorizes the transmission of the visual signal by amplitude modulation (A5) and the accompanying aural signal by frequency modulation (F3).

(b) Standard width television channels will be assigned and the transmitting apparatus shall be operated so as to limit spurious emissions to the lowest practicable value. Any emissions including intermodulation products and radio frequency harmonics which are not essential for the transmission of the desired picture and sound information shall be considered to be spurious emissions.

(c) Any emissions appearing on frequencies more than 3 MHz above or below the upper and lower edges, respectively, of the assigned channel shall be attenuated no less than:

(1) 30 dB for transmitters rated at no more than 1 watt power output.

(2) 50 dB for transmitters rated at more than 1 watt power output.

(3) 60 dB for transmitters rated at more than 100 watts power output.

(d) Greater attenuation than that specified in paragraph (c) of this section may be required if interference results from emissions outside the assigned channel.

[28 FR 13722, Dec. 14, 1963, as amended at 33 FR 8677, June 13, 1968; 36 FR 19592, Oct. 8, 1971; 47 FR 21500, May 18, 1982; 52 FR 31404, Aug. 20, 1987]

§ 74.737 Antenna location.

(a) An applicant for a new low power TV, TV translator, or TV booster station or for a change in the facilities of an authorized station shall endeavor to select a site that will provide a line-of-sight transmission path to the entire area intended to be served and at which there is available a suitable signal from the primary station, if any, that will be retransmitted.

(b) The transmitting antenna should be placed above growing vegetation and trees lying in the direction of the area intended to be served, to minimize the possibility of signal absorption by foliage.

(c) A site within 8 kilometers of the area intended to be served is to be preferred if the conditions in paragraph (a) of this section can be met.

(d) Consideration should be given to the accessibility of the site at all seasons of the year and to the availability of facilities for the maintenance and operation of the transmitting equipment.

(e) The transmitting antenna should be located as near as is practical to the transmitter to avoid the use of long transmission lines and the associated power losses.

(f) Consideration should be given to the existence of strong radio frequency fields from other transmitters at the site of the transmitting equipment and the possibility that such fields may result in the retransmissions of signals originating on frequencies other than that of the primary station being rebroadcast.

[47 FR 21500, May 18, 1982, as amended at 52 FR 31404, Aug. 20, 1987]

§ 74.750   Transmission system facilities.

(a) Applications for new low power TV, TV translator, and TV booster stations and for increased transmitter power for previously authorized facilities will not be accepted unless the transmitter is listed in the FCC's list of equipment type accepted for licensing under the provisions of this subpart.

(b) Transmitting antennas, antennas used to receive the signals to be rebroadcast, and transmission lines are not type accepted by the FCC. External preamplifiers also may be used provided that they do not cause improper operation of the transmitting equipment, and use of such preamplifiers is not necessary to meet the provisions of paragraph (c) of this section.

(c) The following requirements must be met before low power TV and TV translator transmitters will be type accepted by the FCC:

(1) The equipment shall be so designed that the electrical characteristics of a standard television signal introduced into the input terminals will be maintained at the output. The overall response of the apparatus within its assigned channel, when operating at its rated power output and measured at the output terminals, shall provide a smooth curve, varying within limits separated by no more than 4 dB: *Provided, however,* That means may be provided to reduce the amplitude of the aural carrier below those limits, if necessary to prevent intermodulation which would mar the quality of the retransmitted picture or result in emissions outside of the assigned channel.

(2) Radio frequency harmonics of the visual and aural carriers, measured at the output terminals of the transmitter, shall be attenuated no less than 60 dB below the peak visual output power within the assigned channel. All other emissions appearing on frequencies more than 3 megacycles above or below the upper and lower edges, respectively, of the assigned channel shall be attenuated no less than:

(i) 30 dB for transmitters rated at no more than 1 watt power output.

(ii) 50 dB for transmitters rated at more than 1 watt power output.

(iii) 60 dB for transmitters rated at more than 100 watts power output.

(3) When subjected to variations in ambient temperature between minus 30 degrees and plus 50 degrees Centigrade and variations in power main voltage between 85 percent and 115 percent of rated power supply voltage, the local oscillator frequency stability shall maintain the operating frequency within:

(i) 0.02 percent of its rated frequency for transmitters rated at no more than 100 watts peak visual power.

(ii) 0.002 percent of the rated frequency for transmitters rated at more than 100 watts peak visual power.

(iii) Plus or minus 1 kHz of its rated frequency for transmitters to be used at stations employing offset carrier frequency operation.

(4) The apparatus shall contain automatic circuits which will maintain the peak visual power output constant within 2 dB when the strength of the input signal is varied over a range of 30 dB and which will not permit the peak visual power output to exceed the maximum rated power output under any condition. If a manual adjustment is provided to compensate for different average signal strengths, provision shall be made for determining the proper setting for the control, and if improper adjustment of the control

could result in improper operation, a label shall be affixed at the adjustment control bearing a suitable warning.

(5) The apparatus must be equipped with automatic controls that will place it in a non-radiating condition when no signal is being received on the input channel, either due to absence of a transmitted signal or failure of the receiving portion of the facilities used for rebroadcasting the signal of another station. The automatic control may include a time delay feature to prevent interruptions caused by fading or other momentary failures of the incoming signal.

(6) The tube or tubes employed in the final radio frequency amplifier shall be of the appropriate power rating to provide the rated power output of the translator. The normal operating constants for operation at the rated power output shall be specified. The apparatus shall be equipped with suitable meters or meter jacks so that appropriate voltage and current measurements may be made while the apparatus is in operation.

(7) The transmitters of over 0.001 kW peak visual power (0.002 kW when circularly polarized antennas are used) shall be equipped with an automatic keying device that will transmit the call sign of the station, in International Morse Code, at least once each hour during the time the station is in operation when operating in the translator mode retransmitting the programming of a TV broadcast station. However, the identification by Morse Code is not required if the licensee of the low power TV or TV translator station has an agreement with the TV broadcast station being rebroadcast to transmit aurally or visually the low power TV or TV translator station call as provided for in §74.783. Transmission of the call sign can be accomplished by:

(i) Frequency shift keying; the aural and visual carrier shift shall not be less than 5 kHz or greater than 25 kHz.

(ii) Amplitude modulation of the aural carrier of at least 30% modulation. The audio frequency tone used shall not be within 200 hertz of the Emergency Broadcast System Attention Signal alerting frequencies.

(8) Wiring, shielding, and construction shall be in accordance with ac-

cepted principles of good engineering practice.

(d) Low power TV, TV translator and transmitting equipment using a modulation process for either program origination or rebroadcasting TV booster transmitting equipment using a modulation process must meet the following requirements:

(1) The equipment shall meet the requirements of paragraphs (a)(1) and (b)(3) of §73.687.

(2) The stability of the equipment shall be sufficient to maintain the operating frequency of the aural carrier to 4.5 MHz±1kHz above the visual carrier when subjected to variations in ambient temperature between 30° and +50° centigrade and variations in power main voltage between 85 and 115 percent of rated power supply voltage.

(e) Type acceptance will be granted only upon a satisfactory showing that the apparatus is capable of meeting the requirements of paragraphs (c) and (d) of this section. The following procedures shall apply:

(1) Any manufacturer of apparatus intended for use at low power TV, TV translator, or TV booster stations may request type acceptance by following the procedures set forth in part 2, subpart J, of this chapter. Equipment found to be acceptable by the FCC will be listed in the "Radio Equipment List" published by the FCC. These lists are available for inspection at the FCC headquarters in Washington, DC or at any of its field offices.

(2) Low power TV, TV translator, and TV booster transmitting apparatus that has been type accepted by the FCC will normally be authorized without additional measurements from the applicant or licensee.

(3) Applications for type acceptance of modulators to be used with existing type accepted TV translator apparatus must include the specifications electrical and mechanical interconnecting requirements for the apparatus with which it is designed to be used.

(4) Other rules concerning type acceptance, including information regarding withdrawal of type acceptance, modification of type accepted equipment and limitations on the findings upon which type acceptance is based,

are set forth in part 2, subpart J, of this chapter.

(f) The transmitting antenna system may be designed to produce horizontal, vertical, or circular polarization.

(g) Low power TV, TV translator, or TV booster stations installing new type accepted transmitting apparatus incorporating modulating equipment need not make equipment performance measurements and shall so indicate on the station license application. Stations adding new or replacing modulating equipment to existing low power, TV translator, or TV booster station transmitting apparatus must have a qualified operator (§ 74.18) examine the transmitting system after installation. This operator must certify in the application for the station license that the transmitting equipment meets the requirement of paragraph (d)(1) of this section. A report of the methods, measurements, and results must be kept in the station records. However, stations installing modulating equipment solely for the limited local origination of signals permitted by § 74.731 need not comply with the requirements of this paragraph.

[28 FR 13722, Dec. 14, 1963, as amended at 33 FR 8677, June 13, 1968; 36 FR 19592, Oct. 8, 1971; 37 FR 25844, Dec. 5, 1972; 41 FR 17552, Apr. 27, 1976; 43 FR 1951, Jan. 13, 1978; 46 FR 35465, July 8, 1981; 47 FR 21500, May 18, 1982; 47 FR 30496, July 14, 1982; 52 FR 31404, Aug. 20, 1987]

§ 74.751   Modification of transmission systems.

(a) No change, either mechanical or electrical, may be made in apparatus which has been type accepted by the Commission without prior authority of the Commission. If such prior authority has been given to the manufacturer of type accepted equipment, the manufacturer may issue instructions for such changes citing its authority. In such cases, individual licensees are not required to secure prior Commission approval but shall notify the Commission when such changes are completed.

(b) Formal application (FCC Form 346) is required for any of the following changes:

(1) Replacement of the transmitter as a whole, except replacement with a transmitter of identical power rating which has been type accepted by the FCC for use by low power TV, TV translator, and TV booster stations, or any change which could result in a change in the electrical characteristics or performance of the station.

(2) Any change in the transmitting antenna system, including the direction of radiation, directive antenna pattern, antenna gain, transmission line loss characteristics, or height of antenna center of radiation.

(3) Any change in the overall height of the antenna structure, except where notice to the Federal Aviation Administration is specifically not required under § 17.14(b) of this chapter.

(4) Any horizontal change of the location of the antenna structure which would (i) be in excess of 152.4 meters (500 feet), or (ii) require notice to the Federal Aviation Administration pursuant to § 17.7 of the FCC's Rules.

(5) A change in frequency assignment.

(6) Any changes in the location of the transmitter except within the same building or upon the same pole or tower.

(7) A change of authorized operating power.

(c) Other equipment changes not specifically referred to in paragraphs (a) and (b) of this section may be made at the discretion of the licensee, provided that the FCC in Washington, DC notified in writing upon completion of such changes.

(d) Upon installation of new or replacement transmitting equipment for which prior FCC authority is not required under the provisions of this section, the licensee must place in the station records a certification that the new installation complies in all respects with the technical requirements of this part and the station authorization.

[28 FR 13722, Dec. 14, 1963, as amended at 38 FR 6827, Mar. 13, 1973; 39 FR 38652, Nov. 1, 1974; 45 FR 26067, Apr. 17, 1980; 47 FR 21501, May 18, 1982; 48 FR 41423, Sept. 15, 1983; 50 FR 23710, June 5, 1985; 52 FR 31405, Aug. 20, 1987]

§ 74.761   Frequency tolerance.

The licensee of a low power TV, TV translator, or TV booster station shall maintain the transmitter output frequencies as set forth below. The fre-

Federal Communications Commission

quency tolerance of stations using direct frequency conversion of a received signal and not engaging in offset carrier operation as set forth in paragraph (d) of this section will be referenced to the authorized plus or minus 10 kHz offset, if any, of the primary station.

(a) The visual carrier shall be maintained to within 0.02 percent of the assigned visual carrier frequency for transmitters rated at not more than 100 watts peak visual power.

(b) The visual carrier shall be maintained to within 0.002 percent of the assigned visual carrier frequency for transmitters rated at more than 100 watts peak visual power.

(c) The aural carrier of stations employing modulating equipment shall be maintained at 4.5 MHz ± 1 kHz above the visual carrier frequency.

(d) The visual carrier shall be maintained to within 1 kHz of the assigned channel carrier frequency if the low power TV, TV translator, or TV booster station is authorized with a specified offset designation in order to provide protection under the provisions of §74.705 or §74.707.

[43 FR 1952, Jan. 13, 1978, as amended at 52 FR 31405, Aug. 20, 1987]

§74.762 Frequency measurements.

(a) The licensee of a low power TV station, a TV translator, or a TV booster station must measure the carrier frequencies of its output channel as often as necessary to ensure operation within the specified tolerances, and at least once each calendar year at intervals not exceeding 14 months.

(b) In the event that a low power TV, TV translator, or TV booster station is found to be operating beyond the frequency tolerance prescribed in §74.761, the licensee promptly shall suspend operation of the transmitter and shall not resume operation until transmitter has been restored to its assigned frequencies. Adjustment of the frequency determining circuits of the transmitter shall be made only by a qualified person in accordance with §74.750(g).

[52 FR 31405, Aug. 20, 1987]

§74.763 Time of operation.

(a) A low power TV, TV translator, or TV booster station is not required to

adhere to any regular schedule of operation. However, the licensee of a TV translator or TV booster station is expected to provide service to the extent that such is within its control and to avoid unwarranted interruptions in the service provided.

(b) In the event that causes beyond the control of the low power TV or TV translator station licensee make it impossible to continue operating, the station may discontinue operation for a period of not more than 30 days without further authority from the FCC. Notification must be sent to the FCC in Washington, DC not later than the 10th day of discontinued operation. During such period, the licensee shall continue to adhere to the requirements in the station license pertaining to the lighting of antenna structures. In the event normal operation is restored prior to the expiration of the 30 days period, the licensee will so notify the FCC of this date in writing. If the causes beyond the control of the licensee make it impossible to comply within the allowed period, informal written request shall be made to the FCC no later than the 30th day for such additional time as may be deemed necessary.

(c) Failure of a low power TV, TV translator, or TV booster station to operate for a period of 30 days or more, except for causes beyond the control of the licensee, shall be deemed evidence of discontinuation of operation and the license of the station may be cancelled at the discretion of the FCC.

(d) A television broadcast translator station shall not be permitted to radiate during extended periods when signals of the primary station are not being retransmitted.

[28 FR 13722, Dec. 14, 1963, as amended at 52 FR 7423, Mar. 11, 1987; 52 FR 31405, Aug. 20, 1987]

§74.765 Posting of station and operator licenses.

(a) The station license and any other instrument of authorization or individual order concerning the construction of the station or manner of operation shall be kept in the station record file so as to be available for inspection upon request of authorized representatives of the FCC.

(b) The licenses or permits of operators employed at low power TV stations locally originating programs (as defined by § 74.701(h)) shall be posted in accordance with the provisions of § 73.1230(b).

(c) The call sign of the station, together with the name, address, and telephone number of the licensee or local representative of the licensee, if the licensee does not reside in the community served by the station, and the name and address of the person and place where the station records are maintained, shall be displayed at the transmitter site on the structure supporting the transmitting antenna, so as to be visible to a person standing on the ground. The display shall be maintained in legible condition by the licensee.

[47 FR 21502, May 18, 1982, as amended at 52 FR 7423, Mar. 11, 1987]

§ 74.769 Copies of rules.

The licensee or permittee of a station authorized under this subpart shall have a current copy of Volume I and Volume III of the Commission's Rules and shall make them available for use by the operator in charge. Each such licensee or permittee shall be familiar with those rules relating to stations authorized under this subpart. Copies of the Commission's rules may be obtained from the Superintendent of Documents, Government Printing Office, Washington, DC 20402.

[40 FR 54794, Nov. 26, 1975]

§ 74.780 Broadcast regulations applicable to translators, low power, and booster stations.

The following rules are applicable to TV translator, low power TV, and TV booster stations:

Section 73.653—Operation of TV aural and visual transmitters.

Section 73.658—Affiliation agreements and network program practices; territorial exclusivity in non-network program arrangements.

Part 73, Subpart G—Emergency Broadcast System (for low power TV stations locally originating programming as defined by § 74.701(h)).

Section 73.1201—Station identification (for low power TV stations locally originating programming as defined by § 74.701(h)).

Section 73.1206—Broadcast of telephone conversations.

Section 73.1207—Rebroadcasts.

Section 73.1208—Broadcast of taped, filmed or recorded material.

Section 73.1211—Broadcast of lottery information.

Section 73.1212—Sponsorship identifications; list retention, related requirements.

Section 73.1216—Licensee conducted contests.

Section 73.1510—Experimental authorizations.

Section 73.1515—Special field test authorizations.

Section 73.1615—Operation during modifications of facilities.

Section 73.1635—Special temporary authorizations (STA).

Section 73.1650—International broadcasting agreements.

Section 73.1680—Emergency antennas.

Section 73.1940—Broadcasts by candidates for public office.

Section 73.2080—Equal employment opportunities (for low power TV stations only).

Section 73.3500—Application and report forms.

Section 73.3511—Applications required.

Section 73.3512—Where to file; number of copies.

Section 73.3513—Signing of applications.

Section 73.3514—Content of applications.

Section 73.3516—Specification of facilities.

Section 73.3517—Contingent applications.

Section 73.3518—Inconsistent or conflicting applications.

Section 73.3519—Repetitious applications.

Section 73.3521—Mutually exclusive applications for low power TV and TV translator stations.

Section 73.3522—Amendment of applications.

Section 73.3525—Agreements for removing application conflicts.

Section 73.3533—Application for construction permit or modification of construction permit.

Section 73.3534—Application for extension of construction permit or for construction permit to replace expired construction permit.

Section 73.3536—Application for license to cover construction permit.

Section 73.3538 (a)(1)(3)(4), (b)(2)—Application to make changes in existing station.

Section 73.3539—Application for renewal of license.

Section 73.3540—Application for voluntary assignment of transfer of control.

Section 73.3541—Application for involuntary assignment or transfer of control.

Section 73.3542—Application for emergency authorization.

Section 73.3544—Application to obtain a modified station license.

Federal Communications Commission   **§ 74.783**

[52 FR 7423, Mar. 11, 1987, as amended at 52 FR 25867, July 9, 1987; 52 FR 31405, Aug. 20, 1987; 56 FR 28099, June 19, 1991; 59 FR 31557, June 20, 1994]

§ 74.781   Station records.

(a) The licensee of a low power TV, TV translator, or TV booster station shall maintain adequate station records, including the current instrument of authorization, official correspondence with the FCC, contracts, permission for rebroadcasts, and other pertinent documents.

(b) Entries required by § 17.49 of this Chapter concerning any observed or otherwise known extinguishment or improper functioning of a tower light:

(1) The nature of such extinguishment or improper functioning.

(2) The date and time the extinguishment or improper operation was observed or otherwise noted.

(3) The date, time and nature of adjustments, repairs or replacements made.

(c) The station records shall be maintained for inspection at a residence, office, or public building, place of business, or other suitable place, in one of the communities of license of the translator or booster, except that the station records of a booster or translator licensed to the licensee of the primary station may be kept at the same place where the primary station records are kept. The name of the person keeping station records, together with the address of the place where the records are kept, shall be posted in accordance with § 74.765(c) of the rules. The station records shall be made available upon request to any authorized representative of the Commission.

(d) Station logs and records shall be retained for a period of two years.

[48 FR 44806, Sept. 30, 1983, as amended at 52 FR 31405, Aug. 20, 1987]

§ 74.783   Station identification.

(a) Each low power TV and TV translator station not originating local programming as defined by § 74.701(h) operating over 0.001 kw peak visual power (0.002 kw when using circularly polarized antennas) must transmit its station identification as follows:

(1) By transmitting the call sign in International Morse Code at least once each hour. This transmission may be accomplished by means of an automatic device as required by § 74.750(c)(7). Call sign transmission shall be made at a code speed not in excess of 20 words per minute; or

(2) By arranging for the primary station, whose signal is being rebroadcast, to identify the translator station by transmitting an easily readable visual presentation or a clearly understandable aural presentation of the translator station's call letters and location. Two such identifications shall be made between 7 a.m. and 9 a.m. and 3 p.m. and 5 p.m. each broadcast day at approximately one hour intervals during each time period. Television stations which do not begin their broadcast day before 9 a.m. shall make these identifications in the hours closest to these time periods at the specified intervals.

(b) Licensees of television translators whose station identification is made by the television station whose signals are being rebroadcast by the translator, must secure agreement with this television station licensee to keep in its file, and available to FCC personnel, the translator's call letters and location, giving the name, address and telephone number of the licensee or his service representative to be contacted in the event of malfunction of the translator. It shall be the responsibility of the translator licensee to furnish current information to the television station licensee for this purpose.

(c) A low power TV station shall comply with the station identification procedures given in § 73.1201 when locally originating programming, as defined by § 74.701(h). The identification procedures given in paragraphs (a) and (b) are to be used at all other times.

(d) Call signs for low power TV and TV translator stations will be made up of the initial letter K or W followed by the channel number assigned to the station and two additional letters. The use of the initial letter generally will follow the pattern used in the broadcast service, i.e., stations west of the Mississippi River will be assigned an initial letter K and those east, the letter W. The two letter combinations following the channel number will be assigned in order and requests for the assignment of the particular combinations of letters will not be considered. The channel number designator for Channels 2 through 9 will be incorporated in the call sign as a 2-digit number, i.e., 02, 03, ..., so as to avoid similarities with call signs assigned to amateur radio stations.

(e) Low power TV permittees or licensees may request that they be assigned four-letter call signs in lieu of the five-character alpha-numeric call signs described in paragraph (d) of this section. Parties requesting four-letter call signs are to follow the procedures delineated in § 73.3550. Such four-letter call signs shall begin with K or W; stations West of the Mississippi River will be assigned an initial letter K and stations east of the Mississippi River will be assigned an initial letter W. The four-letter call sign will be followed by the suffix "-LP." A party holding a low power TV construction permit who requests a four-letter call sign must file with that request a certification that the station has been constructed, that

physical construction is underway at the transmitter site or that a firm equipment order has been placed.

(f) TV broadcast booster station shall be identified by their primary stations by broadcasting of the primary station's call letters and location in accordance with the provisions of § 73.1201 of this chapter.

[41 FR 17552, Apr. 27, 1976, as amended at 47 FR 21502, May 18, 1982; 52 FR 7424, Mar. 11, 1987; 52 FR 31405, Aug. 20, 1987; 59 FR 31557, June 20, 1994]

§ 74.784   Rebroadcasts.

(a) The term *rebroadcast* means the reception by radio of the programs or other signals of a radio or television station and the simultaneous or subsequent retransmission of such programs or signals for direct reception by the general public.

(b) The licensee of a low power TV or TV translator station shall not rebroadcast the programs of any other TV broadcast station or other station authorized under the provisions of this Subpart without obtaining prior consent of the station whose signals or programs are proposed to be retransmitted. The FCC shall be notified of the call letters of each station rebroadcast and the licensee of the low power TV or TV broadcast translator station shall certify that written consent has been obtained from the licensee of the station whose programs are retransmitted.

(c) A TV translator station may rebroadcast only programs and signals that are simultaneously transmitted by a TV broadcast station.

(d) A TV booster station may rebroadcast only programs and signals that are simultaneously transmitted by the primary station to which it is authorized.

(e) The provisions of § 73.1207 of part 73 of this chapter apply to low power TV stations in transmitting any material during periods of program origination obtained from the transmissions of any other type of station.

(Sec. 325, 48 Stat. 1091; 47 U.S.C. 325)

[28 FR 13722, Dec. 14, 1963, as amended at 47 FR 21502, May 18, 1982; 52 FR 31405, Aug. 20, 1967]

—2—

The Screen Over the Fence

The Evolution
of Neighborhood Television
in America

The Roll Out

According to broadcast researcher Janet Hill Keefer, the idea of a low-power television medium dates back to the early 1960s when the communications subcommittee of the Senate Committee on Interstate and Foreign Commerce conducted hearings concerning the availability of television in remote areas of the West—the so-called "TV-deprived" areas of the country. However, as stated in Chapter 1, it was not until 1982 that low power television was formally authorized by the Federal Communications Commission. By that time the FCC had been flooded with applications from translators requesting permission to carry originating programming. With VHF frequencies virtually saturated throughout the United States, the number of UHF stations continued to grow. The costs of putting them on the air in relatively low population areas were very high, however, considering the availability of advertising funds both nationally and locally for limited audiences. In many cases an investment in an available full-power UHF channel simply would not earn the income necessary to pay off capital costs, even less the continuing operating costs. It was estimated that at that time a full-power UHF station would cost between $2 and $2.5 million to construct, while an LPTV station would cost as little as anywhere between

$50,000 and $300,000, and even with state-of-the art equipment usually not more than $500,000. Capital costs for many of the LPTV stations put on the air by non-commercial groups were between $150,000 and $200,000.

There were thus so many entities that wanted LPTV licenses that the FCC found itself unable to meet all the demands, simply because there was not sufficient spectrum space available. As stated in Chapter 1, because of the continuing huge number of applications, the FCC decided to hold lotteries for the available channels. Each month, beginning in the fall of 1983, the FCC selected a given market for the issuance of construction permits through a lottery.

Many of those who wished to put LPTV stations on the air represented segments of the population that had generally been denied equal access to the television industry by reason of color, ethnicity, or gender. These groups, out of the mainstream of the "old-boys" network of media financing sources, could in many cases afford only the limited capital costs and operating expenses of LPTV. Recognizing the financial limitations and the previous lack of equal opportunity for such groups, the FCC had an additional reason for using a lottery: to open up the LPTV spectrum to a broad population. This precluded the likelihood that all the licenses would be grabbed up by those who had the most money, the power, and the lawyers able to last through a comparative hearing. (Comparative hearings take place at the FCC when a mutually exclusive, or "mx," situation arises; that is, when two or more applicants apply for the same frequency in the same market, thus requiring an FCC decision as to which one is most qualified. This is determined through hearings, sometimes extensive, before the FCC.)

Peoplevision

> *The mission of our LPTV stations was and still is to serve the people and the local community.*
>
> —Ken Carter

The FCC decided to give preference for LPTV licenses to racial minority and women applicants. One reason was that these groups' constituencies were not being fully served by the existing broadcast industry. Another was that representatives of these groups had traditionally and systematically been discriminated against in seeking employment in the industry, and this preference would open some doors for their entry into the field. Most of the large broadcasting and media companies, and their associations, objected to this affirmative action approach. They insisted that the groups involved— mainly African-Americans, Latinos, and women—were already being adequately served by cable channels, if not by the more broadly oriented television broadcast stations, and therefore they did not need special access to LPTV licenses or station signals in order for their programming and media employment needs to be adequately met. Those in favor of special minority and women's access to LPTV pointed out that cable was not available on a broad scale to many of the minority group members because of their generally lower economic level compared to that of the white majority society, and cable's frequently high cost. The same reasoning was applied in regard to other potential viewers living on limited incomes, such as many elderly and disabled persons. It was planned that the LPTV stations would target such constituencies, which (because they were not high-level consumers) were not adequately served by the programming of full-power LPTV stations.

As early as 1980 a number of minority groups began planning for LPTV operations. In Washington, D.C., for example, a group of former FCC lawyers and engineers who were African-American formed an organization to apply for an LPTV license. A consortium of eleven non-profit groups did the same, in order to seek a channel for instructional, cultural, and educational programming not being provided to their constituencies by the existing full-power stations.

The FCC affirmative action policy was challenged in the courts and was ultimately found to be constitutional by the Supreme Court. When the first LPTV station went on the air in 1983, the FCC had already received more than 12,000 applications for licenses.

In the Beginning. . .

In 1982, LPTV's first year of authorized operation, the FCC had granted licenses to more than 150 LPTV stations, issued construction permits (CPs) to almost 200 more, and had almost 8,000 applications for CPs pending. Concomitantly, the Commission continued to authorize translators. Some 4,400 translators were already licensed, and about 900 new ones had received CPs.

LPTV rules were issued by the FCC on April 26, 1982. The huge number of applications had prompted the FCC to put temporary brakes on the new service. It effected a freeze on all new LPTVs. A year before the rules were issued, in April of 1981, the FCC was already so deluged by applications that it had put a freeze on new applications. The commission set up a three-tiered market size plan as a basis for controlling applications. Tier 1 was designated as rural areas that were not being adequately served by full-power stations; tier 2 was designated as smaller markets and small suburban areas, where the LPTV transmitter would be within 55 miles of markets 102–212 in size; tier 3 comprised medium-to-large cities and larger suburban areas, the top 100 markets, with LPTV transmitters within 55 miles of these centers. To facilitate its principal purpose in authorizing LPTV stations—serving areas without adequate service—the FCC exempted tier 1 from the freeze.

The FCC hoped for a diversity of local ownership in order to serve targeted audience needs. In addition to prospective owners who wanted to operate LPTVs for strictly commercial purposes, a large number of applicants represented local non-profit civic and citizen groups, and colleges and universities. Some groups, principally commercial but also in some instances civic and educational, established formal and informal networks of LPTV stations through off-air retransmission. In addition, a number of school districts were seeking means of TV instruction on a broad basis, and LPTV was an affordable way to meet that need.

Certification

The process for obtaining an LPTV license was (and is) essentially the same as that for a full-power TV station: (1) filing an application for a construction permit (CP), (2) approval by the FCC and issuance of a CP, (3) construction of a facility in accordance with the specifications on the construction permit, (4) notification to the FCC when construction has been completed, (5) holding of technical and program testing, and (6) issuance of a license by the FCC. The application form is similar to that for full-power stations. It requires data in four major categories: legal qualifications, financial qualifications, proposed programming, and full engineering information on transmitting and operating equipment including the antenna and the antenna site. The FCC imposed several major restrictions. The top 212 markets were protected from an incursion of LPTV stations. This meant those markets could not be the city of license, although there was no prohibition against someone with a super-antenna or cable picking up an LPTV station's signal from another town. This restriction was established in part because the frequencies in major markets were already saturated, and any additional signals, even low-power, would likely cause interference. A second restriction required LPTV transmitters to be a minimum of 55 miles distant from a major city. A third restriction required a minimum of 210 miles between transmitters when an LPTV station operated on a co-channel frequency with a full-power station. An exception was made for LPTV stations if closer proximity to the full-power station did not interfere with the latter's grade B signal contour (grade B refers to a signal's weakest area of coverage). Use of directional antennas permit LPTV stations to avoid interference with grade

B contours in the 210–mile zone. Waivers and exceptions, based principally on noninterference criteria, did permit the establishment of LPTVs in a number of major markets.

To deter frivolous applications, but to avoid hampering serious applicants who had little economic backing, the FCC established a token application fee of $376. Prospective licensees could apply for any channel between 2 and 69 with the exception of channel 37, which was reserved for radio astronomy. An LPTV station on a VHF channel was authorized 10 watts of power; on a UHF channel, 1,000 watts of power.

Rules of the Game

Many of the rules governing operation of an LPTV station were carried over from translator operations. Essentially, LPTV, like translators, was considered a "secondary" service, which means that an LPTV signal not only would not be permitted to interfere with the signal of a full-power station, but, more important to LPTV operators, if a new full-power station were licensed in an area (on an available VHF or UHF frequency), that full-power station had priority. The LPTV station would have to discontinue operations if the full-power station's signal crossed into the signal coverage of the LPTV station, causing interference in reception, and the LPTV station operator was not able to correct the LPTV signal to eliminate the interference. It did not matter if the LPTV station had gone on the air first; the full-power station still had priority. The principal saving grace for the LPTV station was the requirement that before the LPTV station was forced to go off the air, both the full-power station and the LPTV station had to cooperate in conducting tests to determine if there were some way to solve the problem of signal interference. While an LPTV cannot interfere with a full-power TV signal, and a new LPTV cannot interfere with the signal of an already existing LPTV, two LPTV stations can agree to permit minimal interference of their two signals. An LPTV, in addition, may not interfere with land mobile radio signals.

LPTV stations also had to conform to the FCC's equal employment opportunity (EEO) and affirmative action requirements for full-power stations. LPTV stations with five or more full-time employees working at least 30 hours per week were required to supply the commission with an EEO policy statement and report each year on the conduct of and adherence to that policy. In addition to minority preference, the FCC gave preference to applications from rural areas, which clearly had less service than did urban areas, principally because of their distance from markets large enough to support full-power stations. Full-power stations could not draw enough advertising to survive in the sparsely populated rural areas.

An LPTV license automatically permitted the operator to originate programming, unlike a translator license, which permitted only retransmission
of signals from another source. The new FCC rules encouraged translators
to become LPTV stations, by permitting them to do so simply by notifying
the FCC by petition that they wished to begin program origination. As
further encouragement, the FCC did not apply the broadcast stations' multiple ownership restriction to LPTV stations, permitting the latter to be
owned and operated as independent entities or as part of an unlimited network or group-owned system. Licenses were issued for five-year terms.
(See figure 2.1.)

While the FCC was not lax when it came to some engineering standards,
it did not impose the same technical requirements on LPTV stations that it
did on full-power stations, although all LPTV equipment had to meet FCC-
approved specifications. Thorough tests of LPTV transmission equipment
were required at least once each year to ensure continued compliance with
FCC standards and license specifications. The LPTV signal had to be moni-
tored for at least ten minutes every day to guarantee that it remained on
frequency. Frequency deviation was considered a potentially serious problem for LPTV because a number of technical requirements that guaranteed
a steady and consistent signal in full-power stations were not required of
LPTV. Engineering personnel requirements were also not as stringent for
LPTV as for full-power stations. LPTV stations were required to have
someone with at least a Restricted Radiotelephone Operator's permit (dif-
ferentiated from the full-power station requirement of an engineer with a
First Class permit) available for its transmitter, remote control, and program
origination sites. Transmitter (technical) logs were required of LPTV, but
program logs were not.

The LPTV Advantage

LPTV had a number of other advantages not afforded full-power stations.
As mentioned, there were few ownership restrictions. And, as noted earlier,
no limit was placed on the number of LPTV stations any one entity could
own, except where the signals of co-owned stations might overlap. Broadcast stations and cable companies were permitted to own and operate
LPTVs, but not in the same market where they held a broadcast license or a
cable franchise. However, any one applicant could not apply for more than
fifteen CPs at one time. Broadcast networks were barred from owning
LPTV stations.

There was a minimal anti-trafficking rule: LPTV licensees had to hold
on to the license for one year before they could receive authorization to sell.

Figure 2.1 Coverage Map of a Multiple LPTV Operation in Louisiana Bayou Country. Courtesy KLAF.

No limits were set on the number or on the minutes per hour of commercials. No minimum number of required hours of operation per day was imposed. No specified amounts of certain types of programs (such as news and public affairs, educational, and so on) were required.

Some rules similar or identical to those for full-power stations did apply. For example, LPTV stations were expected to follow Fairness Doctrine practices; that did not last long, however, inasmuch as the Fairness Doctrine was abolished in 1987. LPTV stations did and still do adhere to the equal-time rules for political candidates. The indecency, obscenity, and profanity clause of the Communications Act of 1934 applies to LPTV stations, as does the V-chip provision of the Telecommunications Act of 1996. Like full-power stations, LPTVs may not conduct lotteries. Like other stations, they must honor copyrights of any materials they use; they do not fall under the educational "fair use" provision. Perhaps most disappointing for LPTV stations was their exemption from the "must-carry" rule: cable systems are not obliged to carry them.

Almost immediately the LPTV stations formed their own association, not necessarily to compete with the National Association of Broadcasters (NAB) or the National Cable Television Association (NCTA), but for reinforcement of each other and for mutual protection from the objections and, in many cases, anger of broadcasters and cable companies that saw LPTV as unnecessary and a threat, however small, to their share of the available ad dollars in any given market. The National Association of Low Power Television (NALPTV) was organized in Washington, D.C., by John Reilly, a provider of public television seminars and himself an applicant for fifteen LPTV licenses.

The Name Game

For some years LPTV stations expressed displeasure with the FCC's call-sign regulation. They wanted call signs that more closely approximated the signs of full-power stations so the public would not think of them as lesser or inferior stations. Reported *Broadcasting* in 1991:

> Low-power television stations do not want to be called low-power television stations anymore. In an effort to improve the status of their service among potential viewers and advertisers, the Community Broadcasters Association last week asked the FCC to change the name of the program-originating stations it represents from "low-power" to "community" television stations.[1]

As might be expected, the NAB opposed what it perceived as the leveling of the playing field between full-power and low-power television outlets, arguing that such a move was a "thinly veiled attempt to convert low-power TV stations, which are intended as a secondary service and licensed by lottery, into full-service facilities."[2] In 1994 the FCC finally let LPTV stations use the standard four-letter call signs, adding only the suffix LP to indicate their low-power designation (something the NAB lobbied for). LPTVs were against the suffix but felt mostly positive about the ruling.[3] The change in name did little, however, to alter their ascribed lowly or subordinate status in any given television market.

Indeed, LPTV had initially developed as an alternative to the full-power stations, providing local coverage that the larger stations, because of network affiliation or the need for income-producing broad-interest syndicated programs, could not. In this sense, the local LPTV station was akin to the local radio station that concentrated on serving a narrow local population. However, as LPTV grew, more and more LPTV stations became part of LPTV networks or part of loose confederations sharing syndicated programming. In some cases the local coverage and service factor became secondary.

LPTV began with high hopes, to provide a service to viewers who had not previously been adequately served, to open up the television medium as it had not been before to people of color, ethnic groups, and women, who had not been afforded equal opportunity to enter the media mainstream, to create diversity in programming and service that reflected the special and varied natures, needs, and interests of the American people, and, many hoped, to move away from the "lowest common denominator" of programming that dominated U.S. television. Whether these hopes and potentials have been realized is another matter. This alternative to the full-power stations moderated its purposes with its growth.

LPTV stations' growth and importance made them competitors not only to full-power stations in their communities, especially non-affiliate independents, but to local cable systems as well. New rules and regulations designed to enhance other delivery systems sometimes ignore the needs of LPTV, still considered a secondary system. The FCC's 1997 rule making regarding digital television bypassed the potential impact on LPTV. Rep. Billy Tauzin, chair of the House Subcommittee on Telecommunications, noted that the new digital systems, as proposed, would harm LPTV. "The prospect of losing 50 to 60 percent of the LPTV broadcast service and more than 10 percent of the translator stations is neither good public policy nor an acceptable result."[4] (More on this topic may be found in Chapter 6.)

Neighborhood Views

The basic idea fueling the creation of LPTV was the improvement of service to the viewing public, especially those segments of the population whose needs were not being fully met by mainstream video signals. It was argued that even in large cities with several full-power television outlets, parts of the viewing audience felt orphaned and disenfranchised, often because of language and social barriers. In areas far away from regular television service, the same situation existed. The *Los Angeles Times* termed this segment of the population the "forgotten viewers," adding that LPTV outlets were helping to change this and citing numerous examples:

> In small Indian communities from the Rockies to the desert Southwest, low-cost television "mini-stations" are broadcasting political debates, giving native language instruction and airing documentaries on Indian art and culture. . . . In the Bronx, in neighborhoods so poor cable operators are afraid their copper wires will be stripped by scavengers, at least 300,000 Haitians tune in to a [low-power] station broadcasting in the patois that most islanders speak. . . . A Buffalo, New York, station owned by Ralph Nader's Citizen's Television System . . . features school board meetings, ballet performances, documentaries, city council meetings and community festivals.[5]

Increasing community identity was the plan of many LPTV licensees, according to Channel 43 station manager D.J. Everett, whose operation brought unique local programming to Hopkinsville, Kentucky. "The only significant television that people in our area have been able to get has been either Tennessee television or Indiana television. Well, you know there's just a normal thing that people do; they identify with their own town and their own state."[6] LPTV operator Richard Bonner concurred with Everett, adding that tailoring programming to a very specific audience—the inner city, for example—is a public service that ultimately strengthens the whole community. "We have a large ethnic audience because we're the only station that broadcasts in the *patois*. [This audience] is sometimes willing to watch a marginal color picture in their language, rather than a great picture on CBS if they do not understand it."[7]

Promoting local identify is also the mission of the County of San Bernardino Special Districts Department, which operates low-power television stations and thirty-seven television translator channels at six geographically dispersed sites within the county. Says District Manager L. Craig Duckworth:

> The mission of each of [our] low-power TV stations is to provide local, community based television that is informative and entertaining. LPTV in San Bernardino County provides a medium that enables smaller rural communities to maintain and promote their own unique identity within the constraints of limited funds. Programs are locally produced and aired and cover important local events or services that enlighten and support community

spirit. Two recent programs covered a senior citizens' center and services related to seniors and Calico Ghost Town Days—an entertaining reenactment of activities of an old gold mining town.[8]

LPTV's strong rural agenda is evident throughout the country, especially in areas of the West and Midwest. Notes Redwood TV Improvement Corporation's Rich Penkert: "Our mission is to provide over-the-air UHF television programming to over 1,000 farm families in rural Minnesota. These farm families have no other way to get most of the local networks because they live outside the range of the big city broadcasts."[9]

Local school systems around the country have recognized the potential of low-power television in realizing their educational objectives and agendas. One such example is Channel 14 in Clearwater, Florida, which went on the air in 1989. The mini-station programs educational material throughout Pinellas County, stated Glyndell Hadaway, director of media services for the UHF outlet. "We felt we wanted to branch out and do something new and innovative. We decided that we needed more programming for a school system this size."[10] The station designs its broadcast schedule for elementary students. Other educational LPTV stations around the country serve a vast range of levels, from pre-school to college.

The local television service concept attracted other players as well and inspired partnerships between some well-established media groups. One such alliance brought United Press International into the LPTV fold. The idea behind this union was the formation of "an extensive network of LPTV stations." In a press release, the newly formed company stated its objective:

> Our principal focus will be to . . . provide local television to those parts of the country which are underserved by existing conventional TV stations. . . . With low-power television, smaller markets can have the sort of TV service previously limited to big cities. . . . We contemplate the Community TV Network will have station affiliates broadcasting in 30 or more markets within the next 24 to 36 months. . . . We expect to become a principal force in the LPTV industry.[11]

To Protect and Advance

To ensure the neighborhood orientation of the low-power video medium, a number of organizations have been formed. However, the one with the longest track record for supporting local LPTV stations has been the Community Broadcasters Association (CBA). The trade association formed in 1984 and was incorporated as a not-for-profit entity, whose sole purpose is the protection and nurturing of LPTV, the newest video medium. According to Robert G. Allen, an attorney with a Washington law firm, the association was formed because "There really hasn't been an umbrella organization to represent the interests of LPTV broadcasters."[12]

Several other organizations have attempted to lobby for the benefit of the LPTV industry, among them the American Low-Power Television Association, the National Translator Association, and the National Association of Low-Power Television. Each has had a measure of success, although some ultimately shut their doors.

Upon its creation, CBA listed its six principal goals as:

1. To promote and exchange ideas for those involved in community television
2. To increase the public's knowledge and awareness of LPTV
3. To encourage effective management, research and marketing
4. To promote legislation favorable to the LPTV community
5. To conduct seminars, trade shows and publish news and information
6. To encourage the entry of minorities and women in the business

CBA's president, Sherwin Grossman, succinctly states the aim of his organization: "To provide, conserve, protect, and foster local broadcasting in the United States."[13]

As the LPTV industry has grown, observes Grossman, so has its need for an association to champion its cause and to represent its needs to the highest levels in Washington. In this respect, CBA's mandate resembles those of other broadcast organizations, namely the National Association of Broadcasters (NAB) and the National Cable Television Association (NCTA), which seek to promote the well-being of their member outlets.

Cable Ready

Among the most significant challenges engaging LPTV during its brief existence has been the quest for cable carriage. The value of this cannot be overstated. Perhaps the most important benefit of cable adoption is the enhancement to low-power, over-the-air signals. On cable the playing field is, indeed, level. Equality reigns, at least to a degree. LPTV stations can enter the homes of subscribers with the comparable signals—if not production values—of their full-service counterparts, since all transmissions received by a cable system's headend are given signal parity via the coaxial lines that enter viewers' living rooms. Thus, the disparity between low- and full-power stations is all but eliminated, something the latter are not thrilled about.

From the inception of LPTV it was obvious that cable adoption was a key to the further development of the medium, but must-carry rules as applied to full-power stations did not include the more diminutive outlets. LPTV was on the outside looking in, so to speak, although many of its proponents and supporters were intent on getting the FCC to require local cable systems to carry its signals. John Kompas, a principal architect of CBA, viewed the issue as a top agenda item of the newly formed organization. Declared Kompas in 1984, "The top legislative priority [of CBA] is to resolve LPTV's must-carry problem with cable."[14] Meanwhile, to many media observers, this seemed an unlikely outcome. In particular, the NAB felt LPTV should just accept its secondary status and nature, which also meant living with greater strictures than those imposed on the "big guys." Wrote *Business Week,* federal regulations would continue "to make it difficult for many low-power stations to be carried over cable systems, as their full-power competitors are."[15]

Prior to Congress's 1992 prohibition denying LPTV must-carry cable rights, low-power operators had launched carriage battles around the country, winning most of them in local courts. One such example was reported by *Multichannel News:* "An Austin, Texas, low-power television station owner, who filed suit over the local cable system's alleged 'cherry-picking' of his programming, has won an agreement for full-time carriage of his signal as an off-air channel."[16] Dozens of such lawsuits were filed against cable systems by the early 1990s with the support and efforts of CBA (among others), which "lobbied for language in the Senate cable bill S 12 establishing some criteria under which LPTV stations [could] demand carriage from local operators."[17] Regarding this successful attempt to get low-power recognition from the cable industry, CBA president D.J. Everett joyfully, if not cautiously, remarked, "This may not be Christmas, but it's pretty close."[18]

The legal skirmishes to get LPTV on cable continued in the mid-1990s, with the NAB still the primary voice of the opposition. "The NAB's highly paid lobbyists continue to fight to deny 'must carry' to stations like WAV-TV and WKOG-TV in the new telecommunications act being debated in Congress. The villain keeping stations like WKOG off the air is not local cable systems, but America's major broadcast networks and station owners."[19]

As the millennium approaches, the tensions between the full-power and cable TV industries and LPTV operators have decreased only slightly, if at all. From the perspective of CBA, cable is overprotected by the FCC in a way that ultimately discriminates against low-power television, while full-power operators continue to prevent programming diversity to preserve their cherished bottom lines. Summing up CBA's perspective on the situation, its attorney, Peter Tannenwald, observed that the opposition is very misguided in their actions against LPTV. Lamented Tannenwald to *Broadcasting,* "They're [all] looking at the wrong goal."[20]

On the whole, LPTV has done well in penetrating the coaxial curtain. Today the majority of LPTV stations reach viewers through the medium of cable.

—3—

See LPTV Run

Its Organization and Structure

The Micro-Organism

Low power television stations are essentially smaller versions of full power stations, most of them operating the same way for the same commercial purposes. The principal differences are determined mainly by their smaller base of potential viewers and, concomitantly, less advertising, which results in lower budgets. This, in turn, affects the size of their staffs, the extent and orientation of programming, and the amount of technical facilities.

Ownership Categories

As noted earlier, there are several types of ownership of LPTV stations, reflecting the general categories of ownership of full-power stations, but differing in the extent of ownership in each different category. LPTV stations may be applied for and owned by virtually anyone, including individuals, small businesses, large corporations, associations, groups, organizations, institutions, colleges, and high schools—virtually anyone who wishes to be a television entrepreneur, either to make money, to provide a public service, or even for the self-indulgence or self-satisfaction of being a television producer.

Some of these stations are independently owned and operated. These may be commercial stations, principally providing entertainment in order to draw as many viewers as possible and as many advertising dollars as possible. Some LPTV commercial stations are comparatively large, some are small. Some independent owners are seasoned professionals in the media field; others are amateurs, learning as they go along.

Many individually owned and operated LPTV stations are "mom-and-pop" operations. That is, they are owned and operated by an individual, and the owner himself or herself takes one or more of the traditional staff positions, aided by family members or friends who fill some of the other positions. These LPTV stations are similar to the small-market, low-power radio stations that once made up a fair proportion of radio licensees. "Mom" and "pop" are frequently the principal (and in a few cases, the entire) operating staff. The high cost of constructing and operating any full power television station, even in the smallest market, has eliminated any mom-and-pop full-power TV operations. Although family-operated stations are typical of the mom-and-pop station, there are some that are virtually one-person operations; that is, the owner essentially handles all the functions, even taping local events, editing them, and putting them on the air, as well as filling out the schedule with tapes from other sources.

Another type of individually owned LPTV station is that which has a sufficient budget (to a greater or lesser degree) to hire a professional staff, obtain state-of-the-art equipment, and produce or buy first-class programming. Some of these operations are relatively small, with only a few staff members. Others—especially those in large markets where even a limited range has a large potential audience or where there is an immediate specialized audience and consequently a steady flow of advertising dollars—are able to afford larger staffs, better facilities, and choice programming.

Individually or family-owned stations frequently produce a fair amount of local programming, inasmuch as they are not part of a larger conglomerate ("multiple system owners," similar to the term "MSO" used for cable system ownership), receiving system-wide programs through satellite. An LPTV station that serves local needs may in fact require a larger staff than does an LPTV station that receives virtually all of its programming from its group owner. Some individually owned stations affiliate with other stations for the purposes of program exchange. A number of Spanish-language LPTVs fall into this category.

Another category of LPTV ownership is the totally non-profit, noncommercial licensee. Fifteen percent of full power TV stations are owned and operated by such entities, principally colleges and universities, community groups, and state communication or educational systems. The majority of LPTV stations fall into this category. Some of the licensees are not formal educational institutions or organizations but are minority, ethnic, or women's groups that have incorporated as non-profit educational organizations. Others are non-minority organizations, community groups, and a large LPTV category, religious entities. These stations are interested in providing a service to a targeted audience, and although some of them seek advertising as a necessary means for staying on the air, others are subsidized by their owner group and operate virtually or completely as non-commercial stations. Some of these groups have formed networks to share programs of mutual interest. For some years this category of station completely dominated the LPTV field. It was not until 1987 that commercial LPTV stations began to go on the air in significant numbers.

College- and university-owned LPTV stations have both an advantage and disadvantage. Those licensed as non-commercial stations may not carry any advertising and therefore do not have the commercial income to hire large staffs. On the other hand, most use college students who are majoring in some area of communications as staff members, thus providing a large, if inexperienced, non-paid pool of employees. Because most of these students intend to work professionally in a communication field, they not only are motivated and dedicated, but are applying their classroom theory to a real-life situation; thus they may be competent if not professional staff members.

A further major category of ownership is the group-owned station, where economic efficiency may result in the downsizing of the operations at each station. One group-owned cost-saving approach is feeding member stations programming that has been bought by the group owner at lower rates than if it had been purchased by each station individually. Another is the centralizing of some of the stations' operations, such as regional and national sales (where individual station representatives are not employed), accounting, and overall business supervision. There are exceptions, of course, depending on the orientation of the management of a given group-owned system.

In some instances an owner who has been able to obtain several channels in a community has turned his or her group of stations into a subscription TV alternative to cable systems. While the number of channels available to a subscriber is limited—more than ten channels is a rarity, and fewer than that is the norm—the ability to provide programming designed or dedicated to smaller viewer groups' special interests and lower fees have made multi-channel LPTV subscription services feasible.

Staffing

The staffs of LPTV stations are similar to those of full power stations, with the exception that size and job areas are determined by the more limited budgets of LPTVs as well as by the LPTV general narrow-casting approach to programming.

The most important departments in low-power stations are sales, programming, and engineering. Some stations fill all three positions with full-time employees. Others use part-timers. Non-commercial stations, of course, do not need a time-sales staff. Unless top management is located at a specific group-owned station or the station depends solely on films or syndicated programming, the individual station will have a station manager. The smaller the operation, the better the likelihood that the station manager will also be the sales manager or the program director or both—and will fill any number of other positions at the same time. The general manager is responsible for overseeing all the operations of the station, including business and financial matters, sales and advertising, capital cost planning, budgeting, programming, engineering, and public relations and promotion. The general manager is the key implementor of federal rules and regulations and must see to it that the station complies with FCC directives. The general manager must also set the goals for all of the departments and personnel of the station and must evaluate their achievements or shortcomings.

The larger the station, the greater the likelihood that there will be a separate business manager. The business manager takes care of accounts receivable and accounts payable and sees to it that the proper bookkeeping is done and records are kept for tax and fee reports. The business manager must be certain that proper accounting policies and procedures are maintained and that corporate balance sheets and IRS filings are prepared. Any work or personnel in the categories of accountants, bookkeepers, human resources personnel, or billing clerks usually report to the business manager.

In commercial LPTV stations, the sales manager is the most important person. Frequently, the sales manager is also the general manager of the station, inasmuch as sales is the key to the station's existence. In a very small station one person may go out and sell time, write the commercial spots, produce them, even portray the talent on them, schedule them, and make sure they go on the air. The larger the station, the larger the sales staff.

The program director is responsible for developing the program schedule for the station and acquiring the programs that will go on the air, whether they are produced locally, to serve local community needs for targeted audiences, or whether they are acquired through syndication or some other source. A key part of this job in a commercial station is to schedule programs that appeal to a sufficient number of viewers in a given time slot to attract enough advertising to keep the station going. Because small stations generally do not have a promotion and/or public relations director, the program manager frequently takes on the responsibility of serving as liaison to the community and determining what kinds of local events and issues are important to cover. Some stations that produce a fair amount of local programming may have a production manager, in addition to a program director, to handle the development, design, and execution of such shows.

The promotion and public relations director should develop promotion and publicity activities that will draw viewers to the station, establishing a positive image for the station itself, as well as hyping individual programs. One difficult part of the job is getting other media, particularly newspapers, to carry the station's program schedule. LPTV stations are largely ignored by the other media in large markets and even in some of the smaller towns, where there is not a plethora of station or cable listings. For example, *TV Guide* does not carry independent LPTV station program schedules.

Every LPTV station needs an engineer on call. Larger stations may have a full-time engineer. Others may have part-time technical personnel who show up only when there is a technical problem. The chief engineer or other supervisory technician is charged with making sure that all technical facilities, including studio, transmitter, and remote equipment, are functioning properly, and the engineer must arrange for immediate repair or purchase of parts or equipment if anything goes wrong.

Other positions that are usually found in larger stations—set designers, lighting experts, makeup and costume heads, studio supervisors, technical directors and control board operators, researchers and audience analysts, public liaison people, news reporters and editors—are generally not available in the limited budgets of smaller stations. However, some of these slots are sometimes filled with volunteers from the community or by internes from local colleges who earn class credits for their work at a station.

Examples of LPTV Stations

Individually Owned Stations

Some individually owned or family stations specialize in a given type of programming to fill a niche in their viewing areas, and they structure their organizations accordingly. One example is W25AN (the official FCC call letters) or, informally, WBZN (for purposes of easier audience recognition) in Trenton, New Jersey, where brothers Louis and Gregory Zanoni together fill the roles of owner, president, and general manager. They operate the station principally as a news outlet for Mercer County in central New Jersey, employing a director of news and three reporters, two full-time and one part-time. The station attempts to cover breaking stories as they happen, putting on daily the events in its service area. It pays special attention to politics, provides coverage of local elections, and presents features on politicians and political issues. In addition, the station has two time-sales representatives.

Some LPTV stations provide less service to their communities, some are able to provide more. One of the latter is in Fruitport, Michigan, which uses its local channel number, 40, for its primary identification for its viewers. It is on twenty-four hours a day, with a mixture of local programming and feeds from cable and satellite networks. It produces more than forty hours of local programming each week, a prodigious amount that one no longer finds on full-power stations. Among locally produced programs is an early morning show that provides features, commentary, and news of the community. A weekly bingo game using telephone call-ins for participation is oriented to senior citizens who are unable to leave their homes to attend bingo games in person. The station attempts to cover all significant local events.

The owner and president of Channel 40 , with twenty years of personal experience in media, has a staff reflective of full-power stations: a general manager, a sales manager, a technical director, a program director, and a news director who also handles public service announcements (PSAs). Other staff members include field and studio camera operators, a control board operator, and equipment technicians. The station rounds out its personnel with interns from nearby colleges and high schools. The operation is large enough to warrant weekly sales meetings and monthly staff meetings.

Many individually owned LPTVs are religious stations. Some are operated by a particular religious organization or association. Some, such as WO7BN in Bruce, Mississippi, are family owned and operated. Its staff of general manager, news director, program director, sales manager, part-time master control operator, and part-time bookkeeper are mostly relatives of the owner. Its programming serves the strong religious interests of the small community in which it is located. Much of its programming is locally produced, and the remainder comes from syndicated sources, reflecting the religious and "family-value" concerns of its viewers. Its Baptist-oriented program schedule includes nightly local news programs, church services, religious education and bible programs, and a Christian music show. To fill out its schedule it carries syndicated reruns consistent with its audience's tastes, such as the *Ozzie and Harriet* show and old western movies. Like most small-town LPTV stations, it attempts to interact to a greater degree with its community's beliefs and interests than do larger market stations, which have a broader base of viewers to draw on for potential advertisers.

Other examples of the mom-and-pop individually owned station are the two LPTVs licensed to a husband and wife team in Michigan, the Crandells. Not typical of the traditional mom-and-pop owner, Judy Crandell is chair of the Alliance for Community Media. The Crandell's studio for one LPTV is in the basement of their home. They bought the license from the United Auto Workers union for $15,000 and spent only $25,000 for equipment. Their program schedules are flexible; they run their own self-produced programs whenever they want to. However, they plan to develop both stations in time, turning one into a public access station for people who have no other outlet through which to reach the public, and making the second station into an outlet for local government and community groups that are unable to obtain sufficient cable time to inform and educate the people about municipal and community functions and services available to community residents.

College and University LPTV Stations

In some instances, such as at the University of Florida at Gainesville's College of Communications, an LPTV station is used as a curriculum resource. The students' station work is graded and counted as credit toward graduation. This station, WLUF, could serve as a model for other educational institutions' LPTVs in its use, staffing, and signal distribution.

At WLUF students are paid for their work, albeit usually at the minimum wage. The operations, program, and personnel directors are paid higher stipends. At some university LPTVs the station manager, and frequently other department heads such as the personnel director, are sometimes full-time staff or faculty members. A qualified engineer is usually hired as an on-call director of technical operations.

At WLUF programming comes from a number of sources, but principally from productions by students at the station's studios and material produced by students in television classes. So that the station can reach more viewers, the university has arranged for its signal to be distributed over the campus-wide closed-circuit television system and for a local cable company to carry it. Because there is no cable must-carry requirement for LPTV stations, few cable systems in the country carry low power TV signals. Since its signal is extended beyond its over-the-air range by cable, WLUF carries live classes to distant learners, mainly from the university's College of Business Administration. The station also airs some syndicated programs, mostly from PBS.

Group-Owned LPTV stations

One example of group ownership is Kaleidoscope Affiliates, which owned eighteen LPTV stations nationally in 1996. While some group owners maintain generally the same format for all of their stations and similar organizational structures, Kaleidoscope stations are divided into three different principal program formats, resulting in some differences in staffing and operations.

One type of LPTV station operated by Kaleidoscope is the Video Juke Box station, which receives calls (over a 900 toll number) from viewers requesting the playing of a given music video. Another type of Kaleidoscope station is oriented to programming for children and for viewers with disabilities, such as blindness and hearing impairment. These stations generally have open-captioned and signed programs. The third type of Kaleidoscope station is oriented to the more traditional TV offerings, but is targeted to specialized audiences; it is similar in programming format to most cable networks. The key person at each of these stations is the sales manager. Because virtually none of the programming at the Kaleidoscope stations is locally produced but programming is brought in through satellite feeds from outside sources, few permanent staff members are needed at any given station.

In the midwest a group of eight LPTV stations is owned by Howard Shapiro, president of the Weigel Broadcasting Company in Chicago. Although commercially oriented, these stations provide special service to ethnic groups not adequately served by full-power television. Stations in Chicago and Rockford, Illinois; Milwaukee, Wisconsin; and South Bend, Indiana, air programming that includes the languages of Arabic, Chinese, Greek, Hindi, Polish, and Spanish. The fact that public service programming can be combined with commercial success is exemplified by these stations. Some advertisers, such as Coca-Cola and McDonalds, who get a lot of business from minority ethnic groups, buy a fair amount of commercial time on these LPTV stations.

Some stations that appear to be group-owned because they carry programming almost identical to that of a number of other LPTVs are not. They are independently owned but are affiliates of a distribution network of specialized programming for targeted audiences. A large number of Spanish-language stations are in this category. One such station is WCEA, or Cuenavision, in Boston, owned by Cuenca Enterprises of America. It is individually owned by Peter Cuenca, who serves as general manager of the station.

Marketing/Public Relations Director Malena Caceres describes the station as follows:

> WCEA is an independent low power station telecasting on greater Boston's UHF channel 19. The station transmits from the top of the Prudential Tower in downtown Boston with a telecast radius of 16 miles. We are also carried

by Cablevision of Boston and Brookline on Channel A26 and by Warner Cable Co. of Chelsea on Channel 15A. WCEA started in 1987 with the main purpose of serving the Spanish-speaking population of the area. WCEA is the only local TV station in Boston with programming directed toward different ethnic groups with cultural ties to the Caribbean, Central and South America. The station reaches about 400,000 viewers. We are affiliated with SUR, an international Spanish-language network, providing our audience with live news broadcasts from most Spanish-speaking countries.[1]

In sum, commercial LPTV stations operate similarly to commercial full power stations. Cashing in on the unlimited number of stations any one entity may own, many entrepreneurs applied for and received the maximum fifteen-station at-a-time allocation, with some repeating the process several times. In one way, commercial LPTV operators are similar to cable system operators. There are some individually owned LPTVs, but increasingly there are MSOs (multiple system owners) who form networks similar to the cable MSOs for greater economic efficiency in operations and in obtaining programming. Organization and staffing are similar to those of full-power stations but on a small scale.

Appendix 3A: LPTV Application for License Renewal

INSTRUCTIONS FOR FCC 303-S

APPLICATION FOR RENEWAL OF LICENSE FOR AM, FM, TV, TRANSLATOR, OR LPTV STATION

(FCC FORM 303-S ATTACHED)

A. This form is to be used in applying for renewal of license for a commercial or noncommercial AM, FM or TV broadcast station and FM translator, TV translator or Low Power TV broadcast station. It is also to be used in seeking the joint renewal of licenses for an FM or TV translator station and its co-owned primary FM, TV or LPTV station.

B. FCC Form 303-S consists of Sections I, II, III, IV, and V. Those Sections which do not apply to the station license being renewed should not be submitted as part of your application. Submit relevant sections only.

All applicants must complete and submit Sections I, II and V of this form.

Applicants seeking to renew only an AM, FM or TV station license must ALSO complete and submit Section III.

Applicants seeking to renew only an FM translator, TV translator or Low Power TV station license must ALSO complete and submit Section IV.

o Applicants seeking to renew the licenses of both a translator (FM and TV) and co-owned primary FM, TV or LPTV station on the same form should complete and submit ALL sections of this application.

C. References to FCC Rules are made in this application form. Before filling it out, the applicant should have on hand and be familiar with the current broadcast, translator and LPTV rules, which are contained in 47 Code of Federal Regulations (C.F.R.):

    (1)   Part 0 "Commission Organization"
    (2)   Part 1 "Practice and Procedure"
    (3)   Part 17 "Construction, Marking, and
    Lighting of Antenna Structures"
    (4)   Part 73 "Radio Broadcast Services"
    (5)   Part 74 "Experimental, Auxiliary, and Special
    Broadcast and Other Program Distributional
    Services"

FCC Rules may be purchased from the Government Printing Office, Washington, D. C. 20402. You may telephone the GPO Order desk at (202) 783-3238 for current prices.

D. An original and one complete copy of the 303-S renewal
application, including all exhibits, must be prepared for each
station license to be renewed, except that an original and one
complete copy, including all exhibits, can be filed for the
joint renewal of licenses for a translator and the translator's
commonly owned primary station. The application with all
required exhibits should be filed with the Federal
Communications Commission in the manner and at the
location specified in 47 C.F.R. Section 0.401.

E. Replies to questions in this form and the applicant's
statements constitute representations on which the FCC will
rely in considering the application. Thus, time and care
should be devoted to all replies, which should reflect
accurately the applicant's responsible consideration of the
questions asked. Include all information called for by this
application. If any portions of the application are not
applicable, so state. Defective or incomplete applications
will be returned without consideration. Furthermore,
inadvertently accepted applications are subject to dismissal.

F. In accordance with 47 C.F.R. Section 1.65, the applicant
has a continuing obligation to advise the Commission,
through amendments, of any substantial and significant
changes in the information furnished.

SECTION I - FEE INFORMATION

By law, the Commission is required to collect charges for
certain of the regulatory services it provides to the public.
Generally, applicants seeking to renew the license for a
commercial AM, FM, TV, FM translator, TV translator or Low
Power TV station are required to pay and submit a fee with
the filing of FCC Form 303-S. However, governmental
entities, which include any possession, state, city, county,
town, village, municipal organization or similar political
organization or subpart thereof controlled by publicly elected
and/or duly appointed public officials exercising sovereign
direction and control over their respective communities or
programs, are exempt from the payment of this fee. Also
exempted from this fee are licensees of noncommercial
educational radio or television broadcast stations. (This
includes licensees of noncommercial educational FM and full
service TV broadcast stations seeking renewal of the licenses
for their translator or low power TV stations provided those
stations operate on a noncommercial educational basis. Low
Power TV or TV translator stations that rebroadcast the
programming of a primary noncommercial educational
station, but are not co-owned by the licensee of such a
station, are required to file fees. In addition, noncommercial
FM translators operating on a non-reserved channel (CH 221-
300), and that are not co-owned by the licensee of the
primary noncommercial educational station, are also required
to file fees.) Renewal applicants that earlier obtained either
a fee refund because of an NTIA facilities grant for the
stations or a fee waiver because of demonstrated compliance
with the eligibility and service requirements of 47 C.F.R.
Section 73.503 or Section 73.621, and that continue to
operate those stations on a noncommercial basis, are similarly
exempted from this fee. See 47 C.F.R. Section 1.1112. To
avail itself of any fee exemption, the renewal applicant must

indicate its eligibility by checking the appropriate box in Question 2(B), Section I. FCC Form 303-S applications NOT involving the payment of a fee can be hand-delivered or mailed to the FCC's Washington, D. C. offices. See 47 C.F.R. Section 0.401(a).

The Commission's fee collection program utilizes a U.S. Treasury lockbox bank for maximum efficiency of collection and processing. All FCC Form 303-S applications, which require the remittance of a fee, must be submitted to the appropriate post office box address. See 47 C.F.R. Section 0.401(b). A listing of the required fee and the address to which FCC Form 303-S should be mailed or otherwise delivered is also set forth in the "Mass Media Services Fee Filing Guide" which is obtained either by writing to the Commission's Form Distribution Center, 2803 52nd Avenue, Hyattsville, Maryland 20871, or by calling Telephone No. 1-800-418-FORM and leaving your request on the answering machine provided for this purpose. See also 47 C.F.R. Section 1.1104.

Payment of any required fee must be made by check, bank draft, money order or credit card. If paying by check, bank draft or money order, your remittance must be denominated in U.S. dollars, drawn upon a U.S. institution and made payable to the Federal Communications Commission. No postdated, altered or third-party checks will be accepted. DO NOT SEND CASH. Checks dated six months or older will not be acceptable for filing.

Applicants who wish to pay their filing fee by money order or credit card must submit FCC Form 159, together with their application. Applicants who wish to pay for more than one application in the same lockbox with a single payment must also submit FCC Form 159. When paying for multiple filings in the same lockbox with a single payment instrument, you must list each filing as a separate item on FCC Form 159 (Remittance Advice). If additional entries are necessary, please use FCC Form 159C (Continuation Sheet). Those applicants electing to pay in a manner that requires the submission of FCC Form 159 must still complete Section I, question 1, of FCC Form 303-S. Question 2 of Section I need not be completed, but FCC Form 159 must be submitted instead.

Payment of application fees may also be made by Electronic Payment provided prior approval has been obtained from the Commission. Licensees interested in this option must first contact the Billings and Collections Branch at (202) 418-1995 to make the necessary arrangements.

Parties hand-delivering FCC Forms 303-S may receive dated receipt copies by presenting copies of the applications to the acceptance clerk at the time of delivery. For mailed-in applications, a "return copy" of the application can be furnished provided the applicant clearly identifies the "return copy" and attaches it to a stamped, self-addressed envelope. Only one piece of paper per application will be stamped for receipt purposes.

For further information regarding the applicability of a fee,

the amount of the fee or the payment of the fee, refer to the
"Mass Media Services Fee Filing Guide."

SECTION II - QUESTION-BY-QUESTION GUIDELINES

THIS SECTION MUST BE COMPLETED AND
SUBMITTED BY ALL APPLICANTS REGARDLESS
OF THE SERVICE OF THE STATION FOR WHICH
RENEWAL IS BEING SOUGHT.

Question 1.   The name of the licensee applicant should be
stated exactly as it appears on the station's existing license.
The current street address or post office box used by the
applicant for receipt of Commission correspondence should
be set forth.   If this information has been set forth in Question
1, Section I, it need not be repeated here.

Any change in the licensee's name, which does not involve
a change in ownership requiring prior Commission approval,
can be communicated to the Commission by letter.   To report
any change in the mailing address previously used by the
licensee FCC Form 5072, entitled "Change in Official Mailing
Address for Broadcast Station," should be promptly
transmitted to the Commission.   See 47 C.F.R. Section 1.5.

Question 2.   An applicant for an AM, FM, TV, LPTV, FM
Translator or TV Translator station should identify whether it
has been licensed by the Commission as a commercial or
noncommercial educational licensee.   A licensee that merely
elects to operate its station on a noncommercial basis is not
considered to be a noncommercial educational licensee.
The facility should be described by its service, call letters,
and specific community of license or area as listed on the
station's existing license.   See 47 C.F.R. Section 74.1201(a),
74.701(a) and 74.701(f) for definition of an FM translator, TV
translator and low power TV broadcast stations respectively.
For AM, FM or TV stations the location of the facility should
be described in terms of the specific city or community to
which the station is licensed.   Translator and Low Power TV
stations should specify the area the stations are licensed to
serve.

Question 3.   This question must be completed by a radio or
television renewal applicant seeking to continue its authority
to operate an FM Booster or TV booster station in
conjunction with the primary station.   The FM or TV booster
station should be described in terms of its call letters and the
name of the specific community which it serves.

Question 4.   Aliens, foreign governments and corporations,
and corporations of which less than 80% of the capital stock
is owned or voted by U.S. citizens are prohibited from
holding a broadcast station license.   Where a corporate
licensee is directly or indirectly controlled by another
corporation, of which any officer or more than 25% of the
directors are aliens or of which less than 75% of that
corporation's stock is owned or voted by U.S. citizens, the
Commission must consider whether denial of renewal would
serve the public interest.   Licensees are expected to employ

reasonable, good faith methods to ensure the accuracy and completeness of their citizenship representations.

Question 5. Commission policies and litigation reporting requirements for broadcast, translator and LPTV station applicants are directed to focusing on misconduct which violates the Communications Act or a Commission rule or policy and on certain specified non-FCC misconduct. In responding to Question 5, applicants are advised that the parameters of the Commission's policies and requirements regarding character qualifications are fully set forth in Character Qualifications, 102 FCC 2d 1179 (1985), reconsideration denied, 1 FCC Rcd 421 (1986), as modified, 5 FCC Rcd 3252 (1990) and 7 FCC Rcd 6564 (1992).

For the purpose of this question, the term "parties to the application" includes any individual or entity whose ownership or positional interest in the applicant is cognizable under the Commission's multiple ownership rules. See in this regard Report and Order in MM Docket No. 83-46, 97 FCC 2d 997 (1984), reconsideration granted in part, 58 RR 2d 604 (1985), further modified on reconsideration, 61 RR 2d 739 (1986).

Question 6. NOTE: Radio applicants may find it helpful to refer to the License Renewal Booklet for Radio Stations and the RF worksheets in the Booklet before responding to this Question.

Each applicant should check the appropriate box to indicate whether a Commission grant of the proposed communications facility(ies) may or may not have a significant environmental impact as defined by 47 C.F.R. Section 1.1307. Briefly, Commission grant of an application may have a significant environmental impact if any of the following are proposed:

(a) A facility is to be located in sensitive areas (e.g., an officially designated wilderness area, a wildlife preserve area, a flood plain) or will physically or visually affect sites significant in American history.

(b) A facility whose construction will involve significant changes in surface features.

(c) The antenna tower and/or supporting structure(s) will be equipped with high intensity white lights and are to be located in residential neighborhoods.

(d) The facilities or the operation of which will cause exposure of workers or the general public to levels of radio frequency radiation in excess of the "Radio Frequency Protection Guides" recommended in "American National Standard Safety Levels with respect to Human Exposure to Radio Frequency Electromagnetic Fields, 300 kHz to 100 GHz," (ANSI C95. 1-1982), by the Institute of Electrical and Electronics Engineers, Inc., 345 East 47th Street, New York, New York 10017.

NOTE: In answering this question, applicants for renewal of FM translator stations which transmit.with an effective radiated power of 100 watts or less are excluded from the

standards set forth in subparagraph (d) above. However, in
determining the appropriate response to this question, such
applicants must still perform an analysis of the subject
facilities in the context of the matters set forth in
subparagraphs (a) - (c) above.

If you answered No, a brief statement explaining the reasons
why there will not be a significant environmental impact must
be submitted.   With respect to RF radiation exposure, the
required statement must include a description of the steps
that have been taken to protect the general public, station
employees, and other persons authorized access to the tower
from exposure to RF radiation levels in excess of the specified
safety standards and that these steps comply with those
required by OST Bulletin No. 65, October, 1985, entitled
"Evaluating Compliance with FCC-Specified Guidelines for
Human Exposure to Radiofrequency Radiation." The
applicant must take into account ALL non-excluded
transmitters at and around the station's transmitter site; that is,
contributions to environmental RF levels from all nearby
radio and television stations, not just the applicant's station,
must be considered.

If you answered Yes, submit the required Environmental
Assessment (EA). The EA includes for antenna towers and
satellite earth stations:

(a) A description of the facilities, as well as supporting
structures and appurtenances, and a description of the site, as
well as the surrounding area and uses. If high intensity white
lighting is proposed or utilized within a residential area, the
EA must also address the impact of this lighting upon the
residents.

(b) A statement as to the zoning classification of the site, and
communications with, or proceedings before and
determinations (if any) made by, zoning, planning,
environmental or other local, state or federal authorities on
matters relating to environmental effect.

(c) A statement as to whether construction of the facilities
has been a source of controversy on environmental grounds
in the local community.

(d) A discussion of environmental and other considerations
which led to the selection of the particular site and, if
relevant, the particular facility; the nature and extent of
alternative sites or facilities which have been or might
reasonably be considered.

The information submitted in the EA shall be factual (not
argumentative or conclusory) and concise with sufficient
detail to explain the environmental consequences and to
enable the Commission, after an independent review of the
EA, to reach a determination concerning the proposal's
environmental impact, if any. The EA shall deal specifically
with any feature of the site which has special environmental
significance (e.g., wilderness area, wildlife preserve, natural
migratory paths for birds and other wildlife, and sites of
historic, architectural or archeological value). In the case of

historically significant sites, it shall specify the effect of the
facilities on any district, site, building, structure or object
listed in the National Register of Historic Places, 39 Fed. Reg.
6402 (February 19, 1974). It shall also detail any substantial
change in the character of the land utilized (e.g.,
deforestation, water diversion, wetland fill, or other extensive
change of surface features). In the case of wilderness areas,
wildlife preserves, or other like areas, the statement shall
discuss the effect of any continuing pattern of human
intrusion into the area (e.g., necessitated by the operation and
maintenance of the facilities).

The EA shall also be accompanied with evidence of site
approval which has been obtained from local or federal land
use authorities.

To the extent that such information is submitted in another
part of the application, it need not be duplicated in the EA,
but adequate cross-reference to such information shall be
supplied.

An EA need not be submitted to the Commission if another
agency of the Federal Government has assumed
responsibility: (a) for determining whether the facilities in
question will have a significant effect on the quality of the
human environment and, (b) if it will affect the environment,
for invoking the environmental impact statement process.

SECTION III - QUESTION-BY-QUESTION GUIDELINES

THIS SECTION MUST BE COMPLETED AND
SUBMITTED ONLY BY APPLICANTS FOR
AM, FM OR TV BROADCAST STATIONS.

Question 1(a). Licensees of noncommercial educational and
commercial radio and television broadcast stations are
required by Commission regulation (47 C.F.R. Section
73.2080) to afford equal employment opportunity to all
qualified persons and to refrain from discriminating in
employment and related benefits on the basis of race, color,
religion, national origin or sex. In conjunction therewith,
every station with five or more full-time employees must file
an employment report (FCC Form 395-B) on or before May
31 of each year, identifying the station's staff by gender, race,
color and/or national origin in each of nine major job
categories. See 47 C.F.R. Section 73.3612.

In addition, all AM, FM and TV stations must file an original
and one copy of an Equal Employment Opportunity Report
(FCC Form 396) with their renewal application. This EEO
form is required of all such licensees even where they do not
employ five or more full-time employees or where there are
less than 5% minorities in the labor force (however, in such
cases you need only complete the first 2 pages of the EEO
form).

Question 1(b). Each noncommercial educational broadcast
station licensee is required to submit a current and complete
ownership report (FCC Form 323-E) with its station's renewal

application. See 47 C.F.R. Section 73.3615(d). In such
cases, the question should be answered affirmatively.
However, if the Form 323-E submitted with the station's last
renewal application is "up-to-date" and has not been
amended, a new ownership report need not be filed with the
current renewal application. The applicant should then
answer the question negatively and supply the filing date of
that report and the call letters of the station for which it was
submitted. An "up-to-date" Form 323-E ownership report is
one that is current for each question on that report.

A commercial broadcast station licensee is required to submit
a current and complete ownership report (FCC Form 323)
once each year on the anniversary of the date that its license
renewal application is required to be filed. See 47 C.F.R.
Section 73.3615(a). Licensees of multiple commercial
broadcast stations with different renewal anniversary filing
dates may elect a single date to submit information, but the
ownership reports may not be submitted more than one year
apart. If no changes have occurred, the licensee may submit
a written certification to that fact, instead of filing a new Form
323 each year. In addition, where the licensee is a
partnership composed entirely of natural persons, the annual
reporting requirement does not apply. Similarly, sole
proprietorships are exempt from the requirement to file
annually.

All commercial broadcast station licensees that are not
exempt from the annual reporting program are required to file
Form 323 SEPARATELY from their renewal applications. The
annual ownership report (Form 323 or written certification),
accompanied by its requisite fee payment for each station
covered by that report, should be sent to the U.S. Treasury
lockbox bank at the appropriate address and in the manner
specified in the "Mass Media Services Fee Filing Guide."
Additional information regarding the submission of this report
is set forth in the Commission's Public Notice of June 6,
1990, entitled "Broadcast Annual Ownership Report."

Question 2. A licensee must maintain certain documents
pertaining to its station in a file which is usually kept at the
station's main studio or other accessible place in the
community of license. The file must be available for
inspection by anyone during regular business hours. The
documents to be maintained generally include applications
for a construction permit and for license renewal, assignment
or transfer of control; ownership and employment reports;
and quarterly lists of the community issues most significantly
addressed by the station's programming during the preceding
three months. In addition, commercial television licensees
only are required to maintain and make available to the
public certain records regarding children's programming and
the amount of commercial matter aired during the station's
broadcast of children's programming. A complete listing of
the required documents and their mandatory retention
periods is set forth in 47 C.F.R. Sections 73.3526 and
73.3527. Applicants who have not so maintained their file
should provide an exhibit identifying the items that are
missing/late filed, and identifying steps taken to reconstruct
missing information, and to prevent such problems in the
future.

Question 3. This question should be completed only by a
commercial radio or television renewal applicant. Licensees
for these stations should note that anytime it finds it necessary
to cease broadcasting it must notify the Commission's
Washington, D.C. office, by letter, not later than the 10th day
of discontinued operation. Further, if a licensee finds it
necessary to cease broadcasting in excess of 30 days, it must,
no later than the 30th day of the station being silent, submit
a letter request (no filing fee is required) to the Commission's
Washington, D.C. office for temporary authority to remain
silent. The request must include the date the station ceased
broadcasting; a detailed explanation of the reasons why it
was necessary to take the station off the air; efforts being
made to restore service; and the date by which resumption of
operation is anticipated. The request must also include a
certification relating to Section 5301 of the Anti-Drug Abuse
Act of 1988 (See, as an example, Section V, Certification (1),
of this Form). Extensions of temporary authority to remain
silent must be timely requested if station operations do not
resume within the time given. Licensees must notify the
Commission's Washington, D.C. office, by letter, once
operations have resumed, giving the date that operations
resumed. See 47 C.F.R. Sections 73.1740 and 73.1750.

Question 4. This question should be completed by
commercial TV applicants only. Programming directed to the
educational and informational needs of children is an
identifiable unit of program material that is not a commercial
or promotional announcement, that is originally produced
and broadcast for an audience of children 16 years of age
and under, and that furthers the positive development of the
child in any respect, including, but not limited to, the child's
cognitive/intellectual or emotional/social needs.

Questions 4(b) and (c). Commercial television licensees must
limit the amount of commercial matter in "children's
programming", which is defined for this purpose as
programming originally produced and broadcast primarily for
an audience of children 12 years of age and under. The
children's programming commercial limitations are no more
than 12 minutes of commercial matter per hour on weekdays
and no more than 10.5 minutes of commercials on weekends.
The commercial limits also apply pro rata to children's
programs which are 5 minutes or more and which are not
part of a longer block of children's programming. There are
no restrictions on how commercials within the limits are
configured within an hour's block of children's programming,
i.e., it is not necessary to prorate the commercial limits for
separate children's programs within the hour.

                SECTION IV - QUESTION-BY-QUESTION GUIDELINES

THIS SECTION MUST BE COMPLETED AND
SUBMITTED ONLY BY APPLICANTS FOR
FM OR TV TRANSLATOR OR LPTV BROADCAST
STATION.

Question 1. An FM or TV translator or LPTV station is
expected to provide continuous service except where causes
beyond its control warrant interruption. Where causes

beyond the control of the licensee make it impossible to
continue operation, the station may discontinue operation for
a period of 30 days without further authority from the FCC.
However, notification of the discontinuance must be sent to
the FCC in Washington, D.C. no later than 10 days after the
discontinued operation. (See Section III, Question 3 of these
Instructions for procedures for requesting temporary authority
to remain silent if the licensee finds it necessary to cease
transmitting for more than 30 days.) Failure to operate for a
period of 30 days or more, except for causes beyond the
control of the licensee, shall be deemed evidence of
discontinuation of operation and the license of the translator
or LPTV station may be cancelled at the discretion of the
FCC.   See   47 C.F.R. Sections 74.763 and 74.1263

Questions 2 and 3.   Section 325(a) of the Communications
Act of 1934, as amended, prohibits the rebroadcast of the
programs of a broadcast station without the express authority
of the originating station. Where the renewal applicant is not
the licensee of the originating station, written authority must
be obtained prior to any rebroadcasting. Also, where the
licensee has changed the station being rebroadcast, written
notification must be made to the Commission in accordance
with 47 C.F.R. Section 74.784 or 74.1251.

Question 4. This question should be answered by licensees
of Low Power TV broadcast stations only. Licensees of Low
Power TV broadcast stations are required by 47 C.F.R.
Section 73.2080 to afford equal employment opportunity to
all qualified persons and to refrain from discriminating in
employment and related benefits on the basis of race, color,
religion, national origin or sex. In conjunction with these
provisions, every station with five or more full-time
employees must file an employment report on or before May
31 of each year, identifying the station's staff by gender, race,
color and/or national origin in each of nine major job
categories. See 47 C.F.R. Section 73.3612.

In addition, LPTV stations must file an original and one copy
of an Equal Employment Opportunity Report (FCC Form 396)
with their renewal application. This EEO form is required of
all such licensees even where they do not employ five or
more full-time employees or where there are less than 5%
minorities in the labor force (however, in such cases you
need only complete the first 2 pages of the EEO form).

Question 5(a). (FM TRANSLATOR APPLICANTS ONLY) The
provisions of 47 C.F.R. Section 74.1232(d) provide that an
authorization for an other area FM translator (i.e., FM
translator station whose coverage contour extends beyond
the protected contour of the commercial primary station) will
not be granted to the licensee of a commercial FM radio
broadcast station, or to any person or entity having any
interest or connection with a primary FM station. For the
purposes of this rule, interested and connected parties extend
to group owners, corporate parents, shareholders, officers,
directors, employees, general and limited partners, family
members and business associates.

Question 5(b). The provisions of 47 C.F.R. Section
74.1232(e) provide that an authorization for an other area FM

translator (i.e., FM translator station whose coverage contour extends beyond the protected contour of the commercial primary station) shall not receive any support, before, during or after construction, either directly or indirectly, from the commercial primary FM radio broadcast station, or from any person or entity having any interest or connection with the primary FM station. For the purposes of this rule, interested and connected parties extend to group owners, corporate parents, shareholders, officers, directors, employees, general and limited partners, family members and business associates.

Federal Communications Commission
Washington, D. C. 20554

—4—

And Now the News

Programming for the 'Hood

We concluded that something had to be done to preserve
local broadcasting.

—John Kompas

LPTV Programming Plan

LPTV began with dual programming purposes; the minds of some entrepreneurs were diametrically opposite to those of others. As a result of the
metamorphosis of translators into stations, LPTV was considered by some
to be merely a formalized extension of existing distant signals. To others,
the new low-power stations were designed to provide a special narrow-casting
service to audiences that were deemed not to have been adequately served
by the full-power television stations. Some critics and practitioners believed
that LPTV should follow the approach taken by some of the early cable
networks, providing special programming for targeted audiences, in this
case specific communities and subgroups within those communities. It was
also believed that such an approach would provide an excellent opportunity
for direct community involvement in the programming of the LPTV station.

While about 30 percent of LPTV licensees still use their stations for the
extension of distant signals or for the carriage of general programming not
necessarily oriented to specified groups within the given community, the
majority of LPTV operations do serve as alternative sources of video materials for their viewing areas. Many of the stations are designed to reach

minority racial or ethnic groups. Some stations are aimed at political, philo-sophical, social, or religious interest groups. Most LPTV stations do offer an alternative to the "lowest common denominator" fare offered by most full-power TV stations, especially those affiliated or owned by a major network. They provide programming not deemed commercially advantageous by full power stations, programming aimed at small interest groups in a circum-scribed community. (This is not to suggest that a commercial approach has not been taken by some low-power outlets. For example, in 1993 Gregory and Ernest Schimizzi launched TV-23 in Southampton, New York, offering advertiser airtime.) Audiences are sometimes clearly defined, such as a spe-cific religious sect or occupational group (for example, workers in an indus-trial plant that is the basis for the economy of the community), or they may be amorphous, held together only by a general interest (for example, as parents of elementary and secondary school students in the town). The key term, however, is "narrow-casting," or "targeted audiences."

Getting Local

As discussed in chapter 2, the mission of many LPTV outlets is to offer a locally oriented programming schedule. More than half of the LPTVs on the air do so (63 percent, according to a 1994 study by Mark Banks). Perhaps no more obvious an example of this is station RFD [rural free delivery]-TV in Omaha, Nebraska, which markets itself as "all-rural TV." More than half of LPTVs with a local orientation concentrate on religious programs with a local flavor. Several religious groups, most notably Protes-tant fundamentalist organizations, own multiple stations, with Trinity Broadcasting, for example, the licensee of more than sixty LPTVs. About one-third of the LPTV stations have their signals picked up and distributed by local cable companies; these LPTVs tend to produce more local pro-gramming than others. Local news, politics, and public affairs are staples in community coverage.

One consultant to the LPTV industry, John Kompas, states:

> Rather than looking for the lowest common denominator, which is what full-power stations that cover large areas have to do, LPTVs respond to the local needs of the communities they serve—which really amounts to a niche market.[1]

Explaining why there is no "typical" LPTV programming, Kompas adds:

> Missions vary widely, from spreading the gospel to delivering off campus educational programming. But one thing most LPTVs have in common is a local programming focus.[2]

This local focus is based in practicality as well as altruism and community-mindedness. The sheer density of the competition, especially in metropolitan areas, provides a compelling reason for LPTV operators to target those traditionally ignored by mainstream electronic media programming schedules. In an interview in *Broadcasting,* Oak Media's Craig Schneider "urged LPTV operators to pay special attention to marketing their programming, which he said ought to consider local elements"[3] in light of the increasing presence of cable and other broadcast media. Taking this suggestion to heart, several LPTV stations have invested themselves heavily in the presentation of what has been called "community television," and by some—with less than friendly views about low-power television—"Flea-TV."

For instance, Akron, Ohio, was due to get its first all-local television station as this book was being written. Slated to begin in the fall of 1998 was an LPTV outlet run by Raymond Burgess, which planned to devote its entire broadcast schedule to information related to one of the Buckeye State's northernmost cities. Not far to the east, another Great Lakes city, Buffalo, New York, has been served by local television since the late 1980s. Channel 58's license is held by consumer crusader Ralph Nader, who put the station on the air with the purpose of engaging the average citizen in the media process.

> [Nader] calls [Channel 58] community television, and viewers see such varied fare as regular broad-casts of the Buffalo Common Council, the Board of Education and the Erie County Legislature, university lectures and international programs. . . . Channel 58 is also the only television station in Buffalo that still offers Mayor James D. Griffin a regular spot. Mr. Griffin has had a stormy relationship with the news media in Buffalo, and has declined to do regular interviews with other stations.[4]

In Ashland, Kentucky, some 300 miles south of the two Lake Erie industrial cities just mentioned, low power station WCB-TV also dedicates itself to the interests and needs of the "town's folk," says station manager Bob Gillum. "Our call letters stand for 'We're Community Broadcasting.'"[5] According to Gillum, his station will serve the public "around the clock with down-to-earth programming very much like that on most Eastern Kentucky radio stations—including obituaries and free ads."[6]

Today, as has been the case since LPTV's inception, localism is at the heart of the mission statements of most LPTV stations. This has been its rallying call as the medium has come under attack by countless broadcast and cable industry groups that would rather see "Flea-TV" scratched out of existence.

The Programming Mix

Whatever the process or approach, the key for most LPTV stations is to show so-called original programming; that is, programming at least somewhat different from what viewers can obtain from their full-power stations' signals. Ideally, that means programming that the target audience literally cannot find on any other channel. Some LPTVs, for example, concentrate on clarifying the mysteries of the stock market for the average untutored investor; some emphasize local sports, such as the football games of the community's high school or the town's Little League baseball games; many stations in rural areas replicate what early radio stations did and present information to farmers, such as crop and weather reports and descriptions of new techniques and products for more efficient farming.

Some LPTV stations orient much of their programming to disability groups, for example, showing people with a given handicap how to overcome the obstacles they encounter in everyday society. Some stations do local infomercials. They are similar to the shopping channels in large markets, but oriented to local audience purchasing habits and to local products and establishments. Many stations also pick up the regional or national home shopping channels. Music videos are an important item if younger viewers are to be attracted to LPTV. A number of LPTV stations put on local versions of music videos or video music, nineties versions of the old Dick Clark show in the early days of TV in Philadelphia. Several dozen rural UHF LPTV operations also offer viewers subscriber services, such as CNN, TBS, ESPN, HBO, and pay-per-view.

Indeed, LPTV programming is eclectic if it is anything at all. In an age of boutique programming and narrowcasting, LPTV is an exemplar. Anyone who doubts this needs simply to survey the medium's programming schedules. Imagine a television station devoted to the hearing impaired, and you have an LPTVoperation. It is called the Silent Network, and it beams much of its signal to the hearing impaired in the Los Angeles area. Cartoons in Polish, soaps in Spanish (four LPTVs target Hispanics in the Orlando area alone), and news broadcasts in Chinese; again you have low-power television. Add programming in Korean, Romanian, and Vietnamese, and you are just beginning to scratch the surface of LPTV's programming services to the nation's foreign and ethnic populations. The all-news format has found a place at some LPTV stations. One is KBI-TV in San Francisco, which offers Bay Area viewers "a satellite-delivered news service operated by Minneapolis-based Conus Communications."[7] As stated above, music television has also found a home at certain LPTV outlets. Programs such as *USA Music Today* became available to low power audiences around the country in the early 1990s.

Despite the apparent diversity offered by LPTV channels around the country, some critics of the medium feel that it has failed to live up to programming expectations and predictions. In 1990 the *Los Angeles Times* concluded that the jury was still out on low-power television's contribution. Reported the newspaper, "There is little original or locally produced programming on most . . . LPTVs." The same issue of the newspaper also went on to observe that, "Despite reduced start-up costs, less government regulation, and the large number of the estimated 4,500 new licenses available, the industry says minority ownership of privately operated LPTVs is less than 10 [percent]—which still dwarfs minority ownership of other TV media."[8]

Public perceptions of LPTV programming on the part of those who are not members of the targeted audiences of LPTV and never or almost never watch an LPTV station are not very favorable. The general public thinks of LPTV programming, if they have heard of it at all, as boring or innocuous or weak. In *The New Television Technologies,* Lynne Gross states that low-power television "doesn't have much respect. Part of this is due to its name. Low power implies just that—weakness."[9] To the extent that LPTV programming does not receive the promotion and the press attention of full-power station programming; to the degree that it does not have the stars nor the big-budget excitement of full-power TV programming; and because LPTV stations are forced by economics to buy the less expensive and therefore usually older or more mundane syndicated series and films, it is understandable that it would be considered weak or second-class by most non-LPTV viewers.

As noted above, the single most pervasive kind of fare on LPTV stations is religious programming. In addition to local programs, such as church services, educational and proselytizing lectures by local clergy, and religious discussion groups, LPTVs are able to use regional and national syndicated religious shows and even live feeds. For example, a popular LPTV program is *The 700 Club*, which is principally seen on Jerry Falwell's Family Channel cable network. Several religious organizations employ satellites to down-link their programs to LPTV stations.

Political groups, especially those with a conservative agenda, have found the low-power medium useful in getting their messages across to the public. For instance, in the 1980s, the Republican National Committee launched GOP-TV, down-linking a weekly hour-long program to stations around the country. Later the far right also found the medium particularly useful to get their extremist views onto the airwaves.

Because a number of LPTVs are operated by educational institutions, principally colleges and universities, there is a fair amount of formal as well as informal educational programming on LPTV. In some instances univerity classes are offered for credit. In other instances special events, such as speakers, academic lectures, recitals, plays, roundtable discussions, and similar campus happenings, are presented.

Some LPTV stations provide time for community access, similarly to the community channels on many of the cable systems throughout the country. The programming on the LPTV community access channels is mostly eclectic, representing about as many different interests as there are producers. Some of these programs are amateurish; others are of high quality, produced by professionals who wish to test their new works in a relatively noncritical setting, similar to the trying out of Broadway plays in regional theaters. In some cases the programs submitted by independent producers are good enough to be shown as part of the regular schedule, prime-time offerings of the LPTV station.

Again, ethnic programming and programming for people of color is another key type of LPTV offering. Such programming is not only usually produced locally, involving representatives from the target audiences, but is often supported and distributed on state, regional, and even national levels. When LPTV first began to grow, several groups believed that it offered a special opportunity for such programming, granting an opportunity traditionally denied by TV networks and most TV stations. A group called Community Television Network provided programs oriented to African-American audiences. In Washington, D.C., a group of African-Americans who had formerly been members of the FCC staff sought to develop an LPTV network that would serve racial minorities. In New York an applicant representing the city's Chinese population sought an LPTV channel for the purpose of airing Chinese-interest and -language programming.

A further source of programming is vested interest or special interest organizations and similar entities. For example, in some areas resorts provide their local LPTV stations with information about their services for tourists and potential customers; Chambers of Commerce seek to air promotional information about their cities or regions; in fact, at one time, on the national level, the U.S. Chamber of Commerce provided LPTV stations with a regular series entitled *Ask Washington*.

Joining the Syndicate

Local programming on a continuing basis becomes expensive, too much so for many LPTV stations, which operate either as non-profits or with limited advertising income, given the limited audiences these stations reach. Therefore, many LPTVs, even those dedicated to serving narrow local needs, must frequently fill their schedules with syndicated shows and films. Many of them, however, are very careful in their selection of movies and syndicated programs, making as certain as possible that the contents of these offerings are oriented to their local audiences' needs and interests. Some of the stations add syndicated shows and movies of a general nature so that they may reach out to a wider audience in order to develop a larger base for potential advertisers.

Because most full-power stations are affiliated with or owned by a national network or are part of a group-owned system, their programming is frequently determined in large part by forces outside of their geographical areas of service. LPTV stations generally, however, have much more leeway in determining their programming than do full-power TV stations, even those that are group-owned or are affiliated with a national, cable, or low-power network. They also generally have more leeway as to the sources of their programming, which can be through satellite, syndication, microwave, tape, or local production. Most LPTV stations may offer any mix they choose of live programming and prerecorded programming. Some LPTV stations offer specialized subscription programming, requiring viewers to purchase descrambling equipment from the station to decode the signal at their sets.

Syndicated programs can be expensive when bought individually by each LPTV station. Buying a package for multiple use by many stations reduces costs. LPTV group owners do this, in the same way that cable MSOs (multiple system owners) do for cable network programs. The Community Broadcasters Association (CBA) is an organization of some 600 television stations with a cooperative arrangement to purchase syndicated programs for its member stations. One bargaining point used by the CBA is that in many areas of the country the LPTV station is the only "live" station in a given community; all other stations are received through cable, satellite, or off-the-air if their transmitters are not too distant. This gives the syndicator a local outlet for his or her product, distribution that otherwise might not be available.

Some syndicators develop special relationships with and rates for LPTV stations at the beginning of the low-power service. Viacom, for example, continues to offer LPTVs special packages, ranging from feature films to special programs that meet an individual LPTV station's targeted audience's particular interests, such as game shows or country music specials. In more recent years other major syndicators such as Lorimar Productions, Turner Entertainment Network, Republic Pictures, and 20th Century Fox have provided special deals for LPTV stations.

The bottom line, relating to service or profit, drives LPTV syndicated selections as much as it does full-power stations. Local nonprofit community stations can seek appropriate specialized programs without special attention to the need to reach a broad audience. Religious LPTVs fall especially in that category, particularly in strong religious areas such as the "Bible Belt." Most stations that are dependent on advertising for survival (and, they hope, profit) seek broad-based first-run syndicated programs or off-network reruns that have performer names and program name recognition strong enough to draw the largest possible audience.

Stations that are group-owned frequently receive syndicated programming through the group's purchase arrangements with producers and distributors. This, of course, obviates one of the principal programming contributions of LPTV station: serving local needs. However, since the cost of purchasing satellite or syndicated programs is much less than that of producing programs locally, syndication is likely to increase—unless station incomes increase to the point where they decide they can afford to serve the public interest as their primary responsibility (Figure 4.1).

Those LPTV operations that do dedicate themselves to local needs and service find a special excitement and satisfaction in what they do. In an interview with researcher Katie Siska, Ron Bourque, director of an LPTV station in Pelham, New Hampshire, stated: "The good thing about local television is that it expands every year. There is always a new trend. This year it was computers, last year it was Karate. They were both geared toward kids and they were both very successful programs."[10]

Casting the Net

In the early days of LPTV, niche or specialty networks (such as the Financial News Network and the Satellite Program Network) recognized the potential of the newest video medium for expanding their audience base and thus made their programming services available to this unique type of station. Likewise, over the years, more and more LPTV stations became affiliates of national TV networks, especially in areas where no cable service or full-power stations were available. Some LPTV stations are affiliated with FOX, which, as the fourth-place major network, made special efforts to obtain affiliates, even LPTVs, in areas where the other stations were already affiliated with the three front-running networks, ABC, CBS, and NBC. UPN and WB, as the two newest national networks attempting to build a respectable base of affiliates, have worked out agreements with a number of LPTV stations and with some LPTV group owners, since these LPTVs in some cases are the only stations in many markets not affiliated with one of the top four networks. In 1989 there was only one LPTV affiliated with a national real-time network, Oregon's Metrocom with FOX.

Figure 4.1. Montana LPTV Station Program Schedule. SKC Public Television, April 16—22. Courtesy SKC-TV

Time	Sunday 16	Monday 17	Tuesday 18	Wednesday 19	Thursday 20	Friday 21	Saturday 22
6:45	Barney & Friends (7:30)	Homestretch & Business	Homestretch & Business	Homestretch & Business	Homestretch & Business	Homestretch & Business	T. Brown's Journal (7:30)
8:00	The Puzzle Place	Lamb Chop	Lamb Chop	Out of Ireland	Across Indiana	Outdoor Wisconsin	Tennessee Crossroads
8:30	Reading Rainbow	Reading Rainbow	Florida File	Today's Japan	Today's Japan	Today's Japan	Embroidery Studio
9:00	Texas Parks & Wildlife	Mr. Rogers	Today's Japan	Mr. Rogers	Mr. Rogers	Mr. Rogers	Technopolitics
9:30	Quilting for the '90's	Shining Time Station	Mr. Rogers	Shining Time Station	Shining Time Station	Shining Time Station	Ciao Italia
10:00	The Art of Sewing	Lamb Chop	Shining Time Station	Lamb Chop	Lamb Chop	Lamb Chop	Julia Child-Cooking
10:30	Gourmet Cooking	Barney & Friends	Lamb Chop	Barney & Friends	Barney & Friends	Barney & Friends	The Victory Garden
11:00	The New Garden	Masterpiece Theatre	Barney & Friends	The Secret of Life	Charlie Rose	Mystery! Rumpole VII	Frugal Gourmet
11:30	World:Comm	Martin Chuzzlewit	Charlie Rose	Mouse...Golden Egg		Miscarriage of Justice	This Old House
12:00	World of Collector Cars	Barney & Friends	Barney & Friends	Barney & Friends	Barney & Friends	Barney & Friends	TBA
12:30	Quilt in a Day	The Puzzle Place	Extension Focus	The Puzzle Place	Extension Focus	The Puzzle Place	Hometime
1:00	American Vacations	Mr. Rogers	The Puzzle Place	Mr. Rogers	Mr. Rogers	Mr. Rogers	Journal
1:30	American Vacations	Sesame Street	Mr. Rogers	Sesame Street	Sesame Street	Sesame Street	The Everyday Gourmet
2:00	Strip Quilting w/Kaye W.		Sesame Street				Inside the Law
2:30	Sewing Connection	Ghostwriter	Ghostwriter	Ghostwriter	Ghostwriter	To the Contrary	Small Business Today
3:00	The Perfect Palette	Carmen Sandiego	Carmen Sandiego	Carmen Sandiego	Carmen Sandiego	Carmen Sandiego	Mystery! Rumpole VII
3:30	The Magic School Bus	Bill Nye the Science Guy	Bill Nye the Science Guy	Bill Nye the Science Guy	Bill Nye the Science Guy	Bill Nye the Science Guy	Miscarriage of Justice
4:00	Firing Line	Masterpiece Theatre	Charlie Rose	The Secret of Life	Charlie Rose	Mr. Rogers	In the Mix
4:30	Creative Living	Martin Chuzzlewit		Mouse...Golden Egg		Mystery! Rumpole VII	Media Watch
5:00	The Ghostwriter Hour	MacNeil/Lehrer	MacNeil/Lehrer	MacNeil/Lehrer	MacNeil/Lehrer	Miscarriage of Justice	McCuiston
5:30		News Hour	News Hour	News Hour	News Hour	McLaughlin Group	Successful Women
6:00	Wild America	Heartbeat Alaska	America's Children	Grand Entry	Ronan Sports Week	Wash Week in Review	Austin City Limits
6:30	The Frugal Gourmet	Valley Viewpoint	Montana Serenade	Denver Mar. Pow-wow	Mission High Chronicle	Wall Street Week	Mark Cohn/Leo Kottke
7:00	National Arts	MacNeil/Lehrer	MacNeil/Lehrer	MacNeil/Lehrer	MacNeil/Lehrer	MacNeil/Lehrer	Mystery! Rumpole VII
7:30	Wild America	News Hour	NewsHour	NewsHour	NewsHour	NewsHour	Miscarriage of Justice
8:00	Nature	Baseball	The Secret of Life	The Human Quest	Mystery! Rumpole VII	...Talking with	Austin City Limits
8:30	Nomads of the Wind	Our Game	Mouse...Golden Egg	Consciousness	Miscarriage of Justice	David Frost	Mark Cohn/Leo Kottke
9:00	Masterpiece Theatre	Eyewitness: Reptile	The Human Quest	The Way of Science	Pole to Pole	Charlie Rose	Thinking Allowed
9:30	Martin Chuzzlewit	Local Messages	Nature of Human Nature		Mediterranean Maze		Stained Glass
10:00	Mystery! Rumpole VII	D. Attenborough's World	The Social Brain	Great Performances	I'll Fly Away	The Nobel Legacy	Ciao Italia
10:30	Children of the Devil		Mouse...Golden Egg	Talking with	Realpolitik	Mr. Jacobs	Julia Child-Cooking
11:00	Masterpiece Theatre		The Secret of Life		Mystery! Rumpole VII	...Talking with	The Victory Garden
11:30	Martin Chuzzlewit		Mouse...Golden Egg	The Frugal Gourmet	Miscarriage of Justice	David Frost	Frugal Gourmet
12:00	Mystery! Rumpole VII	Charlie Rose	Charlie Rose	Charlie Rose	Charlie Rose	Charlie Rose	This Old House
12:30	Children of the Devil						New Yankee Workshop

In the 1990s more and more LPTV stations were being approached by national networks—that is, LPTVs that did not have full-power affiliates or were not carried by cable systems—that decided to use low-power stations, at least on a temporary basis, to try to fill in market gaps throughout the country. Newer, fledgling networks were, understandably, most interested in such affiliations. In 1995 UPN bought four low-power stations as key affiliates. The new WB network was also sanguine about LPTV. Steve Coe, writing in *Broadcasting and Cable* magazine, quoted a WB official as follows: "I certainly wouldn't minimize the importance of low-power stations. . . . Remember, some time ago we wrote off UHF stations and look where they are now." In 1995 WB contracted with four LPTV stations to be its affiliates; in Baltimore (a university-owned station), Baton Rouge, Cincinnati, and Yakima, Washington. In one market in Arkansas the FOX network established affiliations with a group-owned conglomerate of seven LPTV stations.

Whether the initial need for LPTV affiliates by new networks will continue is problematical. Whether it will be a boon to LPTVs or only a passing opportunity also remains to be seen. With the distribution landscape changing from day to day, some of these networks may find more effective means for distributing their products. Network contracts with LPTVs are usually for short terms, with options for renewal and the opportunity not to renew if a full-power station in that market becomes available for affiliation. For example, Steve Coe also quoted FOX's senior vice-president for distribution, Adam Ware: "Low-power stations are not a long-term strategy for us. They serve as a temporary situation for us until regular stations become available . . . I don't want to sell them out . . . [they] have done a terrific job. But it's a means to an end for us."[11]

Although cable systems have fought the growth of LPTV stations, economics have dictated, in some instances, cable-LPTV affiliation. In 1994 the largest cable MSO (multiple system owner) in the United States, Tele-Communication, Inc. (TCI), bought the Main Street Television Network, a low-power TV group. The arrangement was made by a TCI subgroup, Liberty Sports, with the new network called America One. Rich Brown, writing in *Broadcasting and Cable* magazine, quoted America One's vice-president, Jay Feingold: "the main purpose behind launching America One was to deliver Liberty Sports programming to 'white areas' not served by Liberty's regional sports cable networks."[12]

Perhaps more long-lasting will be the networks established especially to service LPTV. However, many excellent ideas early in the history of LPTV went by the boards because they were premature for a still fledgling industry without a large enough station and viewer base. One network that had the right idea, but entered the market too early for there to be sufficient number of LPTV stations on the air to be successful and eventually ceased operations, was the American Television Network. This network offered basic staple programming designed to attract a general audience: films, cartoons, and game shows. Another early attempt was an operation set up nationally by Acrodyne, which offered packages of identical programs to LPTVs to be broadcast at the same time. In a sense, then, the participating LPTV stations were operating as if they belonged to a national real-time network.

Microband, which operated MMDS (multi-channel multi-point distribution system, or, as it is more popularly called, wireless cable) stations, at one time planned to offer interactive services through LPTV, including public opinion surveys and home shopping from video catalogues. Microband went out of business in the early 1990s. An offshoot of this plan was proposed by the Channel America Television Network, which offered LPTV stations viewer participation game shows. Channel America began offering programming to low power stations in 1988 and soon had eighty-eight affiliates. The network also provided member LPTVs with vintage movies, classic sitcoms (*Hazel* and *Gidget*) and dramas (*Matt Helm*), and talk shows. The International Television Network similarly offered alternative popular fare, including MTV-type locally oriented programs.

One of the more successful and innovative networks is the LPTV Association, located in Panama City Beach, Florida. The Association has a number of owned and operated LPTV stations (O-and-Os) as well as LPTV and even full-power TV affiliates. The association calls its programming "tourist television." It provides information for tourists on a variety of topics, ranging from accommodations, restaurants, car rentals, and tourist attractions to area hospitals, first aid, and religious services. One 24–hour-a-day program is *Food for Thought*, a listing of restaurants; another is *Fun & Sun*, which airs between 10 A.M. and 2 P.M. and provides information on shopping, events, recreation such as scuba diving, and similar activities. The video presentations are usually in segments of 15 seconds to 15 minutes, paid for by the establishment or service being shown. One example of a regular client is the Captain Anderson restaurant chain, which presents a 10–minute video on its operations, including its menu, the preparation of its food, its wine and liquor list, and the type of entertainment available to its guests.

The network's affiliates can be seen by anyone within range of the stations' signals and through cable systems in their areas of service; special arrangements have been made for all of the association's stations to be carried by cable, for which the association pays an appropriate fee, in some cases a substantial one. Virtually every hotel within reach of the LPTV signals or serviced by the cable systems carries these programs. In the mid-1990s the LPTV Association service areas included Atlanta, Georgia; Duston–Fort Walton, Key West, and Panama City Beach, Florida; Myrtle Beach and Hilton Head, South Carolina; and New Orleans, Louisiana. The Association has estimated that its programs reach over four million tourists every year.

Regional LPTV networks have been formed around the country with varying degrees of success. A particularly noteworthy example is the network developed by the Wiegel Broadcasting Company. In the early 1990s, the company had seven LPTVs in, and north (Milwaukee) and south (South Bend) of, the Chicago area, with plans to launch an eighth designed to feature ethnic programs in Hindi, Greek, Arabic, Chinese, and a wide assortment of other languages. The station, Channel 23, was slated to broadcast from atop the Sears Tower with the potential for reaching over six million viewers. The company's president, Howard Shapiro, indicated in a September 14, 1992 interview in *Mediaweek* that he had plans to expand his LPTV network holdings.

Meanwhile, religious networks, some regional, are among the most successful in LPTV-land. The American Christian Television System, as early as 1981—even before LPTV was officially authorized—was transmitting religious programming to several hundred stations. Other special interest networks with regional orientations surfaced as well. For example, in the early days of LPTV the United Auto Workers union announced plans to form a network of several stations in various areas of the country designed to promote its agenda to the viewing public.

While the affiliation process and structure is similar between networks and full-power or low-power stations, some financial differences exist. In some cases, as with the principal national networks and their full power affiliates, the stations are given some compensation from the network to carry its programs. In other cases, however, the advertising revenue is so low for the network, as with the limited audiences of LPTV coverage, that the station pays a fee for the programming, earning its income through local ads, or, as is increasingly the case, taking the programming on a barter basis; that is, carrying the programs with no compensation and sharing the "avails"—or advertising spots— with the distributor, whether syndicator or network, or getting the programming for a little cash plus barter.

Program exchange as a means of obtaining and distributing programming is growing for LPTV stations. As noted earlier, some one-third of the country's LPTV stations are carried on local cable systems; the corollary is that a substantial number of LPTVs also carry some local cable channels. Some of the cable networks themselves offer their programs—at a fee, of course—to LPTV stations. The Learning Channel, for example, has licensed its programs to a number of LPTV stations. This arrangement—of cable programs on LPTV—is not only helpful to the LPTV station, by providing it with an additional source of programming, but is of value to the cable system or channel by giving it the possibility of reaching some of the homes that do not subscribe to a cable service.

Si, Hablo LPTV

Foreign language networks are also highly successful, capitalizing on the generally similar interests of a given language group throughout various areas of the country. One key example is SUR, an international network which provides, through satellite feeds, programming from its headquarters in Miami, Florida, to LPTV stations everywhere in the United States. Its most popular offerings include live news broadcasts and soap operas ("novellas") from Central and South American countries, the original or ancestral homelands of the vast majority of its viewers—countries such as Argentina, Columbia, Ecuador, the Dominican Republic, Peru, and Puerto Rico (Figure 4.2).

Spanish-language LPTV stations may well be described as making up a national broadcasting system of their own. By and large the programming on these stations is in formats similar to those of any major TV network. Included are dramas, the extremely popular "novellas" or soap operas, news and sports, special events, films, game shows, music programs (sometimes called salsa MTV), discussions and interviews, talk shows, children's programs, sitcoms—everything one sees on any substantial national network. The only difference is that on these LPTV stations it is all in Spanish (Figure 4.3).

The Spanish-speaking population of the United States is now about 15 percent of the country's 250 million residents and is growing rapidly. Some sociologists predict that in twenty years about one-fourth of Americans will be Latino, with the Spanish language itself widespread. Concomitant with Latino population growth is economic growth. As Latino purchasing power has grown, so has the attention paid to this demographic group by advertisers. Not only are there more commercials aimed at Latino buyers on standard TV stations, but some LPTV Spanish-language stations have become excellent advertising outlets and, therefore, lucrative properties for their owners (Figure 4.4).

While programs oriented toward the Latino population for years straddled the fence between Hispanic culture and North American culture, reflecting the concept of assimilation into the dominant culture, the rise of

Figure 4.2 **Miami LPTV Profile Sheet. Courtesy WJAN-TV**

**TELEARTE
WJAN**

WJAN / CHANNEL 41

Miami's only television station exclusively geared to serve the
majority of the Hispanic Community, filling the void left by the
giant Hispanic Networks, portraying the real needs of the people
in South Florida...

Channel 41 is a quality station that offers spectacular
programming made to order without sparing efforts, the
broadcasting excellence of its programming is further enhanced
by its affiliation with Telearte, South America's largest
production company making Channel 41 the intelligent choice
for South Florida viewers...

Channel 41 programming includes soap operas, dramas,
comedy, variety shows, late night shows and the best in local
and international news. The international resources of CNN, the
world's leader, providing four daily newscasts from thr CNN
International headquarter in Atlanta.

WJAN-Channel 41 is the independent network free to reach,
serve and react by its own rules and regulations, always ready to
feel the beat of our audiences, aimed at the pulse of South
Florida.

Spanish-language LPTV stations dedicated almost exclusively to Latino
viewers has made it possible for LPTV programmers to strengthen the
Hispanic content of their shows. While promoting economic, political, and
social assimilation, but not wanting to destroy a heritage of value for all
Americans, more and more programs are reflecting Hispanic culture, not

only in breadth, but in depth, stressing the values of this culture and inculcating pride in it for the viewers. WCEA in Boston, discussed earlier, states that it is

> committed to promote quality of life and positive values and to present role models and leaders as examples to follow. Our mission is to show them [the audience] that there is hope and opportunity for anyone who is responsible to their family and to the members of our society. We are also committed to divulge, maintain and reinforce our customs and traditions in order to preserve our identity as a group within our society.[13]

A major reason for the increase in both quantity and quality of Spanish-language programming is the development in the United States of two major distribution networks, Telemundo and Univision. While reflecting Anglo formats, the content of their programming is Latino. Through the distribution strengths of these two networks, stations can get Spanish-language copies of popular mainstream shows like *60 Minutes* and *Entertainment Tonight*.

Manuel Martinez-Llorian, as vice-president and general manager of the Telemundo Station Group, explained to researcher Raphaela Logullo in 1996 the mission of his organization:

> The Hispanic community in the United States can relate themselves to our programs, even through we follow the American style in programming. Our main goal is to provide our viewers with a variety of programs that could satisfy every Hispanic man, woman, and child.[14]

As might be expected, Spanish-language LPTV stations are strongest in Florida, and both Telemundo and Univision have their headquarters in Miami.

On a final note regarding ethnic broadcasting, CBA's John Kompas reiterates the medium's commitment to minority viewers. "We're really the only local TV in the United States. This is a strong commitment of our medium, and it's reflected in the fact that 46 percent of LPTV outlets are minority owned."[15]

Figure 4.3 Foreign Language LPTV Station Program Schedule. Courtesy WJAN-TV

TELEARTE 41 WJAN

PROGRAM SCHEDULE
WJAN-TV

051198

	MON	TUE	WED	THU	FRI	SATURDAY	SUNDAY
3:00pm	INFOMERCIAL					INFOMERCIAL	INFOMERCIAL
3:30pm	FLACA ESCOPETA (Children)					Infomecial	Ventanas al Futuro
4:00pm						CINE ARGENTINO CLASICO(Movies)	COMENTARIOS ECONOMICOS
4:30pm	RICO Y PICANTE (International Cooking)						CINE ARTE (Movies)
5:00pm	TODO DULCE (International Bakery)						
5:30pm	CNN NEWS (First Edition)					Show Business	
6:00pm	LOS HEREDEROS DEL PODER (Soap Opera)						En Una Hora
6:30pm							
7:00pm	CNN NEWS (Second Edition)					Mundo Turistico	Corte Tropical
7:30pm	RICOS Y FAMOSOS (Soap Opera)						ZIG ZAG
8:30pm	CNN NEWS (Third Edition)					Noticiero CNN	Panorama Mundial

							Los Casados Felices Game Show
9:00pm	LOS ANGELES NO LLORAN (Soap Opera)						
10:00p	Quo Vadis (Miniserie)	Te Quiero Te Quiero (Comedia Familar)	Que Pasa Ana Margo	Poliladron (Action)	Alta Comedia (Drama)	Las Gatitas De Porcel (Musical Variety)	El Preciodel Poder (Serie dramatica)
11:00p	A OSCURAS PERO ENCENDIDOS					Como ser Feliz en el Matrimonio.	
11:30p					A Oscuras Pero Encendidos	Aqui Brazil	Rompenueces
12:00am	CNN NEWS (Evening Edition)						
12:30am	INFOMERCIAL				Noticiero CNN		
1:00am	INFOMERCIAL						

Figure 4.4 **News Coverage in Spanish as Offered by an LPTV Station.
Courtesy WJAN-TV.**

Appendix 4A: Localism and Low-Power Public Television

Frank H. Tyro

Media/Teleproductions/Public Television, Salish Kootenai College

The history of regulation of broadcasting has been closely tied to two schools of thought as to the forces affecting policy. These two schools basically divide between "market economics" and "social value" ideology. The local service objective is key to the understanding of low-power television and its daughter, low-power public TV. This paper will briefly trace the origins of regulation and of these two perspectives and then apply them to low-power public TV's future.

Several assumptions are made in this examination. First, it is accepted that regulation is necessary for broadcasting to survive and that total market deregulation would lead to a chaotic situation. Second, the assumption is made that localism is desirable. Localism can foster diversity, competition and tolerance. Localism can also foster elitism, racism, and a narrow worldview. However, if given the choice between a melting pot and retention of distinct cultures and views, localism seems more likely to allow for diversity than nationalism. In this paper, localism is equated with local-expression programs presenting discussion of local policy issues, public affairs, cultural expression, and policies that may be unique to geographic areas.

Regulation of Broadcasting

The chaotic situation caused by the lack of regulation of electronic broadcasting in the early 1920s promoted the passage of the Radio Act of 1927. This act was necessitated by interference among radio stations and a decision in *U.S. v. Zenith Corporation* that the Secretary of Commerce lacked authority to assign frequencies or deny licenses for transmission. The famous "public interest, convenience and/or necessity" standard contained in the 1927 act was actually borrowed from the regulation of railroads (Corn-Revere 1993). The Communications Act that followed in 1934, which is the basis of nearly all policy today, was extremely noncommittal as to specifics of regulation, leaving interpretation of this new medium to the Federal Communication Commission and the courts. The Supreme Court was soon called upon to interpret the open-ended approach toward public interest and it stated that the public interest standard was sufficiently precise and a "supple instrument for the exercise of discretion" *(FCC v. Pottsville Broadcasting 1940)*.

The factor underpinning many of the policy decisions since broadcasting began in the 1920s, has been based on the scarcity of frequencies. Historically, it has been felt that the limited number of frequencies and accessibility made it necessary for the government to regulate broadcast more stringently than the press. A factor of major relevance to this paper is the local service objective. This ideal is related to the power to grant licenses in the public interest as well as three other objectives: achievement of an acceptable level of diversity, fulfillment of the public servant role of broadcasting, and maintaining a level of competition. In many situations, these objectives conflict. Noll, Peck, and McGowan (1973) argue that the primacy of local service is how the FCC thinks TV should operate, as an instrument of community. As this paper will show, this ideal is seldom realized. Localism is directly counter to the original television policy in Britain, where the government acts as a distributor of national programming for economic efficiency and social purpose. The FCC's hand was clearly evident in the DuMont decision in the early 1950s. The DuMont Corporation wanted to become the fourth network but needed unused frequencies,which had been assigned to rural areas, reallocated to large metropolitan areas. They argued that their plan would provide more competition and diversity. "In the Commission's view as many communities as possible should have the opportunity of enjoying the advantages that derive from having local outlets that will be responsive to local needs" *(FCC Sixth Report and Order 1952)*. This decision affirmed that the FCC placed increased stock in more local stations than in expanded options in large cities. Our broadcast system is driven by the idea that the identity of states, cities, and towns could be destroyed by a mass communication system with only a national focus.

Local Service Objectives

Localism vests itself in many FCC policies including the restrictions on multiple ownership and preference for owner-managers. It would be incorrect to assume, however, that this support for localism by the FCC has resulted in a TV station for every town. The ideal supported by the FCC has never been fully realized. Programming is dominated by national programs, even on PBS affiliates and LPTV providers. Other than providing local news, weather, and sports, few stations seriously attempt to serve small and diverse populations, let alone really serve as a conduit for local expression. In the Philadelphia area, WYBE provides the highest percentage of programming that could be characterized as local expression in a broadcast outlet; however even it rarely exceeds 10 percent. Attempts to force stations to program more local expression have failed as stations simply buy more syndicated programs to fill the non-network hours. The ratings indicate that the majority of viewers will not sacrifice even a small part of national entertainment to be better informed about local issues and concerns.

In a statistical analysis of awards of TV licenses, Noll and colleagues (1973) revealed that in instances in which two or more applicants vied for the same assignment, applicants promising more local programming were actually less likely to be granted a license. The study also noted that an application by local residents was 25 percent less likely to be granted than a competing application by an applicant with no local connections. The one variable that improved chances of success in a comparative hearing was an offer of more programming hours than the number offered by another applicant. A rational explanation of this ostensibly contrary behavior is that economic reality works against localism.

It is also interesting to note a content analysis study by Entman (1989) that showed one station devoted more time to banter among news personalities and previews of upcoming stories than to local policy issues. While the study is not representative, several other studies had similar results, indicating that it is a valid concern.

Market Economics and Social Value

Many flip-flops in policy concerning AM and FM radio nonduplication rules as well as financial interest and syndication restrictions and UHF–VHF considerations have been based on economics. Many argue that broadcasting better serves the public when broadcasting is a lucrative business. Although broadcast and cable may not be comparable in many aspects, a case can be made that the imposition of few restrictions on cable did not increase service and diversity, only profits.

The market economics position is probably best described by its central assumption; that analyzing communications policy issues can be most fruitful if problems are viewed through maximization of economic efficiency

(Entman and Wildman 1992). Market economists believe that economic efficiency promotes a vigorous and diverse marketplace of ideas and that nurturing and protecting competition is fundamental to good policy.

Social value theorists see competition as often manifesting undesirable effects for society. The market process itself is often suspect and government intervention potentially beneficial (Mosco 1990). The social-value school sees regulation as essential to broadcast diversity. Competition plays into the lowest-common-denominator approach rather than increasing true diversity of ideas. An example often cited is that of the "fairness doctrine." While it was in effect, it had a chilling effect on presentation of diverse issues because stations did not want to be called to task for not allowing both sides of issues to be presented. It was easier not to present any controversial issues. With the repeal of the "fairness doctrine," this impediment has been withdrawn. However, some argue (Entman 1989) that the shallowness of mass audience taste means more of the same rather than new, challenging ideas.

Low-Power Television

Translators are transmitters that pick up the signal of a TV or FM station and rebroadcast that signal on another frequency. Translators are mainly used to bring service to communities that are hidden from a primary broadcast signal by topography. In the early 1950s translators had been operated illegally to bring TV signals into areas plagued by poor reception of television service in states such as Oregon, Pennsylvania, and Montana. The state of Montana in fact had issued licenses for translators within its borders, a clear violation of federal precedent established by the Communications Act of 1934. As the number of illegal transmitters increased to nearly 1,000 in the 1950s, the FCC became concerned about the possibility of interference with legal stations (Mayeda 1981) and initiated licensing of translators.

In 1956, the FCC authorized 10–watt UHF translator stations. In 1958, UHF translators were allowed to increase transmitter power to 100 watts. In the late 1980s there were over 5,000 translators in legal operation (Head and Sterling 1990). Currently, LPTV stations are limited to 10 watts transmitter output power (TOP) on VHF and 1,000 watts TOP on UHF.

In late summer, 1980, the Federal Communications Commission (FCC) adopted a Notice of Proposed Rule Making that would establish a new class of television service to be called low-power television (LPTV). It was envisioned as an evolution of the existing translator service. The only difference between LPTV and translators is the ability to originate programing. Transmitter regulations are identical. LPTVs originate programs via videotape or live programs, whereas translators only pick up and rebroadcast another station. Prior to the early 1980s, only full power, full-service stations originated programming. The FCC hoped these small stations would create a local, community-based and -controlled media that would provide an alternative to the major networks. The FCC saw LPTV as a way of providing the public and minorities with a tool to broaden diversity and ownership competition (Singleton 1983). Two classes of LPTV exist: commercial stations and noncommercial (educational, nonprofit). Gross (1986) sees commercial LPTV as competition primarily for local radio stations and cable TV, not full power television. There were few populations unserved by the major networks. Only a few western states were lacking in coverage by public television. These included Nevada, Montana, and Wyoming. The major networks did not see a need, but did not want to be left out in case LPTV was the wave of the future. *Broadcasting* magazine headlined their article "FCC Opens Pandora's Box on Low Power" leaving little doubt about how their editorial staff viewed this new service (*Broadcasting* 1980, p. 29).

The proposed rule making of 1980 quickly came under attack by the National Association of Broadcasters (NAB), an industry association controlled by large, full-power broadcasters. The NAB saw LPTV as a threat to their world of control and hegemony by people who might have fewer restrictions. The NAB was specifically upset by the proposed ownership limitations. In cases of multiple applications for the same frequency in low power, the rules made it difficult for large existing stations to have the same standing as people from outside the industry . The NAB was also disturbed with processing procedures and much less stringent operating procedures: LPTV had no minimum number of hours of operation, no news or non-entertainment requirements, no limit on commercials, no cross-ownership restrictions, and no community-needs ascertainment requirement. Other ownership restrictions that they felt unfair were preferences for allocation of licenses based on first application filed, minority preference, and noncommercial service preference. Due to the backlog of applications for LPTV, the FCC also requested and was granted authority use a weighted lottery system to determine licenses in cases where two or more applicants vied for the same frequency. Weighting used minority and noncommercial preferences. The possibility of LPTV's originating programming was also a thorny issue with large stations. The NAB's members had been accustomed to oligopoly (Alexander, Owers, and Carveth 1993), no real competition other than among the major networks, comparative hearings, costly attorney fees, and long time periods that allowed competing applications to be filed months after initial applications for licenses. The FCC denied the petition but then was hit with another request for postponement of a cutoff date of early January 1981 for acceptance of new applications for LPTV facilities. The NAB felt the FCC was prejudiced against the traditional broadcasters' entry into this new market (Lampert and Stern 1983). In April 1981, the FCC "froze" applications due to an avalanche of requests for permission to construct LPTV facilities.

In March 1982 the FCC adopted a Report and Order that established low-power television service. The report continued the freeze to give the commission time to process applications already filed, but did allow one-week "window" periods for acceptance of applications once per year. The final regulations clearly established LPTV as a "secondary service," a major concession to the NAB. This secondary designation means that if there is a full-power station proposing a mutually exclusive frequency, the LPTV could be required to cease operation or find another frequency, essentially giving way to a "full service" provider. It also means that in a dispute involving a full-power station, the burden of correcting interference to another station rests with the LPTV. "Full power" means that the power of transmitters exceed levels determined by the FCC as minimums (10 watts VHF and 1000 watts UHF).

"Full service" has an entirely different meaning. To the commercial broadcaster it usually means offering local programs, news, and announcements. To the public TV station it has become synonymous with CPB (Corporation for Public Broadcasting) qualification. CPB qualification simply means a PBS affiliate has twelve or more employees and a budget over a level set by CPB. It has nothing to do with local service or responsiveness to its viewers. Many large PBS stations do very little or no local programming, relying on programs from PBS and the regional public networks and other purchased programming like old movies. Although public television stations must be nonprofit, that status is often questioned. For example, the general manager of WHW, the Wilmington/Philadelphia PBS affiliate, is paid more than the head of PBS.

The secondary nature of LPTV became a major issue with the introduction of high definition television (HDTV). The HDTV service that is being proposed and has undergone testing is a threat to LPTV. The FCC has decided that during the changeover period from the television standard we now have (NTSC, National Television Standards Committee) to HDTV, stations will be required to broadcast in both systems to allow time for people to purchase television sets capable of decoding the new HDTV system. NTSC television sets are incapable of receiving the new system. In order for television stations to broadcast in two systems, they have to have two television channels. Full-power stations will be assigned a second channel and broadcast NTSC on one of these channels and HDTV on the other. The channels that would be used as the second channel reside in the UHF band, and many of them are currently being used by LPTV stations and translators. This could mean that LPTV stations would be bumped off the air since they are considered a secondary service by the FCC.

When LPTV is the vehicle for distribution of educational programming, specifically PBS, another problem arises. In Montana, Nevada, Arizona, California, and New Mexico there are currently twenty-seven stations that are part of the RTS (Rural Television System) consortium, a nonprofit group. These stations broadcast PBS programming to their communities. RTS-affiliated, community-based stations came about because of the inefficiencies of maximum service ideology that has been the pervasive force behind commercial and public broadcastng for fifty years. The RTS stations provide service to areas that are considered too rural for large stations to cover on a cost-effective basis. These stations also come much closer to providing the localism ideal in real-world situations. Although the low-power public stations receive the majority of their programming from the national network (PBS), they provide an avenue for the community to communicate to itself through locally produced programs, messages, and announcements.

An example of the difficulties encountered in providing public television service is evident in looking at Montana, the last state in the United States to construct a public television station. In the Big Sky, the first public television station was low power. The second public television station was low power and served an Indian reservation. The third public television station was a "full-service, full-power" station that covered a geographical area the same size as one of the low-power stations. How could this be? A look at the history of the state reveals a convoluted and unusual set of circumstances.

In the mid 1950s the State of Montana commissioned a study of ways to link the state together educationally via the new medium of television. The Jorgenson Plan, as it was called, foresaw a centralized system using microwave transmitters to tie together a grid of stations that would serve the major population centers. It was never built. After many fits and starts, a statewide system was initiated in 1973. Operating space was leased, and equipment was ordered. Before the system could get off the ground, questionable dealings and kickbacks were discovered that shelved the project. That left a bitter taste in the mouth of the state's legislature and government. It was not until the mid-1980s that the Montana University System decided to attempt to provide public television service to the state.

In 1990, Montana commissioned another study that became known as the Lambda Report. It essentially outlined another plan that was never implemented.

Even though the population of Montana is less than 800,000, the state covers 147,000 square miles and it is the fourth largest state in the United States. Long ago other PBS stations that took note of the lack of PBS service started to serve Montana from the outside. KSPS, a Spokane, Washington station separated from Montana by Idaho, installed microwave links and translators to bring their signal to western Montana. KUED, Salt Lake City, Utah, two states to the south, had the good fortune of being near the headend of a large cable system that used a massive microwave network to daisy-chain its entry into Montana's largest cities. TCI Cablevision continues to use this backbone of microwave repeaters to feed its cable systems, although its usefulness is declining due to satellite-based distribution and fiber-optic technology. However, the microwave system that provided viewers with KUED in the larger cities of eastern Montana happens to pass near Bozeman, the home of Montana State University. By replacing KUED with a Montana-based signal at the point the TCI microwave enters Montana, an instant audience can be accessed without putting up expensive transmitters. This is what happened over a three-year phase-out of KUED/phase-in of KUSM, Bozeman.

From the mid-1980s to the present, LPTVs that broadcast PBS increased in number, serving small communities that were too expensive to cover with cable or large transmitters. The federal government encouraged this service through the U.S. Department of Commerce's NTIA/PTFP (National Telecommunications Information Assistance/ Public Telecommunications Facilities Program) grants. These grants were available to any nonprofit entity wishing to provide public television or radio to unserved areas. Since a very high percentage of Montana and several other states were unserved by a public television network, the government funded a large number of stations that served small communities and provided a local voice. There are currently twenty-seven RTS stations in the West, twelve in Montana. Even with these twelve and a "full-service" station, fewer than 30 percent of Montanans are able to receive public television free over the air.

PBS/CPB Involvement

In the early 1980s when LPTV was coming about, PBS was concerned that it would be swamped by LPTV stations wanting to join the system. PBS feared that they would be pressed to provide services to a large number of stations that did not have large staff and facilities similar to those of existing stations. To avoid dealing with these local, community-based stations directly, they decided to give the authority to do so to existing stations in the states where they occurred. This led to the pass-through concept and the ability of a full-service station to sublicense the PBS signal to other stations and LPTVs. The concept also led to commercial stations' access to popular PBS programs in areas that did not receive public TV, although this seldom happens today. The "full-service" station is not limited as to what it can charge for PBS programming:

> The public television licensee will pay PBS a reasonable fee for its right to relicense the PBS Program Service and will in return be free to charge the requesting entity a fee determined at the licensee's discretion. (PBS policy guidelines 1992)

The PBS policy also allows the "full service" station to decline permission for PBS programming to other providers (LPTV) if they are able to serve an area. This effectively supports an ideology capable of causing the demise of low-power public TV.

> If the area served by a non-public television entity under these licensing arrangements becomes served by a public television licensee then, within a reasonable time period, the non-public television entity's authorization to use the PBS Program Service must be withdrawn. (PBS policy guidelines 1992)

This policy has led to an unfortunate result. Some stations that are broadcasting the PBS signal free, over the air to large (by rural standards) audiences, have received federal funding (NTIA/PTFP) for construction. These are licensed nonprofit educational stations that are producing many hours of local programs and that are in jeopardy of being shut down by the "full-service" station due to disputes between "full-service" and low-power stations. PBS has categorized stations that provide the same programs to their audiences as "full-service" public stations and as "other." The irony is that many large "full-service" stations make no attempt to serve their local areas, opting instead for a fare of national programs. One government agency funds low-power public stations (NTIA/PTFP), while the policies of other agencies (FCC, PBS, CPB) discourage their existence and allow the power of life and death to "full-service" stations that answer to no one.

The Future of Localism in Low-Power Television

If the ideal of localism, access to information within a community, and community-based media is to survive, a fundamental change needs to occur at the federal level, specifically at the FCC and PBS. The FCC needs to affirm the value of localism by removing the secondary status of LPTV. With the new technologies of compression and digital transmission on the verge of making frequency scarcity obsolete, LPTV should be allowed to compete on a level field. With more competition from cable, satellite, and fiber delivery methods, PBS is in no position to quibble over who serves an audience their signal. As long as their signal is getting to the public, they should not be concerned with whether the transmitter is operated by a CPB member or not.

A fundamental change in outlook may also be necessary. Market economic considerations predominate and have been unsupportive of localism. A more balanced view that incorporates the social-value school would be more supportive of local service objectives. U.S. society is not homogeneous. The increasing percentage of Hispanic and Asian people in America as well as the number of distinct indigenous cultures make media clinging to a narrow or one-view perspective out of step with reality. Respect for the diversity of cultures and views needs to be supported by governmental policy in the area of public mass media. The Apache, Blackfeet, Flathead, and Navajo public TV stations as well as low-power public television in general should be encouraged by the federal government rather than threatened with extinction by conflicting ideology.

References

Alexander, A., J. Owers, and R. Carveth, eds. 1993. *Media, Economics, Theory, and Practice.* Hilldale, NJ: Lawrence Erlbaum.

Broadcasting. 1980. "FCC Opens Pandora's Box on Low Power." September 15.

Corn-Revere, R. 1993. "Economics End Media Regulation." In *Media Economics, Theory, and Practice,* ed. A. Alexander, J. Owers, and R. Carveth. Hillsdale, NJ: Lawrence Erlbaum.

Entman, R.M. 1989. *Democracy Without Citizens.* New York: Oxford University Press.

Entman, R.M. and S.S. Wildman. 1992. "Reconciling Economic and Noneconomic Perspectives on Media Policy: Transcending the 'Marketplace of Ideas.' " *Journal of Communications* 42, no. 1: 5-19.

FCC Sixth Report and Order. 1952. Vol. 17.

FCC v. Pottsville Broadcasting Company. 1940. 309 U.S. 134, 470.

Gomery, D. 1993. "Who Owns the Media?" In *Media Economics, Theory, and Practice.*

Gross, L.S. 1986. *The New Television Technologies.* Dubuque, IA: W.C. Brown.

Head, S.W. and G.H. Sterling. *Broadcasting in America,* 6th ed. Boston: Houghton-Mifflin.

Lampert, D.N. and L.C. Stern, eds. 1984. "Low Power Television" in *Broadcasting and Government: Review of 1983 and Preview of 1984.*

Mayeda, D.M. 1981. "High Potential in Low Power: A Model for Efficent Low Power Television Service." *Federal Communications Law Journal* 33, no.5: 419-469.

Mosco, V. 1990. "The Mythology of Telecommunication Deregulation." *Journal of Communications* 40, no.1: 36-49.

NAB. 1980. *Broadcasting and Government: Review of 1979 and Preview of 1980.*

Noll, R.G., M.J. Peck, and J.J. McGowan. 1973. *Economic Aspects of Television Regulations.* Washington, DC: Brookings Institution.

Singleton, L.A. 1983. *Telecommunications in the Information Age.* Cambridge, MA: Ballinger.

Appendix 4B: On Being a Neighbor

David A. Tucker

Our low-power television station believes in the concept of "neighbor to neighbor" communication. Locally originated programs, if carefully produced, can generate a great deal of interest for the station by attracting new viewers. This allows the station to expand its base of support. We categorize our community's support of the station in two ways: (1) in *finances*—we rely on viewers to help us in our semiannual fundraising campaigns—and (2) in *volunteers*—we train and utilize volunteers for video tape and live productions. We have always felt there is a direct correlation between financial support for the station and local programs produced by volunteer production workers. The more community-interest programs we produce, the more volunteers we gain and the more financial support we receive. Although we do not have a large newsroom budget, we have featured many industry, community, and local political leaders in our broadcasts. Recently one CEO of a large lumber mill stated that he preferred the hour-long format of our news program because it enabled him to speak clearly and fully about the decisions he had made about his company without being subject to the usual editing that resulted in the altering of text to soundbites. This he felt separated our station from others because things were not taken out of context. We are a neighbor, so we should be telling it like it is, not modifying it to suit our production agenda.

—5—

The Bottoming Line

Subsidizing the Hidden Screen

LPTV Economics

While the capital and operating costs for an LPTV station are moderately to considerably lower than for a full-power station, the smaller viewer-cum-advertising base for the LPTV means that even a modest investment may be difficult to recoup, and even a mom-and-pop or other small staff operation may be hard to support from month to month. Sophisticated LPTVs may cost from $200,000 to $300,000 to put on the air; some investors have spent up to a million dollars. The idea that low-power TV is a cheap startup venture is inaccurate, wrote pioneer LPTV operator John Boler: "[Those who] read about building a station for $10,000 will find [it] a terrible shock."[1] Adding to Boler's view in an early edition of *LPTV* magazine, reporter Kay Albright observed that "In order to have good-quality productions, you must have state-of-the-art equipment and quality personnel. That costs considerably more than $70,000."[2]

There were many misconceptions surrounding the advent of the LPTV medium. Perhaps the greatest mistake at the start was the idea that the new medium was a guaranteed "get rich quick" opportunity. It was anything but that. In fact, just as many new LPTV operations seemed to go bankrupt as remained on the air. Despite the obvious, wishful thinking on the part of many in the new industry helped create an inaccurate portrayal of LPTV's revenue potential. Throughout the 1980s and well into the 1990s, reports of

TV's "hot" new properties often appeared in newspapers. Reported the *Orlando Sentinel* in 1994, "Low-power television stations have become hot properties because they are comparatively inexpensive to build and operate and they face fewer regulations than full-power stations." However, in the very same story, the downside was revealed as well: "At least four of the eight low-power stations in the Orlando-Kissimmee market are losing money or just breaking even."[3] Many involved in the new LPTV venture found things less than rosy too. In the *Philadelphia Inquirer:* "low-power television station owner Ronald Caponigro report[ed] on his devotion to [the medium] noting [the] low interest by cable companies and general public fails to deter his enthusiasm and commitment."[4]

Clearly, for many new video venturers, it took considerable intestinal fortitude and grit to be in the LPTV business. There were as many skeptics regarding LPTV's earning potential as those who raved about its promise. In fact, a vast number of low-power stations were mere turn-key operations with little or no income. "Like most of the seven other low-power TV stations begun in the area," reported the *St. Louis Post-Dispatch,* "Channel 18 amounts to nothing more than a satellite receiver and rental space on an antenna." Compounding the problem for LPTVs over the years has been their lack of representation in audience ratings reports, raising the broadcast adages "No numbers, no dollars" and "No points, no pay." Further, noted the *St. Louis Post-Dispatch,* "Ratings services pay no attention to LPTV stations, so there's no easy way to gauge the size of their audience—believed to be very small. That makes it difficult to persuade cable systems to carry them,"[5]—not to mention advertisers, who remain very dubious about the value of the medium. On this issue, the Public Relations Society of America concluded that, "many public relations executives . . . are not yet sold on LPTV. One drawback, they say, is that it is difficult to determine how many people are tuning in."[6]

Anticipating shortfalls, some newly licensed LPTV operators chose to sell quickly to recover their investments, while others did so to realize a profit. "Less than 24 hours after signing on the air, Columbus' new low-power television station, Channel 62, said yesterday it has sold the rights to broadcast on its frequency,"[7] reported the *Columbus Dispatch.* "Get in fast and get out faster" was the strategy of many freshly licensed low-power owners. This has not been an unfamiliar practice in other areas of broadcasting as well. For example, during LPTV's startup decade, the 1980s, frenzied turnover buying occurred in the radio medium, too, as the FCC saw fit to eliminate the rule that required new station purchasers to retain frequencies for a minimum number of years to guarantee that the public would benefit from the transaction.

Forging alliances with those interested in the monetary potential of LPTV got many operations off the ground and into the air. Investors were recruited from many professions—mostly non-broadcast in nature, but this gave needed impetus for the medium's continuing development:

> Would-be LPTV owners cover a broad spectrum, from lawyers . . . doctors and retired military officers to mailmen, ministers, newspaper publishers and TV moguls like Ted Turner. Some are wealthy enough to finance construction on their own or by investing jointly with well-to-do colleagues. And one small company, Low Power Technology, Inc., of Boulder, Colorado, recently raised more than $2 million with a penny-stock offering. The most popular method of raising funds, though, seems likely to be the limited partnership. These deals, of course, offer investors tax credits, depreciation allowances and other attractive tax advantages, as well as a share of the profits.[8]

As stated in an earlier chapter, by 1990, groups owned about half of the medium's licenses in the continental United States. Counted among these LPTV partnerships were "Religious broadcasters like Orange County-based Trinity Broadcasting Network and the Home Shopping Network, [which took] advantage of the absence of FCC ownership limits . . . snapping up stations."[9]

Meanwhile, basic LPTV stations set up in no-cost existing structures to reduce overhead as a means of survival—such as the licensee's basement or spare office—may be put on the air for as little as $50,000 or even less. Even in a minimal operation, though, even where the personnel are the owners who delay any personal compensation pending a black-ink ledger, there are such continuing costs as equipment repair and replacement, utilities such as electricity, tapes for dubbing even where there is no local production, and basic communications such as postage, fax, and phone. Although production usually costs much less locally than it does for full-power stations, usually because the quantity and quality of LPTV production resources means lower costs, it still necessitates a budget that has to be met. Further, even the lowest cost syndicated or other source programming requires some outlay of money.

Sourcing the Resources

Where does the commercial station with, at least at first, an inadequate advertising base obtain the income to survive? Considering that some 70 percent of LPTVs are non-profit operations, where do they get the funds to stay on the air? Some non-profit licensees, such as colleges, high schools, and community organizations, buy or otherwise obtain their licenses from commercial stations that are not able to make it financially. In fact, some non-profits have an advantage over commercial stations because they are able to establish a larger base of viewers by being more readily carried by local cable companies, which do not see them as direct competitors to the cable stations' local origination channels for the available advertising dollars in the community.

Noncommercial stations have a number of sources of income. Some non-profits obtain funding directly from their licensee organizations: the community organization; the college or university; the religious group or individual church, among others. Some receive tax moneys appropriated by state or municipal governments with LPTV licenses, such as a state public broadcasting system or a city educational television system. Some LPTVs do what their big-sibling full-power public TV stations do—solicit donations and memberships from viewers. Corporate grants and program underwriting provide some support. Some states and municipalities offer support for specific kinds of programming that serves their larger purposes, such as shows dealing with agricultural information or social services or health needs. Even Neighborhood Assistance programs sometimes have funds available for LPTV, if they serve the organizations' informational and educational outreach purposes. For example, the states of Delaware, Florida, Indiana, Michigan, Missouri, and Pennsylvania, among others, have programs that offer tax credits to businesses that provide support for nonprofit organizations, which may include local LPTV stations.

Commercial LPTV stations also take some of the paths above to obtain revenue. For example, even some commercial LPTVs establish viewer membership clubs and seek viewer contributions. Both commercial and noncommercial stations that have adequate production facilities obtain additional funds by renting out their studios or equipment for local production outfits, including ad agencies that produce commercials for local merchants. Similarly, both types of stations can lease time on their channel to outside organizations, whether nonprofit public-interest groups or home shopping networks; a specified amount of air time is exchanged for a specified amount of money. Both types of stations also seek private grants and contracts in exchange for whatever services the station can provide.

According to LPTV consultant John Kompas, the average monthly income of a low-power commercial outlet in 1994 was in the vicinity of $21,000. Kompas also notes that the emergence of the new networks (UPN and WB) have helped generate income over the last few years.

Local Sales

For commercial LPTV stations, no matter what other sources of income there are, the basic avenue for revenue is the same as for full-power stations: advertising. In its adolescence of rapid expansion, there were high hopes for LPTV advertising income. In 1987 John Kompas, who was president of LPTV marketing and consulting company K-B Limited, predicted that:

> local advertising will be the dominant source of income . . . with some help from paid programming and production services . . . national and regional advertising will ultimately become a significant factor.[10]

Quite obviously, LPTV stations have problems not encountered by full-power stations, insofar as advertising costs are based on how many potential customers an advertiser can reach. Further, even where geography and reception give LPTVs the opportunity to reach a substantial number of a given area's TV homes, only in recent years has Nielsen begun to measure LPTV viewing. This made it difficult previously for LPTV stations to develop even relatively accurate rate cards, which are needed to sell advertisers commercial spots at specified times for specified costs, in terms of reasonably expected rating points.

LPTVs sell their commercial spots in a manner similar to that of full-power stations, mostly in thirty–second packages for runs of one to thirteen announcements, with discounts for multiple "buys" or airings. The costs vary as with full-power stations, dependent on the size of the audience, both in terms of ratings (that is, the percentage of all TV homes in a viewing area tuned in to a given program and accompanying commercials) and shares (that is, the percentage of all TV homes that are watching any program at a particular time and that are tuned in to the specified program and accompanying spots). In small markets or isolated areas, a spot announcement on LPTV can cost as little as $5, which makes TV advertising affordable even to "mom and pop" shops such as grocery stores, hair salons, garages, and so on. In large markets with a large base of targeted viewers, spots can sell for hundreds of dollars. Special events, such as a key football game not aired by other outlets in the area, can warrant higher fees. Writes Adam Shell, "LPTVs are ideal for sending 'specialized' messages to niche audiences not ordinarily featured by local TV stations."[11]

LPTV outlets that can compete directly with local full-power stations through highly competitive programming drawing comparable audiences, such as LPTV station W10AZ, Woodstock, Virginia, can sell commercial spots at virtually full-power station prices. Most LPTVs, however, directly compete more with local radio stations than with TV stations in terms of their audience bases and what they charge for advertising time. (See Figure 5.1.)

Figure 5.1. **Getting an LPTV Signal Out to the Viewing Public Requires Funding. WJAN-TV in Miami Is One of the Medium's Most Successful. Courtesy WJAN-TV.**

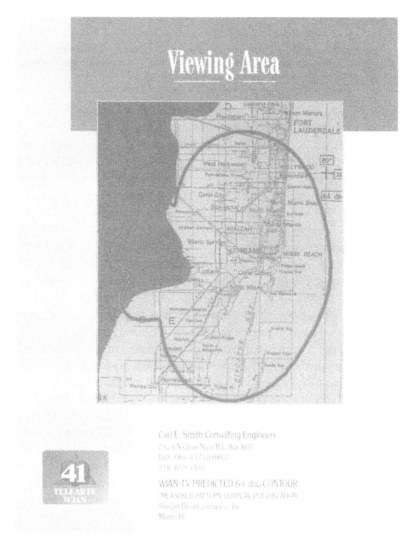

Regional and National Buys

To get regional and national advertisers, local LPTV stations often have to adapt the national campaigns of the potential sponsors to local situations and to the targeted audiences. Usually, this occurs when the LPTV station works out a deal with a local distributor or franchisee of a national company—for example, Goodyear Tire or Blockbuster Video or McDonald's—to get its parent or franchising company to provide money for advertising on the local LPTV station, commercials that are oriented to the company's outlet's specific customer concerns, or a current local promotional campaign. Certainly the local merchant knows the potential customers in the community better than the advertising staff in corporate headquarters in another part of the country! Sometimes an LPTV can get national or regional advertisers by personal contact, showing a given company how one such advertising campaign on the station successfully increased the business of that company's local operation.

LPTV networks, either group-owned-and-operated or established for common program acquisition and exchange, can more easily attract regional and national advertisers by being able to guarantee a larger base of viewers for a given commercial campaign. This point was enhanced in the mid-1990s when Nielsen began to measure LPTV ratings for certain LPTV networks. In 1995 Network One, with forty-two LPTV affiliates, entered into an agreement with Nielsen to measure the network's total audiences. Chandors Mahon, executive vice president of Network One, stated that:

> Network One is primarily concerned with attracting national and primary regional advertisers. The more mainstream, blue-chip advertisers have not been able to advertise with us in the past because there wasn't research available for them to justify to their clients.[12]

Mahon further described how Network One was aware from its founding in 1993 of the need for accurate audience measurement to make spot-selling feasible for his LPTV stations (and, of course, for other LPTVs as well):

> We saw that there was a great potential for advertising sales, but, as a whole, low-power stations were disorganized. We had to get to critical mass and began doing qualitative and quantitative research to prove what we have. We started conversations with K-B Limited in 1994 and knew we had to work with Nielsen on geographic boundaries. The problem in the last was that low-power stations weren't organized, and the Nielsen process didn't have geographical capabilities.[13]

Network operations, however, do not guarantee financial stability. For example, Channel America, based in Florida, had high hopes for a successful LPTV network in the early 1990s. By 1995, however, it had accumulated a loss of $7.9 million, and its stock value had dropped from $2.50 to 7 cents per share, resulting in a delisting by NASDAQ. In 1997 it looked toward an even larger system as a means of financial salvation, with its plans to merge with another LPTV company, Morton Downey Jr.'s LDE Media Techniques, combining entertainment and Downey's revived talk show.[14]

Let's Make a Deal

LPTV stations have always known what full-power stations discovered during the economic recession of the late 1980s and early 1990s: when there is insufficient advertising money available for the purchase of programming—barter. Traditionally, a station, whether low-power or full-power, has paid a certain fee to syndicators to "buy" a given program series or a program special. "Buying" really means "renting"; the station agrees to pay the syndicator, say, a certain amount of money for the rights to show a given number of episodes of the program series a given number of times over a given time period. Within each program are a specified number of minutes that can be used for commercial spots. These spots, or available advertising time, are called "avails." The station sells them to whatever advertisers it can, local, regional, and national.

Once the deal is consummated the station owes the syndicator the amount of money agreed upon, even if the station finds that it cannot sell as many commercial spots as it thought it could and it begins to lose money on the series. With the unavailability of sufficient advertising because of the economic situation or, as from the beginning in the case of LPTVs, because of a small viewer base, alternative means of obtaining programs become necessary. Through barter the station and syndicator agree that the station will be charged less to buy the program if a given number of avails within the program are given to the syndicator. For example, if a half-hour program has space for nine minutes of commercials, in exchange for a lower price for the program the station returns to the syndicator three minutes of avails, which the syndicator then sells directly to national or regional advertisers, keeping that revenue.

The station is now able to afford the program and still has six minutes of avails it can sell. In many cases those six minutes are the maximum it might sell under any circumstances. Therefore, this is a win-win situation: the syndicator sells programs to stations that otherwise could not afford to buy them without barter, and the station obtains programs that it otherwise would not acquire and still makes money through its remaining advertising time. The amount of barter—that is, the percentage of advertising time split between the syndicator and station—varies with each individual station's and syndicator's circumstances.

Subscription Dollars

One of the most creative and logical means for obtaining revenue by LPTVs is relatively new: subscription TV. In areas where viewers receive no cable or limited cable, where the economy does not permit large-scale satellite-receive systems, and where few full-power stations can be received over the air, LPTV stations have an opportunity to provide a special service. Although authorized with the expectation that it would be a community-oriented television service, LPTV was not precluded from receiving direct viewer payment for its local services.

One company with advanced plans for LPTV subscription channels is US Wireless (USW), headquartered in California. In an interview with researcher Stefan Weibel, USW official Mark Silberman stated that USW is targeting sparsely populated rural areas where cable is not available to most of the homes and where television signals can be received only through a satellite dish or a powerful antenna. Silberman stated that an individual household's subscription costs for LPTV programming would be comparable to the basic monthly subscription cost for satellite channels. USW would offer a basic package of broadcast and cable channels plus pay-per-view additional channels. USW believes the cost–income ratio would be a good one for a network of LPTV subscription channels, with LPTV licenses available for under $20,000 each. USW notes:

> First the network stations and their affiliates obtain licenses for a broadcast area, then make their money by building a "subscriber base." With cable TV, the higher the population density the better since the high cost of laying cable to sparsely populated areas is not economically feasible. That's why the broadcast of cable programs over the airwaves and the availability of LPTV channels to carry those programs has opened a window of opportunity for individuals to operate or lease out their own LPTV channels.[15]

Part of LPTV subscription channels' early problems can be traced to their competitive disadvantage to cable. Proffered John Kompas in 1984, "Overall, cable television will represent the most formidable competition for subscription television. If a cable system has penetrated your coverage area, success is doubtful."[16] While cable multichannel capacity was growing, the capacity of LPTV subscription stations was limited to the individual station's single channel.[17] Thrust into a competitive situation with cable by the nature of its local coverage, by 1998 LPTV was still concerned with what it considered inequitable regulations. In 1998 the Community Broadcasters Association (CBA, the organization representing LPTV stations) appealed to the federal courts to overturn FCC rules that protected cable systems, giving them further economic advantage over LPTV stations, by deregulating cable's leased-access rates. CBA made the point that the FCC should promote program diversity by allowing LPTV and cable to be more competitive on an even playing field, rather than indirectly restricting program diversity by giving cable greater financial protection.[18]

The Mini-Minors

LPTV's secondary status is also a key factor in its economic health, resulting in advertisers' concerns that even if a given LPTV program is attracting enough viewers to make commercial placements advisable, that LPTV station or program may have to go dark if it in any way interferes with a full-power signal.[19] As mentioned in an earlier chapter (and discussed at greater length in the next chapter), recognizing this problem in 1997 the Community Broadcasters Association sought primary status designation for LPTV stations that provided a minimum of three hours per week of local programming. However, many of its members, including group-owned and network-affiliated stations, were opposed, stating that such a rule would give those stations that through larger budgets or through necessity produced local programming an unfair advantage over other LPTV stations.[20]

A number of LPTV station owners and managers are concerned about the lack of what they consider equitable economic opportunity for their stations. Ron Bourque, director of a station in Pelham, New Hampshire, states that "unless there is a major change, community television will be eliminated. There is just not enough funding and, sometimes, not enough interest."[21]

As noted earlier, some types of stations, such as Spanish-language stations, operate under special conditions because of the nature of their service and their built-in audience base and loyalty. Telemundo General Manager Manuel Llorian explained to Raphaela Logullo one of the advertising concepts of his station:

> Our viewers will always be very faithful to us, but we are trying to reach even more viewers. Most of our viewers are part of the working class, and have a low income. That is . . . reason why advertisers neglect our importance. There have been many criticisms made to our stations, such as 'the quality of the programs has the same quality as the viewers,' but I tend to disagree. We have invested more money than ever in our programming, and our audience increases every day.[22]

A Latino marketing research firm, Strategy Research, conducted a study a few years ago that found that young Latino viewers have a special affinity for certain brand names and remain loyal to those brands. Given the concentration of this demographic segment in the top ten video markets, advertisers have a ready-made reliable target customer. With Nielsen inclusion of LPTV stations in new ratings research, more and more national advertisers are investing in Spanish-language LPTVs. This increased advertising has, in turn, enabled these stations, in particular, Telemundo and Univision, to strengthen their programming, which has led to more viewers and more advertising. A case in point is Boston's Spanish-language WCEA, which tells potential advertisers in its literature that:

> because of our broad coverage and great awareness, CEA is able to provide our clients with an effective means of reaching the Hispanic market. Advertising with us will definitely provide your business with the exposure and publicity necessary to capitalize your investment.[23]

Given a healthy economic atmosphere for the country, this is an approach that all LPTVs might usefully try to apply.

Appendix 5A: An LPTV Studio Equipment List

(Courtesy Globecom Publishing)

What follows is a low-power television station's (KO7SD-TV7, Rolla, Missouri) first-year equipment acquisitions list, as cited in *LPTV* magazine in its January/February 1984 issue. From this it becomes quite evident that the initial investment in equipment alone requires formidable funds.

2 Ikegami color studio cameras, plus conversion kits
3 Ikegami dual 9–inch monitors
3 JVC 19–inch color monitors
3 Tektronix waveform monitors and a vectorscope
1 JVC production switcher
1 JVC 3/4–inch VTR
1 JVC editor
1 Quanta character generator
1 Laird uniplexer
1 slide projector and filter wheel
1 Videotek demodulator
1 Adda dual-channel time base corrector
5 Grass Valley video distribution amplifiers plus 1 sub- carrier and
2 distribution pulse amplifiers
3 Trompeter video patch panels
1 twelve-input audio board
1 Technics audiocassette recorder/player
1 turntable, cartridge, and shell
4 Sigma audio dual ten-output distribution amplifiers
1 Videotek two-channel audio monitor
1 ADC 2 × 24 patch panel
AKG microphones
1 ClearCom intercom system

Colortran studio lights

2 Quickset tripod dollies

TEC remote controls, access panels, editing console, audio location console, and 4 1/2–bay console

1 Television Technology 10–watt transmitter

1 Scala vertical slot transmission antenna

2 Blond-Tongue satellite receivers

Appendix 5B: A Profile
of Bayou Country LPTV

Dave Pierce

Having had the unforgettable opportunity to help pioneer "underground" FM rock radio in Los Angeles in the late 1960s, I was more than intrigued the first time I heard the term "guerrilla television." By now I was back home in the Bayou Country. It's 1981 and KADN-TV has just signed on as an independent in the Cajun Capitol of the world, Lafayette, Louisiana. I left the sales department at the ABC affiliate to take a job as sales manager working with owner/general manager Charles Chatelain and station manager/program director Eddie Blanchard. We struggled with the fledgling indy until two things happened: Rupert Murdoch decided he wanted a network, and the FCC decided to make LPTV allocations available.

LPTV was meant to fill in the holes in small towns whose network signals from distant urban cities were weak. LPTV would be something like community television on cable access channels. Most broadcasters were just not interested in messing with LPTV. That was the attitude, but not in Lafayette. With KADN stabilizing as a Fox affiliate, Charles Chatelain applied for not one but several LPTV assignments. After all, it was not an expensive process, so why not pick up a double handful? So we started putting LPTVs on the air.

Since there was a Fox affiliation available in Alexandria, we signed on WNTZ Fox 47 on LPTV. Chatelain borrowed the idea from cablecasting and we began simulcasting Fox and syndicated programs to Lafayette and to Alexandria some 90 miles away via a microwave hop. From there another hop (through the town of Frogmore [really], Louisiana) put WNTZ in Natchez, Mississippi. This was such a new idea it took time for the technology to catch up. There was no good automation equipment available. It was mostly cable stuff of low quality and didn't look very good. So part of the LPTV evolution was telling manufacturers what you needed, waiting for them to develop it, and then explaining to them what they did wrong so they would go back to the drawing board and come up with something that worked.

We sent a hard working young salesman named Tom Poehler to open up satellite sales offices in Natchez and Alexandria. Everything else emanated from Lafayette. So with no additional staff (other than sales) and limited additional overhead, we were now operating two stations in three cities.

As program director, Eddie Blanchard realized there was a lot more syndicated programming available that was not being shown in Lafayette's three-station market. Also, local programs, like college and high school sports—a staple of early KADN as an indy—was being squeezed out of primetime by Fox shows. Eddie's goal was the same as the FCC's, to get more programming choices to the public. All he needed was another TV station. Well, we had several LPTVs.

To our knowledge, we were the first broadcasters (certainly down here) to string several LPs together to cover a market with one signal. Locating one tower and transmitter in each of the four largest towns in the Lafayette market, we signed on Channels 46, 56, 62, and 69. Now Opelousas, Church Point, New Iberia, and Abbeville all had television stations in their backyards.

We microwaved the same signal to all four transmitters from our control room at KADN. Along with the WNTZ monitors, our control room began to look like an early-day starship *Enterprise* with switchers firing off commercials and programs to seven different transmitters from a 10 foot by 20 foot room.

A key factor in the viability of this whole idea was the 70 percent cable penetration in our market. Just get a good signal to the cable head-ends. Even an LPTV could do that. In early rock radio jargon "we covered the market like a blanket."

I remember the day Charles Chatelain and Eddie Blanchard laid out the plan to Tom Poehler and myself. They had essentially created one new commercial television station with the call letters KLAF. As sales managers, it was our job to figure out once again how to sell a station with a few viewers, a low profile, and no numbers.

"You've really created another competitor for KADN," I said to them. "We've gone into business against ourselves. We'll be splitting dollars and audience between KADN and these LPTVs called KLAF."

"Sure we will," Eddie replied, "but the cost factor is low and we're bound to get a piece of the ABC and CBS affiliates' business."

"We could sell both products with one staff, positioning ourselves more like consultants than salesmen," I replied, flashing ahead on how to get it done. "We might even slow down the cable."

"Cable bastards want to give away spots for a dollar a holler," Tom

Poehler added, getting into the spirit of things. "We'll sell KLAF to their customers by the bushel basketful."

"I hear Paramount and Warner Brothers are trying to crank up networks. Won't they be hungry for affiliates?" I asked.

"I've already talked to both of them. They've got no place else to go in Lafayette," Eddie said with a smile. "We'll probably get UPN as a primary affiliate and WB as a secondary. We'll start up KLAF with seven nights of network programming. It took KADN and Fox five years to do that."

For some broadcasters, LPTV was a stepchild just as FM radio had been for thirty years until 1968. For the pioneers and entrepreneurs, LPTV was one more golden opportunity. News of our venture leaked to other markets. Owners came to visit, look around, and quiz our staff. Yes, one accounting department did handle it all. Yes, our engineers were overworked. That's right, only one extra traffic girl for each station. Could one promotions department overlap their creativity for KADN, KLAF, and WNTZ? Pretty much. Did Eddie Blanchard do the programming deals for all three stations? You bet. People called from across the country with the big question.

"How do I get programming for my LPTV?" they asked Eddie.

"Well down here I use the Fox for bait," the cagey Cajun responded.

Syndicators may not have been interested in a bunch of LPTVs called KLAF, but adding the Lafayette market for their shows would look good for the barter people. So shows were scheduled for 3 A.M. on KADN Fox and played in the wee hours, but the real audience was at 6 and 10 P.M. on KLAF. Everyone was a winner, including the public, which got a wider variety of programming. Wise folks, those FCC people. Approve a grand idea and leave it to the broadcasters to make it work.

FCC wisdom does have serious limitations, however. In the early 1990s, Eddie and Charles told me the biggest threat to LPTV's future is digital television, and as I write this, the verdict is still out. Anyway, perhaps anticipating this, Charles Chatelain cashed in in the fall of 1997, selling KADN, KLAF, and WNTZ to COMCORP of America, one of the nation's fastest growing small market groups. Charles and Eddie are putting a new ABC affiliate on the air in Monroe, Louisiana and opening other businesses. Tom Poehler is now general manager of KADN/KLAF.

I'm still the local sales manager in the best little town in America. When the sun goes down on the bayou, I edit my memories from the FM underground days while old folk rock lyrics play in my head, and I wonder about guerrilla broadcasters after the millennium when the Rupert Murdochs get it all bought out and consolidated and get the wires and satellites all hooked up.

—6—

Maintaining the Image

Technical Considerations, Other Micros, and the Future

Let me assure you that I share your view that we should explore ways to give low-power stations primary status.
—FCC Chairman William Kennard

LPTV Technicals

The engineering and technical requirements for an LPTV station are the same as for a full-power station, only in smaller numbers. For example, while a full-power station's transmitter must carry at least several hundred thousand watts of power in order to send the signal out to a radius of 40 to 50 miles, the LPTV transmitters are limited by regulation and by the targeted mission of the station and need only a few hundred watts, to reach a radius of 5 to 20 miles. Similarly, the antenna for LPTVs does not have to be as high as for full power stations.

The LPTV technical array consists of a transmitter; a transmitting antenna on either a transmitter tower or, because of the acceptable lower height, on the roof of a building; a place for the transmitter to be housed and protected; a control room with appropriate video equipment; if necessary, even in the smallest operation that does not produce any local programming, a room that can serve as a studio; and lines from the studio or control room to the transmitter. The video equipment can be sophisticated, costing hundreds of thousands of dollars, or basic, costing only several thousand dollars.

Some Sample Costs for Technical Equipment

While the lack of funding for most LPTV stations precludes the use of state-of-the-art technology and equipment, and while "mom-and-pop-spare-room" LPTV operations of necessity seek out used equipment, some of it on the verge of obsolete, at the lowest prices or as giveaways from stations updating their equipment, it is important to remember that the processes in video technology suggest that every attempt should be made to obtain the latest affordable equipment.

Paul R. Beck, director of engineering at Emerson College and a specialist in communications technology, states that "plain vanilla NTSC television, with its arcane 525–line scan, 60 interlaced fields and, worst of all, the conventional 4.3 aspect ratio is as doomed as Henry Ford's Model T. Moreover, the latest new issue being embraced is the ability to send four or more program streams through one Master Control system, rather than the traditional single stream. All the new digital TV systems are planning for minimally four stream."[1] Beck says that most mid- to large-market television stations will be throwing away "tons of older equipment over the next few years as they convert to digital," and that the conventional equipment will be available at probably less than ten cents on the dollar. He gives as an example a Sony BVU-870 professional U-matic videocassette recorded with SLO-MOTION, costing $36,000 when new in 1991, which was selling for less than $3,600 in 1998 and will probably be available for $300 in the year 2000. While Beck touts the availability of such equipment over the next few years as a bonanza for mom-and-pop operations, he cautions those who wish to be technologically competitive in the growing video market to make every effort to get up-to-date equipment.[2]

For professionally competitive new LPTV stations, purchasing state-of-the-art equipment, Beck estimates a total cost for getting on air of between $1,398,000 and $2,495,000, which includes a transmission plant; an origination/control facility, including a basic production studio; a location-portable origination package; a small mobile van; and a film-to-video (telecine) setup. With somewhat cheaper equipment, and without a basic production studio or mobile van, Beck estimates a new modern station's equipment cost at $756,000 to $1,362,000.[3] Of course, these figures can be considerably reduced by reducing the requirements from optimum equipment needed for optimum operation. For mom-and-pop operations and those in between, the total cost, using old and giveaway equipment, could be one-tenth to one-twentieth of these figures, on up.

Figure 6.1 shows Beck's breakdown of LPTV costs "on the really cheap" for a new, professionally competitive station.

Beck stresses the need for satellite receivers for LPTV stations. "The LPTV operator must cluster several of them ... because programming sources are provided at different times from as many as 30 operating satellites with 22 transponders on each bird ... even a small mom-and-pop operation will need at least two satellite receive systems steerable and programmable with an inexpensive PC."[4]

Beck also strongly recommends digital editing and file servers, using a Mac or PC as an engine for picture and sound editing, with a minimum of conventional video or audio recorders, and using a basic computer system as a digital storing facility for full-length programming, with the latter especially useful for unattended LPTV operations.[5] Beck has further advice for the new station: although finding a transmitter location, if possible, on high ground, and installing a tower and antenna there seems like a logical approach, this requires FAA approval, local zoning approvals, and heavy insurance costs. The capital cost can be 40 to 50 percent of the initial capital budget and 25 to 30 percent of the annual operational costs. The principal alternative is renting antenna space on a tall building; in urban areas this cost can be extremely high, too.[6]

The Audience

Nielsen has negatively impacted LPTV.

—John Kompas

As discussed earlier, most LPTV stations have target audiences. Where the signal reaches a narrowly defined geographical area, especially in small-market non-urban areas, it is not difficult for the station to determine the approximate size and some of the demographics of its audience, such as age, gender, and economic status (Figure 6.2). This enables the station to seek advertisers with products or services most likely to be wanted or needed by that target audience, and to determine what kinds of programming would most interest and hold the viewers. With more heterogeneous audiences and a larger viewing base—such as a large-market urban area—the station would find it much more difficult to determine necessary information about its audience. Even where there appears to be a clear target audience, such as for a Spanish-language station, if it is in a large market the demographics of its audience, except for the common Spanish-language thread and some general cultural affinities, might vary in great degree in regard to age, income, education, profession, neighborhood, and other key factors.

116

Figure 6.1 **LPTV "On the Really Cheap." Courtesy Paul R. Beck.**

TRANSMISSION PLANT: $315,000 - $585,000

Transmitter tower (200' estimate) with antenna, with transmission lines $50,000-$100,000
Transmitter security/insurance/maintenance/FAA Tower Lighting $35,000 -$55,000
Transmitter(s) and RF output system (LPTV UHF single array) $75,000-$125,000
Transmitter building structure, land power source, generator & UPS, HVAC $65,000 -$80,000
STL/TSL Relays, with dishes, related RF items $25,000-$50,000
Transmitter Monitoring & Control Systems w/console (Remote Control, as needed) $15,000-$25,000
Transmitter Site Lease/Fees/Rentals/Access/Build-out costs/Development costs $50,000-$150,000

ORIGINATION/CONTROL FACILITY: $290,000 - $ 540,000

Primary building for Master Control/Administration/Public File Office $25,000 - $75,000

Master Control. Console Racks/HVAC/Power Conditioning-UPS $45,000-$85,000
Contract wiring/installation/systems documentation $25,000-$40,000
Basic NTSC equipment package for **single** program stream $75,000- $150,000
(Includes air-play VTRs, systems, switcher, routing, still store)

Satellite Receiver and Dish systems: *(Includes TWO ground-level steerable 12'-14' dish systems,* $30,000- $50,000
with appropriate feed horns, LNA/LNBs, tuners, controllers, PC for positioning and programming control,
audio/video distribution, recording VTRs for delayed broadcast capture)

Basic Production Control Room with Announce Booth: $35,000- $60,000
(For preparing station promos and commercials

Basic Production Studio, (less Control Room): $0 (Deferred)
(Includes small storage and scene-dock area, lighting grid/dimmer system
and three or four economy mini-cameras on tripods)

Basic Editing/Post-Production Control Room. $55,000-$80,000
(Includes simple Racks/VTRs/Monitors/ Switcher/Title/Text Generator/Audio Mixer)

LOCATION PORTABLE ORIGINATION PACKAGE: *(Carry-in "Fly-Pack" configuration)* **$70,000 - $100,000**
(Includes portable mini-racks for table-top control room, three mini-cameras, communications & interphone systems, audio mixer and peripherals, portable lighting packages, portable VTRs, small text generator, portable microwave relay device, AC power UPS system for buffered power on location, general field peripherals.)

SMALL-SIZED MOBILE VAN: *(Local origination capability, including small switcher, monitors, VTRs,* **$0 (Deferred)**
power conditioner, cable reels, four mini-cameras, tripods, audio mixer and peripherals, Video CG/text generator, audio & video distribution, Test and Sync generator/signal routing package, general van-type peripherals.)

ECONOMY FILM-TO-VIDEO (TELECINE): *Projector with built-in camera system, for 16mm and* **$ 6000 - $12,000**
Super 8mm film, for transfer of film w/sound to videotape or for live broadcast. (Consumer-grade quality)

LPTV "ON-THE-*REALLY*-CHEAP"

TOTALS:

TRANSMISSION PLANT:	$315,000 - $585,000
ORIGINATION/CONTROL FACILITY:	$290,000 - $540,000
LOCATION PORTABLE ORIGINATION PACKAGE:	$ 70,000 - $100,000
SMALL-SIZED MOBILE VAN:	$ 0 - $ 0
ECONOMY FILM-TO-VIDEO (TELECINE):	$ 6,000 - $ 12,000
GENERAL CONTINGENCY:	$ 75,000 - $125,000
	$ 756,000 - $1,362,000

Figure 6.2 A Native American LPTV Station Jousts With the State University to Retain Its Sovereignty. Courtesy SKC-TV.

SKC-TV April 1995

Published by the Salish Kootenai College Media Center

PBS

designed by Sam Sandoval, who is now attending the Institute for American Indian Arts in Santa Fe, NM

U of M Blinks

by
Frank Tyro
SKC Media Center
Director

After 6 years of frustration, SKC-TV's position on duplication of public TV programming in Montana has finally been heard. In March, the University of Montana verbally agreed to change the transmitter power and transmitter site in order

to have less of an impact on SKC-TV's operation and ability to fund raise. We trust that the University and Board of Regents will follow through on their plan, although past (and current) experience has shown us that we need to be extremely careful in dealing with the higher education system in Montana. We have learned that agreements can be slippery things, open to interpretation based on political whims. We are still awaiting information from the University on the possibility of a special antenna at their transmitter site to decrease the impact on the Bitterroot Valley Public TV system (BVTV).

Thanks go out to Bill Munoz, SKC-TV Board Chair and the SKC-TV Board, Rhonda Lankford of the Tribal Legal Department, CS&KT Chairman Mickey Pablo, Jay Preston of Ronan Telephone Company, Don Olsson of Ronan State Bank, Jean Morrison of Plains/Paradise Public TV, B.J. Hawkins of Meagher County Public TV and the Executive Director of the Montana Public TV Association. Also to Jacquie Coppage, Jim Parker, Nick Mariana of Bitterroot Valley Public TV. Paul Hart and Annette Brown have worked tirelessly on this issue. Thanks also to Joe McDonald, SKC President, William Marcus and all of you who have called, stopped by, and in many other ways supported our efforts.

The day that this is being written, we received a copy of a letter to Montana State University from PBS telling them that based on the new projections of the U of M signal, SKC-TV, Plains-Paradise and BVTV will be allowed to continue to broadcast. Oh thank you great, kind, benevolent Oz!

April Showers........

The Arlee transmitter has been operating from noon to 11pm during the month of March. By the time you read this, I will have made another visit to Pistol Creek and, hopefully, increased the operation time to all hours that we broadcast programs. If this doesn't occur at the beginning of the month, I would expect that it will by the end of April. Keep thinking sun and rain because we need both!

Some stations measure audiences through direct contact: encouraging phone calls and letters to the station, initiating random phone and mail surveys, putting together focus groups at the station or at community organizations. In a small community this is not too difficult, but it does require the time and effort of station personnel. In a larger community such approaches would be not only more costly, but less reliable. A large, reasonable percentage-of-audience sample is needed to obtain any respectably accurate information for potential advertisers and for the station's program manager. As noted earlier, the initiation by Nielsen of ratings for LPTV stations makes it now possible for more LPTVs to obtain appropriate audience measurements.

Nielsen measurements of LPTV station audiences follow the same procedure as for full power stations, with one exception: Nielsen determines ratings only of those LPTV stations that are affiliated with one of the national networks. Unaffiliated LPTV stations are not part of the Nielsen ratings process. Otherwise the approach is the same, with the inclusion of network-affiliate LPTVs in all 211 U.S. markets. For these LPTV stations Nielsen asks the same questions as for full-power stations: "Who is watching?" and "What are they watching?" The same methods of measurement are used: through Nielsen metered homes, representing a demographically representative sample of all television homes, with the meter's "black boxes" sending in their daily data during the middle of the night; and through diaries. The LPTV measurements are included in the "overnights"—that is, the daily measurements of individual markets—and in the quarterly sweeps, in which diary measurements are taken across the country, in February, May, July, and November. Even though LPTV ratings tend to be considerably lower than those of full-power stations—since they lack a comparable wide range of coverage and potential viewers—Nielsen applies no cutoff or minimum rating requirement in reporting LPTV viewing numbers. The LPTV stations measured use the Nielsen ratings the same way full-power stations do, to establish rate cards for selling advertising time.

Promotion

Because most LPTV stations either have a limited base for advertising income or are owned by non-profit, institutional, or organizational groups whose budget priorities are clearly not for TV programming, these stations usually do not have much money for promotion of the station or specified programs. Ironically, because they are limited in range and do not receive much public exposure, such as the kinds of listings and feature stories in newspapers that full-power TV stations have, LPTVs have a special need for effective promotion to attract an audience.

Some stations have virtually no promotion, their outreach being limited to announcements on their own channels. Some LPTV stations, especially those in larger markets, have intensive promotion campaigns, akin to those of full-power stations. For example, K25AS in Eugene, Oregon, aggressively pursued potential audiences in several ways. Not only was there a public relations campaign to convince audiences to switch to their UHF feed to pick up the station, but the station made UHF tuners available to those TV homes that had discarded or disconnected their UHF antenna input. K25AS advertises the station's image and programming in other media, as well as on its own channel, with ads in newspapers serving their viewing area, spots on radio stations, and placards on the sides of buses. For a while K25AS listings were carried by the local issue of *TV Guide*, but they were dropped when *TV Guide* discovered it was listing an LPTV station—which was against its policy.

Riding the Nets

Other promotional approaches include creative use of techniques for distribution and programming choices. Carriage on a local cable system assures not only an immediately larger audience, but greater exposure of the station and its offerings, to wider geographic and demographic groups of potential viewers. Affiliation with one of the major (ABC, CBS, FOX, NBC) or minor (UPN, WB) national networks enhances an LPTV station's status and exposure in its service area. In the mid-1990s a number of LPTVs found their viewership greatly expanded through affiliation with, principally, FOX, UPN, or WB.

Another approach to promoting an LPTV station is through carriage of network programs not being carried by local affiliates of a given network. Usually this occurs when there are a limited number of stations in a viewing area, with one or more stations carrying the programs of more than one network, thus requiring a rejection of some network programs at given time periods. This also occurs sometimes when the local affiliate finds it more lucrative to carry a locally produced program or a syndicated series at a given time slot. In Pittsburgh, Pennsylvania, for example, the local ABC affiliate dropped *Star Trek: the Next Generation* and *Entertainment Tonight* from its program schedule. LPTV station W63AU picked them up and immediately increased its viewing audience. This happens, as well, where the affiliate's image or community attitudes dictate the non-carriage of a given program series, as when several ABC affiliates in the Bible Belt yielded to pressure groups and refused to carry *NYPD Blue*, even before the first program was aired.

Any programming that fills a gap in the viewing area or that is so popular that it attracts an audience that does not feel saturated by that program type on other channels is fodder for the LPTV operation. For example, in areas with high youth demographics, no amount of music videos seems ever to be too much or too many. In a strongly fundamentalist religious community, the audience is open to almost unlimited religious programming. In some urban areas the economics and the demographics of the viewing audience indicate audience acceptance and desire for more and more shopping programs. Not only does the inclusion of broadly popular program formats enhance the income from the specified type of program, but it serves at the same as a promotional device, attracting viewers to the station who might otherwise not even know of its existence.

LPTV networks and group-owned systems do help promote their O-and-O (owned-and-operated) and affiliated LPTV stations by promotional devices that a given individual station cannot afford by itself. Such promotion includes ads in other media, including radio, newspapers, and national and regional magazines, and conducting or supporting special techniques such as treasure hunts, giveaways, and write-in contests.

Behind the Cyclorama

In the past, as in the present, the LPTV landscape has been marred by various obstacles. Indeed, it has been anything but smooth going for the industry since its launch in the early 1980s. Low-power operators attribute this bumpy ride to a number of factors, and they seem unanimous in the opinion that the very agency designed to nurture and protect broadcast media, the FCC, has proven to be one of its biggest headaches. Comments LPTV's John Kompas, "Surprisingly the Commission has been the most contemptuous of our efforts to establish ourselves as an important medium—a medium whose raison d'être has essentially been public service. There's a real contradiction here, it seems to me."[7]

Concurring with Kompas is low-power owner Phil DeSaro, who runs WRIW in Providence, Rhode Island. DeSaro puts it very succinctly, "The FCC is, and has been, the single greatest threat to our continuing operation. Because of this, our primary mission has simply been survival. How could it be otherwise?"[8] Sarah Evett, known as Granny to her faithful viewing audience in Etheridge, Tennessee, points a finger of blame at the FCC as well, but tempers her view with the assertion that the commission is somewhat naive, if not rather ignorant, in their actions concerning low-power television "You know, the FCC would be very fair if the big dogs (networks, cable and satellite industries) out there would tell them the truth."[9]

Multiple LPTV licensee Ken Carter adds his view to the preceding observations: "Without a doubt the single greatest threat to the continuation of our medium is the FCC. Its declared intent was to enable community-minded individuals to live up to its mandate of public service, but regrettably it has done little to help us realize this worthwhile goal."[10]

Kompas and Evett believe that the Commission has not been LPTV's only formidable nemesis, however. Notes Kompas, "We've been held in equal contempt by the industry as well. The NAB, NCTA, and cable people have been quite hostile toward our existence. The Nielsen ratings company has failed to adequately define our needs, too, and that has been damaging."[11] Adds Evett,

> The satellite and cable outfits have been an ongoing threat to our existence. For instance, the new home dishes compete against us, and the satellite programmers will not put low power stations on them. As we are a rural county, so many think they can get the local station. In fact, they tell them this, but it is not the case. And if cable is going to call itself a community medium, I believe it should be made to carry low power. Cable and satellite people are not above board in their dealings.[12]

These attitudes, say LPTV practitioners and supporters, have kept the medium from realizing its aspirations. In fact, the opposition has had a pretty potent effect on stalling the growth of the industry. "Sadly," notes Kompas, "the low-power field has not blossomed as hoped. Too many full-power operators have feared our unique potential to gather audiences. Ironically, in the end, that has actually hurt the television audience itself, which has not fully benefited from what LPTV could bring to it."[13]

The anti-LPTV campaigns, which, for example, have mired the medium in one form of government red tape or another, have taken their toll. LPTV suppliers and support industries have been among those affected as well.

> For Television Technology Corp., a manufacturer of low-power television transmitters and radio gear, 1985 was not the best of years. By the end of the company's fiscal year 1985 last June, and despite an increase in net sales . . . it had suffered its second consecutive year of losses. . . . The primary source of TV Technology's woes: several years of bottlenecks in FCC approval of permits in the fledgling low-power television industry. . . . TV Technology has not been alone in confronting stalled markets for LPTV transmitters and translators, with companies such as Emcee, Townsend, and Acrodyne also making efforts in the field.[14]

Convergence Concerns

Perhaps nothing to date has challenged the fate of the LPTV industry more than the wholesale convergence of the broadcast media (both radio and

Figure 6.3 Headlines

Digital TV May Squelch Minority-Owned [LPTV] Stations

Low-Power Station WBA-TV in Cincinnati is Booted Off the Air in Digital Move

Digital TV Threatens to Knock Low-Power Stations Off the Air

The above headlines appeared in the *Los Angeles Times* during July 1998. They corroborate the fears of most LPTV operators as the video medium enters the digital age and spectrum space becomes more scarce.

---

television) from the analog to the digital domain. While this has mostly been good news for primary or full-power broadcast services, which are being grandfathered into the new transmission *modus operandi,* LPTV's existence has been threatened, because the frequency space it uses is viewed as integral to the transformation of what Sarah Evett above referred to as the "big dogs." (See Figure 6.3.)

To date the FCC has treated LPTV's interests in the ramifications of convergence in much the same way it originally dealt with the must-carry provisions that were so crucial to the medium's development. Bemoans Rich Penkert, "We are afraid our 13 UHF television frequencies will be taken away and given to the broadcasters to use in their application of HDTV."[15] Echoing Penkert's concern, L. Craig Duckworth adds, "The single greatest threat to LPTV operation is the displacement of channels caused by the FCC re-allocating limited spectrum to HDTV and full power stations."[16]

LPTV operator Myoung Hwa Bae corroborates the preceding views: "The biggest obstacle we currently face is the possible displacement of one or two of our stations by DTV. We hope the petition before the FCC regarding this does not fall on deaf ears. We have invested over 2 million dollars in our LPTV operations, and we risk losing our entire investment if we are purged from the air and not relocated."[17]

In an editorial in *The Arizona Republic,* Alexander Cockburn observed:

> The digital TV "great giveaway" might better be called the "great takeaway." The government in the process of bringing digital TV will be confiscating the channels of legitimate broadcast television. This not only puts low-power television owners out of business, but leaves Big Business in control of over-the-air broadcasting. Senator John McCain has submitted a proposal that eliminates up to one-third of the low-power stations.[18]

In their concern about the impact of DTV, LPTV operators have not been alone, as this 1997 report in *Broadcasting and Cable* reflects:

> House Telecommunications Subcommittee Chairman Billy Tauzin (R-La.) in a March 25 letter to FCC Chairman Reed Hundt expressed concern about the potential impact of the commission's digital TV rulemaking on low-power television. Tauzin's primary concern is that the commission complete rulemakings by April 3. However, the "fundamental engineering exercise the FCC is using to distribute digital channels ignores LPTV stations," he wrote. "The prospect of losing 50 to 60 percent of the LPTV broadcast service and more than 10 percent of the translator stations is neither good public policy nor an acceptable result."[19]

An Air of Hope

Throughout the 1990s the LPTV industry was engaged in a concerted effort to ameliorate its secondary status stigma as a means of thwarting the movement by HDTV and DTV to subsume the medium's precious spectrum space. Wrote Jackie Biel in *Community Television Business* magazine, "LPTV stations have labored under a 'secondary status' label that has barred them from traditional financing, prevented reasonable cable carriage, and provided a snide kind of fuel for full power competitors' dismissive insinuations."[20]

As stated in an earlier chapter, initially a plan championed by CBA sought rulemaking that would, at the very least, enhance the image of LPTV by changing its nomenclature from "low-power broadcasters" to "community broadcasters." For their effort CBA came under fire, as several industry associations, foremost among them the NAB, "smelled a rat" and accused the group "of a veiled attempt to make low-power stations the practical equivalent of full-power stations." Meanwhile, INTV "argued that any change smacking of a secondary to primary status for CBA members would hamper implementation of Advanced Television Systems."[21]

Despite the LPTV industry's formidable efforts to be included in the FCC's allocation of digital frequencies—thereby assuring low power's continued existence—the commission ruled in 1993 that LPTV would not be eligible, at least not at the onset, to participate. The ruling by the FCC prompted Polar Broadcasting Incorporated (a low power television operator) to file an appeal in the U.S. District Court. For the next several years, the debate concerning DTV and LPTV would rage on, with little satisfaction coming to the latter.

Meanwhile, as this book was about to go to press, there seemed to be some feeling among LPTV proponents that their luck must be about to change. "Yeah, its going to happen. I really feel it," commented John Kompas, who based his optimism on what he perceived as support for the medium's bid to gain Class A status for its commercial operators by the new chair of the FCC, William Kennard. "This would give us legitimacy, as well as the necessary transfer to digital space, must-carry privileges, and, most importantly, permanence. The new Chairman seems to me to be much more informed about the value of what we do and therefore more sympathetic than his predecessors, so this bodes well. We'll have to see what happens, but we'll hope for justice."[22]

Indeed, this view was reflected in Kennard's speech before community broadcasters at the 1998 NAB convention. Reported *Community Television Business* magazine:

> [The] Chairman told LPTV that the Commission will begin gathering public comments on the petition for LPTV primary status filed last September by the Community Broadcasters Association. . . Kennard also praised attendees for their commitment to local expression and community service, calling the LPTV industry a "little oasis" of ownership diversity and commitment to community in an increasingly consolidated broadcast industry.[23]

Micro Brethren

Another low power phenomenon caused a stir in the 1990s. This one, however, operated illegally, at least from the initial standpoint of the FCC. (New FCC chair William Kennard was favoring the authorization of low-power radio as this book neared publication.) It called itself many things, but became best known as "micro" or "pirate" radio. In 1998 the battle between the FCC and low power radio was heating up, especially since the NAB had decided to press the feds to purge these unlicensed, "rebel" (as they have been labeled) stations from the airwaves:

This sort of development has commercial broadcasters increasingly alarmed. In January [1998] their main industry group, the National Association of Broadcasters, called on the FCC and Justice Department to create a task force to "eliminate" microradio. It's also been vigorously lobbying against low-power in all its forms recently.[24]

In 1998 nearly 1,000 micro radio outlets transmitted signals in cities and towns around the country, some using as little as one watt. These disenfranchised broadcasters argue that their primary mission is to bring community or neighborhood radio to listeners, which they feel is in short supply in the corporate world of commercial radio. Micro operators contend that their efforts are consistent with the government's mandate that broadcasters should, first and foremost, serve the "interest, convenience, and necessity" of the listening public. Supporting their contention that community radio is becoming a thing of the past in this country, micro advocates point to the media consolidation trend since the 1996 Telecommunications Act and the subsequent decline of local programming:

> "The day of the community station is all but gone," said William Morrison of Friday Harbor, Washington. "The need for what a community station provides still exists, but the large corporately owned, profit-driven stations are not interested in the individual towns and geographical areas."[25]

Meanwhile, various proposals to legitimize micro stations are before the FCC. One would authorize one AM and one FM channel per market. These low power radio outlets would serve an area of a couple of square miles and not exceed one watt of power, therefore avoiding interference with full-power stations. Another proposal seeks three classes of low power radio service on FM. Under this plan, there would be a primary class station authorization, which would permit stations up to three kilowatts of power and a maximum service area of fifteen miles. A second class of station would transmit up to fifty watts and cover less than four miles. The last class, which would be called "special event stations," would put out less than twenty watts, cover under three miles, and be licensed in ten-day increments.

Perhaps as you read this, the matter will have been resolved. At writing, however, it appears to be an uphill battle for those micro radio proponents who want the stamp of approval from the FCC. While the Commission has invited comments on the legitimization of this "rogue" medium, the same forces that have kept LPTV from a fuller realization of its goals appear intent on preventing any new sanctioned entry into the radiowave portion of the electromagnetic spectrum. "The radio broadcast band is already congested. Why compound this delicate situation when those stations that presently exist do a pretty darn good job of fulfilling their role as public trustees?" asks Lynn Christian, senior vice president of the Radio Advertising Bureau during a phone interview with the author.

Regarding the micro radio movement, LPTV's John Kompas observes, "We're fighting a similar battle, and we're a legal medium." Adds Kompas, "You would think the government and industry would, at least, stand behind a broadcast service that is authorized to provide programming to the viewing public. The whole thing is rather ironic and perplexing, not to mention frustrating."[26]

Appendix 6A: The Future of LPTV—A View

Mark Banks

In general, LPTV has fought an uphill battle just to survive, and despite its continued growth and tenacity during its history, its future hinges on several things: regulatory protection, economic stability, competitiveness, audience acceptance, and attention to serving the local programming needs of the LPTV audiences.

Of these, probably the most important is the protection of the service through legislative and/or regulatory protection. LPTV is in a life-or-death battle for a place in the world of advanced television. As full-power stations are awarded additional frequencies for digital television, many LPTV stations face being bumped from their channel berths. Moreover, the role of LPTV stations in digital television, plus the ongoing uncertainly of must-carry provisions, add to the fragility of the low-power service. Until these issues are resolved—as many of them are sure to be resolved soon—LPTV's survival will remain threatened.

Beyond regulatory protections, the two most important factors for survival of the commercial sector of LPTV will be the ability to attract regular audiences accompanied by regular and reliable measurements of those audiences. For the non-commercial sector of LPTV, survival depends on continued underwriting by parent organizations.

If LPTV had come along in 1970 rather than 1980, it might have experienced a very different growth and stabilization. Not really getting started until the mid-1980s, the medium has fought a tremendous battle of competition for audiences. As other media provide greater consumer choice and power, the very moniker of "low power" television has had a negative ring. Moreover, the medium's already frail channel-frequency security is being threatened by impending high definition television service, which may take over many of the existing LPTV channels. Add to all this the prospect of many more programming services through wired services, and LPTV pales all the more, seeming not to be a "new" technology, but rather a retrogressive and somewhat impotent "old" technology.

Perhaps LPTV's unique contribution will be the cultivation and expansion of its service to local or specialized needs and interests. If LPTV is also carried on whatever new wired services provide programming to local audiences, some low-power stations may thrive. But the urge (i.e., economic need) to provide non-local programming may work against that possibility, causing LPTV to get lost in the myriad viewing opportunities as it looks more and more like other channels. Should this happen, the more vulnerable the service will become to the stronger competitive forces in the electronic media world.

However, there is a strong likelihood that some aspects of LPTV will endure. Those stations that serve specialized audiences, such as communities in Alaska or among Native American tribes, some strong ethnic or minority-serving stations, and some that have a large enough economic base as in some large markets, will remain important to their audiences. Some rural stations will also continue to serve the needs of their geographic areas, much as small-market radio has done. And, as multiple station ownership grows, some LPTV clusters will enjoy stability from the advantage of multiple programming outlets.

Appendix 6B: Public Notices

 **PUBLIC NOTICE**

Federal Communications Commission	News media information 202 / 418-0500
1919 - M Street, N.W.	Fax-On-Demand 202 / 418-2830
Washington, D.C. 20554	Internet: http://www.fcc.gov
	ftp.fcc.gov

April 16, 1998

COMMISSION POSTPONES INITIAL DATE FOR FILING TV TRANSLATOR AND LOW POWER TV APPLICATIONS FOR REPLACEMENT CHANNELS

By this Public Notice, the Commission today grants the request of the National Translator Association (NTA) to postpone from April 20, 1998, until June 1, 1998, the first day for filing "DTV displacement relief" applications by licensees and permittees of low power television (LPTV) and TV translator stations. On March 24, 1998, the NTA filed its "Ex Parte Request for Stay of Effective Date of Eligibility for Filing DTV Related Displacement Applications," seeking this delay.

In the digital television (DTV) proceeding, the Commission adopted measures to help LPTV and TV translator operators who will lose their channels due to interference conflicts with DTV stations, including the opportunity to apply on a "first-come" basis for replacement channels and other facilities changes necessary to resolve conflicts or preserve their existing service areas. Operators facing *imminent channel displacement*, for example due to the filing of an application for a conflicting DTV station, may apply for such displacement relief at any time. April 20th was to be the first date on which stations facing *eventual*, as opposed to imminent, displacement could file their channel replacement applications. There is a premium on filing applications on the initial filing date, because displacement applications are filed on a first-come basis and there will not likely be enough channels to accommodate all displaced stations.

The NTA urges that a large number of potentially displaced stations need more time to prepare applications, and that these demands exceed the resources of the relatively small group of engineers who select the replacement channels and prepare the engineering specifications in the applications. It points out that the engineering community is undergoing a "steep learning curve" regarding DTV-related analysis, relevant software for such analysis is only now becoming available and that at least two translator groups need more time to develop area-wide plans. NTA's request is supported by several low power station operators and by engineering consultants who represent hundreds of LPTV and TV translator stations. Two licensees of multiple LPTV stations oppose the request, stating that they have expended substantial efforts and resources to meet the April 20th initial filing date.

The Commission agrees with the reasons given by the NTA and is persuaded that many stations do need more time to prepare applications that may be critical to their survival. Also, without additional time, applicants may be inclined to submit hastily prepared deficient applications, in order to reserve their "place in line", intending to later correct deficiencies identified by the Commission staff. Poorly prepared applications would slow application processing and delay the authorization of needed replacement channels.

The Commission recognizes that a postponement of the initial filing date could disadvantage some LPTV and TV translator stations. During the postponement period, additional full service DTV applications will be filed, thus prompting additional imminent displacement applications and reducing the number of replacement channels available to remaining LPTV and TV translator stations. Nonetheless, we are persuaded that far more stations will benefit from the postponement. Finally, we note that some LPTV or TV translator operators may not learn of this action until after filing their applications on April 20th. Therefore, displacement relief applications of a nonimminent nature filed between April 20 and June 1 will be held at the Commission and given a filing date of June 1, 1998.

For additional information contact Keith Larson, Assistant Chief for Engineering, Mass Media Bureau at (202) 418-2600.

By the Chief, Mass Media Bureau

PUBLIC NOTICE

Federal Communications Commission
1919 - M Street, N.W.
Washington, D.C. 20554

News media information 202 / 418-0500
Fax-On-Demand 202 / 418-2830
Internet: http://www.fcc.gov
ftp.fcc.gov

April 21, 1998

PETITION FOR RULEMAKING FOR "CLASS A" TV SERVICE

(Interested persons may file statements opposing or supporting the Petition for Rulemaking listed herein by May 22, 1998; replies are due by June 8, 1998. An Acrobat version of the full text of this petition for rule making, RM-9260, is available through the Mass Media internet page (http://www.fcc.gov/mmb/)
or the PDF file can be downloaded directly from:
(http://www.fcc.gov/Bureaus/Mass_Media/Filings/rm9260.pdf) .

Documents saved as PDF files can be viewed and printed from any Windows, DOS, UNIX, MAC, or OS-2 platform that has Acrobat reader software (free from Adobe Systems, Inc.) installed and configured for use with the browser. *Get the Free Reader* .

RM NO.	RULES SEC.	PETITIONER	DATE REC'D
RM-9260	Rule Parts 73 and 74	Community Broadcasters Association (CBA) 1600 Aspen Lane St. Cloud, MN 56303	9/30/97, as amended 3/18/98

NATURE OF PETITION

CBA requests amendment of the Television Broadcast Station Rules in Part 73 to create a "Class A" TV service, which according to CBA would, on a prospective basis, avoid unnecessary displacement of low power television stations (LPTV) that provide substantial local programming to their communities.

CBA proposes that Class A station provide interference protection to existing analog TV, DTV, LPTV and TV translator stations. Class A stations would have primary spectrum user status, within their principal service contours, against all later authorized full power and low power stations.

CBA proposes that Class A status be made available to qualified LPTV and television translator licensees initially authorized under Subpart G of Part 74 of the Commission's Rules, who would apply for the status within one year of the effective date of the new service class. As proposed, an applicant would qualify by demonstrating that continuously during the preceding three months its station met the minimum operating schedule for TV broadcast stations and, for each calendar week, aired at least three hours of programming produced in the protected service area of the station or within the combined service area of a group of commonly controlled stations carrying common local or specialized programming not otherwise available to their communities. Additionally, an applicant would certify that on and after the filing date of its Class A application, its station complied and would continue to comply with all requirements applicable to TV broadcast stations, except as limited by the station's power level and the manner in which the channel was assigned to the station under the LPTV rules in Part 74. CBA also proposes that a Class A applicant be required to show that interference would not be caused within the Grade B contour of any analog TV or DTV station operating on a channel specified in the TV or DTV allotment tables as of the date of filing of the Class A application, or within the protected contour of any low power or TV translator station authorized prior to the filing date of the Class A application. According to the petition, an applicant for Class A status could not propose a change in channel or facilities change that would extend the station's current protected service area, nor would initial Class A applications be subject to competing applications.

CBA proposes that a Class A station licensee may at any time apply to convert from analog to digital operations, provided the conversion met the interference protection standards applicable to primary stations or would not cause any more interference to another station under Part 73 of the Commission's Rules authorized prior to the date of the conversion application than was caused by that Class A station's analog operation. The petition also proposes that a Class A station licensee be permitted to apply on a first-come basis for an additional channel for digital operation, provided the application proposal met the interference protection requirements in Sections 73.623 (c) or (f) with respect to earlier authorized DTV stations, and that a Class A licensee be permitted to apply for a channel in the DTV Table for which the eligible full power TV licensee for that channel did not file its construction permit application by the established deadlines in Section 73.624(e).

The petition proposes effective radiated power (ERP) limits for analog Class A stations of 10 kW for stations operating on channels 2-6, 31.6 kW for channels 7-13, and 500 kW for channels 14 and above. CBA proposes that digital ERP limits for Class A stations be the same as the DTV station power limits given in Sections 73.622 (e)(4), (5) and (6) of the Commission's Rules.

For additional information contact Keith Larson, Assistant Chief for Engineering, Mass Media Bureau at (202) 418-2600.

Written comments must be directed to the Office of the Secretary (1800), Room 222, FCC, 1919 M Street NW, Washington, DC 20554, and these comments must clearly reference RM-9260. Public copies of FCC documents are available for reference at the FCC headquarters in Washington, DC. In addition, items adopted by the Commission and other important FCC documents are published in the FCC Record. Hard copy versions of FCC releases may be purchased from International Transcription Services, which can be reached at (202) 857-3800.

Appendix 6C: CBA Factsletter

Sherwin Grossman, President   Mike Sullivan, Exec. Dir
305-592-4141/3808   320-656-5942/255-5276
--June 11, 1998

Displacement Applications

The word is 1,100. This is the number of displacement relief applications filed with the Commission on June 1. The Commission has to first get them filed in their computer system. Estimates for this task range from 1-2 months. Step 2 is an engineering assessment process that places applications into three categories: (i) complete and acceptable for granting (ii) complete but mutually exclusive and (iii) defective which can mean incomplete or requiring waivers for approval. The engineering assessment is computerized. Optimistic FCC personnel estimate an initial grant list of category one applicants in August '98–Is this for real? Category two mutually exclusive applicants have to await the Report and Order (R&O) on the pending Auction Rulemaking. This R&O is expected soon. Category three will be worked one by one with periodic grant lists of completed applications.

Once granted, the operator will have 6-months to build to the CP. There's a **Streamlining** Rulemaking pending that proposes a 3-year construction period for CPs. This R & O could be complete within 6-months. It could be critical to many applicants who are also interested in power increases or other modifications classified as major changes. We must work to eliminate any requirements to "build twice."

June 1 displacement applications have created another procedural change. Prior to June 1, **imminent displacement applications** received priority and the Commission would make grants without consideration of other potential applicants. After June 1, anyone facing imminent displacement needs to file an application for Special Temporary Authority (STA). With the STA, the operator will be able to make a station modification to avoid displacement by the DTV station but will **not** have priority over others who filed on June 1. This could result in future contour changes or an auction after the operator has built to the STA. It's all summarized as "caveat emptor."

Primary Service Rulemaking Process

"On course but hurdles ahead" is probably the best summary of where we are. So many of your filed supportive and constructive comments. Even NAB noted in their reply comments the "detailed community service that is provided by" LPTV (your) stations. But they continued stating that community service is not the issue. It's the added risk we present to the DTV implementation. The next phase is a Notice of Proposed Rulemaking. That isn't a done deal. We'll keep you advised. We may need your help to keep this on track. You can read CBA's reply comments on The LPTV Loop at lptv@loop.com. We're continuing to work very hard on the Norwood/Ford legislation. But the legislative days remaining in the 105th Congress are dwindling and we are up against some problems for which we don't have solutions, yet.

—7—

Studies and Briefs

A Comparative Assessment and Civil Action on Behalf of LPTV

Field Testimony

This chapter consists of two significant documents, one prepared nearly a decade earlier than the other; at the time this period represented nearly the entire lifespan of the LPTV medium. The first is a comparative study compiled in 1984 by Shane Media for Globecom Publishing Ltd. Its aim, as stated in its introduction, was to analyze and document "similarities between [the] operation of standard television stations and [the] operation of new 'Low Power' television stations also on the air in small markets." The second document presented in this chapter is a legal brief of a civil action prepared by attorney Robert T. Perry on behalf of International Broadcasting Network. The case was argued in the United States District Court for the District of Columbia. It challenged the FCC ruling in 1992 that "exclude[d] low power television stations from must carry status." Both documents are offered here as a means of further elucidating what has been presented in the preceding chapters.

Comparative Study of Community Television

Introduction

This research project was conducted by Shane Media Services, Houston, Texas, during the months of August and September, 1984, on behalf of

Globecom Publishing Ltd., of Prairie Village, Kansas. As a publisher of periodicals aimed at the television industry, Globecom was interested in analyzing and documenting similarities between operation of standard television stations in small markets and operation of new low-power television stations, also on the air in small markets.

Documentation of the data would allow Globecom to make management decisions on the subscription base of its *LPTV* magazine and the perception of the new LPTV industry.

Among the initial topics considered for the study:

- Annual cost of operation
- Anticipated expenditures 1985, 1986
- Type of equipment/services to be purchased
- Video and audio quality
- Amount of local origination
- Reaction to the term "LPTV"
- Length of service
- Profitability
- Affiliation with other local media

Based upon these initial ideas, a Research Objective was established, methodology was outlined and tested, and a questionnaire was written and administered according to Shane Media Services specifications based upon our experience researching media use by the public.

Research Objective

The goal stated in the introduction—analyzing and documenting similarities between standard and low-power television operations—assumes that there are such similarities. Therefore, our project begins with a much more basic question: Do the similarities exist? In order to effect full understanding of the study by our clients and by our own research personnel, Shane Media Services has found it useful to devise a single, short question from which all other questions in a study might flow. This question we define as "the Research Objective."

Here is the Research Objective established for the Globecom study:

> What are the comparisons and contrasts that can be identified among full power television stations in small markets and the new low power television stations?

Such a question is developed for guidance purposes only and is not administered to the study respondents.

Methodology

Based on the Research Objective, it was determined that a sample would be drawn representing standard television stations in small markets and another sample would be drawn from licensees of low-power television stations (defined by parameters set by the Federal Communications Commission in assigning channel assignment and maximum operating power).

The sample of standard television stations (referred to as full-power for the purposes of this report) was drawn from stations in ADI 160–212 as defined by Arbitron Ratings Company. We further listed stations in Arbitron's "Supplemental Market" definition, ADIs broken out from major markets to serve smaller population units. Stations from each of these lists were verified by use of the *Broadcasting Yearbook* for 1984.

This station list accumulated from industry sources was then cross-referenced with a *Rand-McNally Atlas* to assure the size of markets. We pursued an initial list of cities of 50,000 and fewer residents to include in the sample as many stations as possible whose service area would afford a reasonable comparison to the market profile of the new low-power stations.

Sample for low-power television stations was drawn from the *Broadcasting Yearbook* 1984; from the mailing list of *LPTV* magazine (a Globecom publication); from a list of LPTV stations collected by the National Association for Community Television Broadcasters (NACT); and from industry advertising by the Southern Baptist Convention (a licensee) and the Spanish International Network (a programming supplier).

We attempted to identify fifty full-power stations serving small communities and an equivalent fifty low-power stations serving small communities in order to conduct the Comparative Study. Our initial research brought us to a list of 107 full-power stations but only thirty-six low-power stations.

The lack of a representative list of Low Power stations is significant not only to this Comparative Study but also the industry. That subject is addressed in the "Summary of Findings," p. 140.

Once the lists of television stations were identified, Shane Media Services developed a questionnaire to explore subjects determined to be of significance in the Comparative Study.

One questionnaire was used for the list of full-power stations. Another, subtly different questionnaire, was used for low-power stations. The differences were subtleties of language, and took into account the fact that most of the full-power stations in the sample were affiliates of traditional networks, that most had been on the air for some period of time, that most had commitments already to local origination of programming.

An additional question was added to the low-power questionnaire about how members of the new industry wished to be identified. This question (no. 21) did not apply to respondents in the full-power category.

The questionnaire for full-power stations was identified as TELEVISION QUESTIONNAIRE for coding purposes only.

The questionnaire for low-power stations was identified as COMMUNITY TELEVISION QUESTIONNAIRE for coding purposes only.

Because of the scope of the questions, high-ranking officials who worked in-house with their properties were used as respondents. General Managers, in-house Owners, in-house Presidents or Executive Vice Presidents were identified and contacted at each of the stations selected for the study. It was determined that only operators at those levels would have access to the richness of information needed.

Respondents were contacted by phone and asked to make a commitment to participate in the study. The questionnaire was described by telephone and some questions were previewed by phone to acquaint the respondent with the breadth of the questioning.

One researcher, a female, made all calls, so that a consistency of approach could be maintained. As the researcher received a commitment to participate in the study, a cover letter, a questionnaire, and a stamped, addressed envelope was sent to the respondent. A deadline was attached to each classification of station (September 21 for "Full Power," October 1 for low-power) in order to effect prompt returns.

In several cases among full-power television operators, reticence was exhibited during the telephone conversation. Nine of these operators received specific letters from Ed Shane, Project Director, referencing the initial conversation and asking for participation.

The difficulty in assembling a list of low-power respondents prompted Shane Media Services to issue a special, personal letter for each low-power respondent contacted. In it we identified the sponsor of the Comparative Study as *LPTV* magazine.

In order to develop as large a sample as possible, multiple tries were made, especially if early attempts resulted in no answer. Phone listings were checked against AT&T Information Services and at least three calls were made to hard-to-reach respondents.

Full Power TV Sample

Full power stations identified		107
Screened out by researcher service area	9	
Weather Emergency*	2	
No phone listing	6	
Called, no answer	4	
Refusals at phone contact	13	
Questionnaire not returned	33	
Questionnaire returned, refused	_1	
	68	−68
Full power in-tab		39

Low Power TV Sample

Low power stations identified		37
Screened out by researcher		
No phone listing	8	
Called, no answer	2	
Off the air	1	
Applicant, not on air	3	
Questionnaire not returned	_7	
	21	−21
Low power in-tab		16
Total full power and low power in-tab		55

*While the study was being conducted, Hurricane Diana struck the Atlantic coast. Two North Carolina stations were eliminated from the list because of hurricane damage.

Summary of Findings

Profile

Because information gathered in the Comparative Study is quantifiable, a "profile" can be drawn of the average respondent. Such a narrative profile is often helpful in gaining understanding of the findings of a study.

Full-Power Station

The average full power station in the study is virtually a full-time operation, with airtime close to nineteen hours a day. Much of that airtime is filled with programming from a major network, and CBS has the edge on primary affiliation.

Almost nine hours a week is produced locally, most of it news and community affairs programming with some sports as part of the local mix. It's unlikely that the amount of local programming will increase substantially during the coming year.

Movies, syndication and other "outside" programming expenses amount to $106,301.04 annually, about 4.5 percent of revenues, based on 1984 projections. Recent equipment expenditures outpaced programming costs, equalling about 6.5 percent of 1984 revenues. Equipment costs during the past year were more than the station bore in previous years, but the 1985 equipment budget calls for expenditures to drop by 8.25 percent.

That equipment purchased in 1985 will most likely be purchased from a Distributor/Systems House or directly from the manufacturer. For many purchases, the station will combine the benefits and buy from both sources. The most likely purchases in 1985 are Videotape Recorders, Editing equipment, Monitors and Test equipment. New camera equipment is possible but less probable. The station will make regular purchases of raw videotape stock.

Management plots the station's audio quality at 6.4 on a scale of 10. Video quality is described as 7.9 on a 10–scale. There seems to be no correlation between the rating of audio or video quality and the projected equipment expenditures.

The station has been on the air twenty-one years and just over three months. It's part of a group ownership but has no co-owned affiliate in town. There are thirty-six full time employees and six or more part timers.

Management relies on *Broadcasting, Broadcast Engineering, Television/Broadcast Communications,* and *TV/Radio Age* for reliable information on the industry.

The future is going to bring increased competition from TV and Cable, but for the near-term business seems to be growing. Even with local newspaper working hard to challenge the station for advertising dollars, revenues for 1984 should top $2.3 million. By 1986, the station expects revenues up 25.3 percent to more than $2.9 million.

Low-Power Station

Compared to the average full power station in the study, the average low power respondent is a newcomer whose economics are represented on a smaller scale.

The low power operator has been on the air for just over 2.5 years and expects just over $100,000 total revenue for 1984. He is confident of the future, however, projecting more than double that amount in 1985 and a 224 percent increase by 1986. Those dollars are challenged by radio, with newspaper viewed as a secondary competitor. In the future, competition for viewers will come from other TV signals and from Cable.

The station broadcasts more than twenty hours a day with more than fourteen hours each week produced locally. Local programming concentrates on sports, then news and community affairs. That local time will definitely increase during 1985.

The station is owned singly and has no other local media affiliation in town. There are nine full-time employees and one or two part-timers.

A variety of programming services is available to the station from CNN Headline News to Country Music Television to Satellite Program Network. An "average" low-power operator has no clear single program service that is "the one," as full-power stations have traditional networks. For the various services that are carried, the monthly cost is $1939.36, or almost 23 percent of 1984's projected revenues.

Also eating into revenues will be equipment costs, budgeted for 1985 at almost $37,000.00, approximately 15 percent of projected revenue. By 1986, the equipment budget will fall to only 9 percent of revenues. These expenditures are in addition to the station's relatively recent start-up expenditure—$290,923.07.

On a scale of 10, management plots audio quality at 6.6. Video quality is at 7.2. Just as with the average full power broadcaster, there seems to be no correlation between the low power operator's rating of his audio and video quality and his proposed expenditures for equipment.

The only product on the shopping list for sure in 1985 is raw videotape. Otherwise, there may be a purchase of a new camera, character generator, lighting equipment and audio/video distribution equipment. The purchase will probably be made from a Distributor/Systems House, but a Dealer or Manufacturer could also get the business.

Management keeps up with the industry through *LPTV* magazine and *Broadcasting. Broadcast Engineering* has high readership but low marks for actually serving the station's needs.

While this description has been written for the average low-power station, the station respondent would prefer another name for his industry, perhaps "Community TV."

Comparison or Contrast?

This project bears the title "Comparative Study," yet it is more a catalog of contrasts than of comparisons. Similarities between standard, or full power, television stations in small markets and the new low power stations are few. In fact, the similarities may begin and end at the fact that each group provides programming and local service by television.

The most drastic contrast between the two groups is the economic scale upon which each works. For instance, the *lowest* revenue projection for

1984 among full power stations is $650,000.00. A low of $12,000.00 among low power stations begins to indicate the gulf between the two industries. The picture is further illuminated by the *highest* projection among low power stations for 1984—$280,000.00. The *highest* LPTV projection is only 43 percent of the *lowest* full power projection.

Not until 1986 do any LPTV revenue projections approach parity with the least of the 1984 full-power projections! Worse, the *total* LPTV projection for 1984 is less than half of the *average* projection for 1984 by full-power television.

To determine how to present the findings of this study, we coupled these disparate revenue projections with the ratios of program expense-to-revenue and equipment budget-to-revenue noted in "Profile," above.

The imbalance made us conclude that overall comparisons could not be drawn and that, with rare exceptions, the two groups of stations should be looked upon as separate.

Even this approach became difficult when we tried to consider those stations in the low-power grouping as one entity, because we found few threads that tie the new stations together. The infancy of the medium is apparent. While one of our LPTV respondents had been on the air for twenty years, that station is the exception to the rule. Of fourteen other stations replying to the question about length of service, only one had been on the air longer than two years (and that one reported 2.5 years service). Another respondent went on the air *the day before* our questionnaire arrived! Eliminating the twenty-year veteran and the day-old new arrival, the average life of an LPTV respondent had been only thirteen months.

Low Power, Low Profile

Our research efforts among LPTV operators were hampered by the fact that many of the operators were not readily identifiable in their own communities. Our researcher was told "No Listing" by AT&T information on many occasions as she sought numbers for LPTV stations by their call signs and by references like "Channel 61" or "TV 30." Because we had the advantage of the lists from which we had drawn our LPTV sample (see "Methodology," page 138), our researcher was able to use names of owners or station officials and receive AT&T listings of respondents at home or at another office. AT&T "Information" charges totalling $18.50 are testimony to the difficulty in making contact with LPTV respondents.

This commentary is included here as neither complaint nor defense. Rather, we believe it constitutes a significant finding of the research that

LPTV has such a low profile. The lack of a representative list and the difficulty in pursuit of those on existing lists of LPTV operators indicate that *there may not yet be a low-power television industry!*

In defense of the low power respondent to this study, we note a greater percentage of return from low power than from full power stations (43.2 percent from LPTV, 36.4 percent from standard television). However, the greater universe of small market full power stations meant that the numerical return from that group far outweighed the numerical return from LPTV

Full Power, Fully Entrenched

Traditional television is blessed with several advantages that go beyond economics. Length of service is chief among them. Only six respondents (15.4 percent) had been on the air less than two years. Twenty-four of them (61.5 percent) were veterans of twenty-five years or longer. The two oldest stations among the full-power respondents had been on the air thirty-one years. Our experience in analyzing these matters tells us that longevity of that sort provides solid local recognition. Further, our researcher noted no difficulties when trying to ascertain phone listings for traditional television stations, a dramatic contrast to her LPTV quest.

Another advantage for traditional television when compared to low power stations is an established group of national program suppliers. Of our full-power respondents, 87.1 percent are affiliates of the three major networks. In all, full-power respondents mentioned only five program sources (SIN and CNN Headline News were the others).

By contrast, LPTV respondents mentioned fourteen specific national services. Others were listed as generic, such as "barter" or "satellite services." Clear leaders among services for LPTV are Satellite Program Network (SPN) and Country Music Television.

LPTV seems to have no single, major, mass appeal program supplier that can provide large blocks of programming.

Thus LPTV local origination fills more hours than local programming on full-power stations. LETV stations that originate locally schedule an average of fourteen hours, five minutes per week. Local programming is 9.8 percent of the programming week of LPTV respondents who provide local service. (Three respondents do not.) Full-power stations devote 6.8 percent of their air time to local programming.

News leads local origination among full-power stations. Sports leads on LPTV. Low-power respondents expect to deliver more local programming in the future, while full-power stations expect no change or only minimum increase.

The greater financial strength of full-power stations allows greater choice in programming acquisitions from syndicators and other suppliers. Four full-power respondents (14.3 percent) indicated programming expenditures of $20,000.00 per month or more. The average *annual* figure for LPTV respondents is $23,272.32.

The dramatic differences between full-power and low-power respondents are demonstrated by comparative average economic figures:

Economic Comparison

	Full power	Low power
Start-up costs	2,250,000.00	290,230.76
Additional	1,333,437.00	87,461.54
Last year	153,235.39	46,666.66
Budget		
1985	140,588.23	36,909.09
1986	192,692.30	29,727.27
Revenue Projection		
1984	2,345,172.40	102,272.72
1985	2,649,814.80	246,750.00
1986	2,939,200.00	331,333.33
Program Costs		
Monthly	8,858.42	1,939.36
Annual	106,301.04	23,272.32

It is difficult to assess the significance of the drop in LPTV budget projections. The average for 1985 drops 57.8 percent from the amount listed as the "last year" figure.

The average from full-power stations is much more reliable, with 34 respondents. Because of the recency of the industry, the question applied to only *three* LPTV respondents, only two of whom listed any "last year" expenditures.

Supply and Demand

The choice of supplier for broadcast equipment showed a much clearer pattern among full-power television respondents. While "Distributor or systems house" received the highest marks, "Direct from the manufacturer" was a close second. LPTV responses were spread over the range of answers.

	Full power	Low power
Direct from the manufacturer	71.8	46.6
Distributor or systems house	76.9	66.6
Dealer	53.8	53.3
Independent rep	28.9	33.3
Other	0.0	6.6

An LPTV respondent added a note: "Local preference where possible for ongoing support." We wonder if once again the recency of the LPTV movement makes finding patterns a thing of the future. We wonder further if the low marks for manufacturers by LPTV respondents indicates a lack of contact with manufacturers.

Quality Consciousness

Audio trailed video in self-analysis of quality among the respondents, one of the few areas where the full-power and low-power groups can be compared.

	Full power	Low power	Combined
Video	7.9	7.2	7.55
Audio	6.4	6.6	6.50

Reading Matter

Broadcasting proves to be the most solid link between the traditional television respondents and the low-power operators in this study. Full-power respondents rated it highest—8.6—on a scale of 10; LPTV respondents rated *Broadcasting* at 6.3, second on the 10-scale and second in the number of mentions.

LPTV magazine was first among low-power respondents. We must caution here that each low-power respondent had been prejudiced by the mention of that magazine in the cover letter. (See "Methodology," p. 138.)

Magazine Evaluations

These titles were listed on the questionnaire in this order.

	Full power	Low power	Combined
Broadcasting	8.6	6.3	7.45
Broadcast Engineering	8.0	4.9	6.45
BME	5.9	4.8	5.35
LPTV	2.0	7.3	4.65
Television/Broadcast Communications	7.8	4.6	6.20
TV/Radio Age	6.3	4.8	5.55
TV World	2.7	4.0	3.35

(continued)

These titles were added by respondents in a place provided for additional evaluations. They are listed here alphabetically.

Advertising Age	8.0	—	4.0
Broadcast Week	8.0	7.0	7.5
Electronic Media	7.1	—	3.55
Low-power Community TV	—	6.0	3.0
Multichannel News	—	7.0	3.5
NTA Newsletter	—	5.0	2.5
Satellite Guide	—	4.5	2.25
Videography	—	6.0	3.0

Competition

A real difference in the perspective of full-power and low-power respondents is in their view of competition.

In terms of competition for advertising revenues, full-power stations are battling newspaper first, other TV second. Low-power respondents see radio as the biggest challenge to dollars.

	Full power	Low power
Newspaper	69.2%	46.6%
TV	35.9%	20.0%
Radio	17.9%	66.6%
Cable	5.1%	6.6%

Responding to a question about viewer competition in ten years, LPTV operators still see radio in the picture, although they agree with full-power respondents that TV, new TV, and cable will provide the greatest challenge.

	Full-power	Low-power
Television	43.5%	40.0%
Cable	41.0%	40.0%
New TV	25.6%	20.0%
Newspaper	12.8%	26.6%
Radio	7.7%	26.0%
DBS	10.2%	—

Conclusions

The absence of a clear-cut low-power television industry indicates that interests hoping to sell goods and services to it must be patient. Very patient.

The same interests would do well to target full-power stations in lower ADIs, since respondents in this study are well aware that competition is heating up from new television and cable.

Our returns from low-power operators show that they are dissatisfied with the term low-power that has been adopted from the FCC designation. However, there is no majority in favor of a new label. The plurality (46.6 percent) favors "Community TV." That name was included because it is a designation heard in personal interviews conducted to test and shape the questionnaire.

Our best recommendation to Globecom Publishing Ltd. is an expansion of service that is narrowly drawn only to LPTV. Redirect toward the smaller ADI and hope to embrace LPTV when it "grows up."

A commonality is not present between the full-power television industry and a low-power television industry. However, there is clear economic commonality among full-power stations in small markets. Therein lies opportunity.

Civil Action Notice for Local Community Broadcasters

IN THE UNITED STATES DISTRICT COURT
FOR THE DISTRICT OF COLUMBIA

TURNER BROADCASTING SYSTEM, INC., et al.,	)
	)
Plaintiffs,	) Civil Action No.
	) 92-2247
v.	) (TJP, SWF, SS)
	)
FEDERAL COMMUNICATIONS COMMISSION,	)
and the UNITED STATES OF AMERICA,	)
	)
Defendants.	)
———————————————————	) Civil Action Nos.
	) 92-2292, 92-2494,
AND CONSOLIDATED ACTIONS.	) 92-2495, 92-2558
———————————————————	) (TPJ, SWF, SS)

INTERVENOR-DEFENDANT APPLICANT LOCAL COMMUNITY
BROADCASTERS' MEMORANDUM IN REPLY TO OPPOSITIONS
TO MOTION FOR SUMMARY JUDGMENT ON CROSS-CLAIM

INTRODUCTION

Intervenor-Defendant Applicant Local Community Broadcasters respectfully submits this memorandum in reply to the oppositions of Intervenor-

Defendant Applicant National Association of Broadcasters ("NAB") and Defendants United States of America and Federal Communications Commission to the Local Community Broadcasters' motion for summary judgment on its cross-claim.

This cross-claim is a challenge to Section 4 of the Cable Television Consumer Protection and Competition Act of 1992 ("Cable Act" or "Act") insofar as it largely excludes low-power television stations ("LPTV stations") from must carry status. The Local Community Broadcasters seek a declaration that certain provisions of Section 4 deny LPTV stations freedom of speech and equal protection under law guaranteed by the First and Fifth Amendments.[1]

The primary opposition to the Local Community Broadcasters' cross-claim comes not from Defendants but rather from the NAB. This is not surprising, given that Congress seems to have excluded most LPTV stations from must carry status only because the NAB vigorously lobbied for such exclusion.

While differential treatment of full and low-power television stations "does not by itself . . . raise First Amendment concerns," *Leathers v. Medlock,* 111 S.Ct. 1438, 1442 (1992), it becomes "constitutionally suspect when it threatens to suppress the expression of particular ideas or viewpoints." *Id.* at 1443. The denial of must carry status to most LPTV stations threatens to suppress their viewpoints because many will fail without cable carriage.

The differential grant of must carry status to full and low-power television stations is also constitutionally suspect because the public "subsidy" at issue here is a public forum. *Rust v. Sullivan,* 111 S.Ct. 1759, 1776 (1991). In allocating cable channels for carriage of local broadcast signals, Con-

---

1. Because the Local Community Broadcasters ("LCB") have not sought a declaration that every single provision in Section 4 differentiating full-power and low-power television stations is unconstitutional, the NAB asserts that LCB lacks confidence in its legal argument. NAB Memorandum at 4, 24. To the contrary, LCB has complete confidence in its argument. LCB has focused its attention on those provisions in Section 4 which will *actually* preclude any of LCB's eight members from gaining must carry status. Other provisions will not pose any major obstacle. For example, even though Section 4 gives full-power television stations priority of access to must carry channels, Cable Act 4(b)(2)(A), most cable systems will soon have triple digit channel capacity, thus ensuring vacant must carry channels for any LPTV station. LCB's draft order inadvertently omitted Section 4(c) as one of the provisions to be declared invalid, insofar as it placed a ceiling on the number of LPTV stations that may have access to vacant must carry channels. LCB did, however, argue that Section 4(c) was unconstitutional in its earlier memorandum. Local Community Broadcasters' Memorandum in Support of Motion for Summary Judgment on Cross-Claim at 30 (January 22,1993).

gress has designated those channels as public fore for a limited purpose. *Perry Education Ass'n v. Perry Local Educators' Ass'n,* 460 U.S. 37, 45 (1983). "When speakers and subjects are similarly situated, the State may not pick and choose [to whom to grant access]." *Id.* at 55. Full-power and low-power television stations are similarly situated; they are both integral components of the nation's network of broadcast television stations.

The FCC authorized low-power television service in the early 1980's because many communities remained unserved or underserved by full-power television service. The Commission recognized that the new service would greatly enhance program diversity and localism, two important service objectives for broadcast television. The secondary status of low-power television stations ("LPTV stations") refers merely to their obligation to prevent or eliminate interference with full-power television stations, not their relative importance in serving the programming needs of the communities in which they broadcast. While LPTV stations operate on a secondary basis, they are the primary source of television programming for many audience segments in rural, suburban and urban areas.

PRELIMINARY STATEMENT

A. Contrary to the NAB's Assertions, Low-power Television Service Is An Integral Component of the Nation's Network of Broadcast Television Stations

The NAB asserts that low-power television service is merely a secondary television service on which the Federal Communications Commission ("FCC" or "Commission") has never relied to provide the diversity and localism expected from full-power television stations. NAB Memorandum at 4-5. That simply is not the case.

When the Commission first considered the need for low-power television service in 1978, it observed that "[o]ur concepts of program diversity and of service needs . . . do not focus necessarily on a paucity of conventional over-the-air . . . signals available in the community. Rather they go to whether identifiable service needs of communities in general are being met by existing television sources."[2] When the FCC proposed to authorize low-power television service in 1980, it noted the potential for such service to "respond [ ] to the needs and interests of particular audiences that are underserved by available television broadcast service, both in urban and

---

2. *Inquiry Into the Future Role of Low-power Television Broadcasting and Television Translators in the National Telecommunications System,* 68 F.C.C. 2d 1525, 1527 (1978).

rural areas."[3] When it approved low-power television service in 1982, the Commission concluded uhat "low-power stations can provide diverse programming" and that "low-power service is particularly suited to carry out" the FCC's "important service objective" of local television programming.[4] A few years later, the Commission observed that low-power television service "significantly expands the information marketplace."[5] In short, contrary to the NAB's assertion, the Commission has relied upon low-power television service to provide the diversity and localism *not* expected from full-power television stations.

NAB also errs in describing low-power television service as a "secondary" programming service. NAB Memorandum at 4-5. The "secondary" status of LPTV stations merely refers to their obligation to prevent or eliminate objectionable interference with full-power television stations, not their status in serving the programming needs of the communities in which they broadcast.[6] As FCC Chairman Fowler observed in 1982:

Low-power television may not have the transmission capabilities of full broadcast television, but its capacity to provide televised programming that is directly responsive to the interests of smaller audience segments makes it truly unique in its ability to expand consumer choices in video programming. From this perspective, the power of these stations may below, but their potential is enormous.[7]

Similarly, LPTV stations may operate on a "secondary" basis, but they are the primary source of broadcast television programming for many smaller audience segments.

The NAB also contends that the Commission never contemplated that LPTV stations would compete with full-power television stations or cable systems. NAB Memorandum at 5. In fact, the Commission has always contemplated such competition:

---

3. *Inquiry Into the Future Role of Low-power Television Broadcasting and Television Translators in the National Telecommunications System,* 82 F.C.C.2d 47, 77 (1980) ("Notice of Proposed Rule Making").

4. *Inquiry Into the Future Role of Low-power Television Broadcasting and Television Translators in the National Telecommunications System,* 51 Rad. Reg. 2d (P & F) 476, 484 (1982) ("Report and Order"), aff'd sub nom. Neighborhood TV Co. v. FCC, 742 F.2d 629 (D.C. Cir. 1984).

5. *Inquiry Into Section 73.1910 of the Commission's Rules and Regulations Concerning the General Fairness Doctrine Obligations of Broadcast Licensees,* 102 F.C.C. 2d 143, 212 (1985).

6. *Notice of!Proposed Rule Making,* 82 F.C.C. 2d at 54; *Report and Order,* 51 Rad. Reg. 2d (P & F) at 486.

7. *Report and Order,* 51 Rad. Reg. 2d (P & F) at *525* (Separate Statement of Chairman Fowler).

We also emphasize ... that while the rules for the low-power service are intended to protect the public's expectation of service from full [power] stations, we do not intend to cater to full [power] licensees' unreasonable fears of competition from low-power stations, and fetter the low-power service for that reason. *We believe low-power can provide competition that stimulates the entire telecommunications marketplace.*[8]

For the past decade, LPTV stations have competed with full-power television stations and cable systems, not only for viewing audiences, but also for local advertising.

The NAB further asserts that the Commission did not consider low-power television service of sufficient value to divert scarce administrative resources from overseeing full-power television service. NAB Memorandum at 6. To the contrary, the Commission limited its regulation of low-power television service not because it deemed the service to lack sufficient value but rather because the Commission assumed that marketplace forces would compel LPTV stations to serve the public interest. The FCC thus imposed "a minimum of program-related regulations [on LPTV stations], so that they might be fully responsive to marketplace conditions. ... [Programming] judgments properly are left to licensees; it is in their interest, and the public's, to garner audience by attempting to serve unmet needs."[9] It was for the very same reason that the Commission later eliminated many of the programming obligations imposed on full-power television stations.[10]

The NAB further disparages low-power television service, noting that the Commission declined to grant must carry status to LPTV stations in 1982. NAB Memorandum at 7. That decision, however, was based upon certain assumptions which later proved false, not on any assessment that low-power television service was of limited value.[11] The Commission, for example, assumed that cable operators with vacant channels would voluntarily carry LPTV stations and that cable subscribers would retain the

---

8. Id. at 488 (emphasis added).

9. Id. at 519.

10. Revision of Programming and Commercialization Policies, Ascertainment Requirements, and Program Log Requirements for Commercial Television Stations, 98 F.C.C.2d 1076 (1989), *on reconsideration,* 104 F.C.C.2d 358 (1986), *aff'd in part and remanded in part sub nom., Action for Children's Television v. FCC,* 821 F.2d 741 (D.C. Cir. 1987).

11. *Report and Order,* 51 Rad. Reg. 2d (P&F) at 521-22. The FCC's 1982 decision was made at a time when cable penetration was below 40 percent. Today, cable penetration exceeds 60 percent, making cable television "a dominant nationwide video medium." Cable Act (a)(3).

ability to continue viewing broadcast signals not carried on cable channels.[12] Neither assumption proved true in the long run. 1992 Cable Act 2(a)(15), 2(a)(17). Moreover, the Commission expressly stated that it would reconsider its decision if its assumptions proved untrue.[13]

The NAB also asserts that the Commission has consistently made clear that success or failure of low-power television service will not affect the public interest. NAB Memorandum at 8. But the few FCC statements which it references merely note the uncertain economic viability of low-power television service.[14] In addition, one of those statements describes the service's "promise of enhanced program service diversity and increased minority ownership"—factors clearly relevant to the public interest.[15]

In sum, notwithstanding the NAB's assertions, low-power television service has become an integral component of the nation's network of broadcast television stations. It has not only well served the public interest by providing the first local television service in many rural areas but also by providing specialized local programming for audience segments underserved by full-power television stations in urban and suburban markets.

B. Contrary to the NAB's Assertions, Must Carry Status Will Ensure That Low-power Television Service Remains A Vital Source of Specialized Local Programming.

The NAB next contends that mandatory cable carriage of LPTV stations would instantly transform them into full-power television stations, thus thwarting the FCC's regulatory plan for low-power television service. NAB Memorandum at 8-9. Not only does that contention ignore the real reasons why LPTV stations seek must carry status (economic survival) but it also misstates the true facts.

Even with must carry status, LPTV stations would continue to operate on a secondary basis. They would still be obligated to prevent or eliminate interference with full-power television stations by, for example, shifting to another frequency or redirecting their broadcast antennas.[16]

In addition, whether must carry status would actually increase the coverage of an LPTV station depends upon many factors, including the size of

---

12. *Id.* at 521.

13. *Report and Order,* 51 Rad. Reg.2d (P&F) at 522.

14. *Report and Order,* 51 Rad. Reg. 2d (P&F) at 486, 513, 526 (Separate Statement of Commissioner Fogarty).

15. *Id.* at 526 (Separate Statement of Commissioner Fogarty).

16. *Notice of Proposed Rule Making,* 82 F.C.C.2d at 54; *Report and Order,* 51 Rad. Reg. 2d (P&F) at 486; 47 C.F.R. 74. 703.

nearby cable systems. There are, for example, many LPTV stations whose coverage areas already encompass entire cable systems. Carriage over those systems would not increase coverage. While contending that must carry status would expand LPTV stations' coverage, the NAB neglects to note that must carry status will greatly expand the coverage of many full-power television stations. A full-power broadcaster may, for example, qualify for must carry status even if it is unable to deliver to the cable headend an over-the-air signal of good quality. 1992 Cable Act 4(h)(1)(B)(iii). *Distant* full-power broadcasters may also qualify for must carry status if they agree to indemnify cable operators for any increased copyright liability. *Id.* 4(h)(1)(B)(ii).

The NAB's assertion that must carry status for LPTV stations would eliminate their incentive to target small unserved and underserved audiences is purely speculative. NAB Memorandum at 9. It is also contrary to the current trend in cable programming service away from mass appeal programming and towards narrowcast programming.[17] Rather than eliminate LPTV stations' incentive to provide specialized programming for small audiences, must carry status will restore that incentive, because without cable carriage LPTV stations cannot attract the advertising revenues necessary to recoup the costs of local productions targeted at small unserved and underserved audiences.[18] A number of LPTV stations have already suspended such productions because they are *not* carried on cable channels.[19]

The NAB suggests that LPTV stations' reliance on satellite-delivered programming reflects their limited interest in local narrowcast programming. NAB Memorandum at 10. This is simply not so. No television station—full-power or low-power—can afford to produce all of its broadcast programming. Indeed, the great majority of full-power television stations devote most of their broadcast time either to broadcast network or nationally syndicated programming.[20]

In sum, must carry status for LPTV stations would not instantly transform them into full-power television stations. Nor would it eliminate their incentive to provide local narrowcast programming for audiences unserved

---

17. "New Channels Vie for Slices of Growing Cable Pie," *N.Y. Times,* Dec. 28, 1992, at D6.

18. Affidavit of John Kompas, President of K/B Ltd. and former President of the Community Broadcasters Association, 10 ("Kompas Affidavit'); Affidavit of Andrew Knapp 22 ("Knapp Affidavit"); Affidavit of Earl Marlar 4 ("Marlar Affidavit").

19. Kompas Affidavit at 10 Knapp Affidavit at 22; Marlar Affidavit at 4.

20. "Most TV stations program from three to five hours of local news, information, and other shows daily." H.R. Rep. No. 102-628, 102d Cong., 2d Sess. 56 (1992) (quoting former FCC Chairman Alfred Sikes).

or underserved by full-power television stations. To the contrary, it would restore their ability to provide such programming.

C. Contrary to the NAB's Assertions, Low-power Television as well as Full Power Television Stations Are Victims of Cable Operators' Refusal to Carry.

The NAB asserts that Congress' purpose in adopting must carry requirements was "to impose a structural solution to a specific antitrust problem," suggesting that only full-power television stations have been victimized by cable operators' refusals to carry. NAB Memorandum at 10. That, of course, is not true. Like full-power television stations, LPTV stations compete with cable systems for local advertisers. For that reason cable operators have the very same economic incentive to refuse carriage of LPTV stations. Many LPTV stations have been denied cable carriage and suffered economic injury as a result. Some have even gone out of business.[21]

The NAB suggests that any injury to LPTV stations should be disregarded because high definition television ("HDTV") will soon displace those stations in urban and suburban markets. NAB Memorandum at 8,11. Contrary to its prediction, LPTV stations in those areas will not soon disappear because of HDTV. It may be years before HDTV becomes a reality. A final HDTV system may not even be selected until late 1993.[22] In addition, the new Chairman of the FCC contemplates a more relaxed schedule of implementation of HDTV than his predecessor.[23] Moreover, the digital technology on which the new HDTV system will be based may actually expand the opportunities for low-power television service:

> Digital technology will operate at lower power levels than present analog broadcast television does; therefore, the interference and channel spacing requirements will be substantially different. According to Zenith's brochure on HDTV, with digital technology it would be possible to authorize consecutive channels in the same market—i.e., Channels 20, 21, 22, 23, 24, 25, etc.[24]

ARGUMENT

I. THE DIFFERENTIAL GRANT OF MUST CARRY STATUS FOR Full-power AND Low-power TELEVISION STATIONS IS SUBJECT TO STRICT SCRUTINY.

---

21. Kompas Affidavit at 10; Knapp Affidavit at 22; Marlar Affidavit at 4; Affidavit of Lee Jackson at 7-8.

22. "Now There Are Four," *Broadcasting,* Feb. 15, 1993, at 6.

23. "James Quello: The FCC's 'Report and Order' Chairman," *Broadcasting,* Feb. 15, 1993, at 6, 34.

24. "EM's Story Added to LPTV Misperceptions," *Electronic Media,* Feb. 11, 1991, at 14.

The NAB argues that the differential grant of must carry status to full-power and low-power television stations is subject to minimal scrutiny unless it can be shown that Congress intended to stifle a point of view. NAB Memorandum at 13-16. To the contrary, differential treatment of speakers is subject to strict scrutiny—under First Amendment or Equal Protection analysis—whenever "it threatens to suppress the expression of particular ideas or viewpoints," regardless of Congress' specific intent. *Leathers v. Medlock,* 111 S.Ct. at, 1443. Such differential treatment is like-wise subject to strict scrutiny whenever it involves a grant of selective access to a public forum. *Perry Education Ass'n v. Perry Local Educators Ass'n,* 460 U.S. at 55. Both circumstances exist here.

A. Strict Scrutiny Is Appropriate Because the Differential Grant of Must Carry Status Threatens to Suppress the Viewpoints of LPTV Stations.

The NAB heavily relies on various cases in which the Supreme Court has considered constitutional challenges to tax laws which differentially treat speakers. NAB Memorandum at 3, 13-14, citing *Regan v. Taxation With Representation,* 461 U.S. 540 (1983) and *Leathers v. Medlock.* Its reliance on tax law cases is, however, misplaced. They clearly show that a suppressive purpose is not the *sine qua non* for strict scrutiny under either First Amendment or Equal Protection analysis.

In *Minneapolis Star and Tribune Co. v Minnesota Comm'r of Revenue,* 460 U.S. 575 (1983), for example, the Supreme Court invoked strict scrutiny to review a special use tax applicable only to large circulation newspapers even though there was "no indication, apart from the structure of the tax itself, of any impermissible or censorial motive on the part of the legislature." *Id.* at 580. Similarly, in *Arkansas Writers' Project, Inc. v Ragland,* 481 U.S. 221 (1987), the Court invoked strict scrutiny to review a state sales tax scheme that exempted special interest but not general interest magazines published in the state even though "there [was] no evidence of an improper censorial motive." *Id.* at 228.

In both cases strict scrutiny was invoked by the Court because the tax laws under review threatened to suppress viewpoints, even absent any suppressive purpose. Such laws "impose[ ] a particular danger of abuse by the State." *Id.* That "danger of abuse" arises from the weakened "political constraints that prevent a legislature from passing crippling taxes of general applicability . . ." *Minneapolis Star and Tribune Co. v Minnesota Commissioner of Revenue,* 460 U.S. at 585. Likewise, in *Leathers v Medlock* the Supreme Court made clear that differential taxation of speakers will receive scrutiny if it is "directed at, *or presents the danger of suppressing*, particular ideas." 113 S. Ct. at 1447 (emphasis added).

Regan v. Taxation With Representation, on which the NAB principally relies, is not to the contrary. Despite Congress' decision to only subsidize the lobbying efforts of veterans' organizations, there was no danger of suppression of the lobbying efforts of other tax-exempt charitable organizations. They remained free "to receive deductible contributions to support . . . nonlobbying activit[ies]." 461 U.S. at 545. At the same time, they could create separate affiliates with tax-exempt status for their lobbying efforts. *Id.* at 544.

The NAB correctly observes that Congress adopted must carry requirements for reasons unrelated to suppression of speech. NAB Memorandum at 16. But the same cannot be clearly said about Congress' decision to exclude most LPTV stations from must carry status. While the adoption of must carry requirements redressed a competition imbalance between full-power television stations and cable operators, the exclusion of LPTV stations from must carry status maintains a competitive imbalance between low-power television stations and cable operators. In addition, the denial of must carry eligibility to LPTV stations established a new competitive imbalance between full-power and low-power television stations.[25] The "structure" of Section 4 of the Cable Act thus suggests a possible suppressive purpose. *Minneapolis Star and Tribune Co. v. Minnesota Comm'r of Revenue*, 460 U.S. at 580. That inference is buttressed by the complete absence of an explanation for denial of must carry eligibility to LPTV stations in the Cable Act's legislative history.[26]

In any event, regardless of Congress' intentions, the denial of must carry status to most LPTV stations imperils their economic survival and thus threatens to suppress their viewpoints. The NAB cites various cases in which the Supreme Court upheld differential treatment of speakers despite the practical consequences for the disadvantaged group. NAB Memorandum at 17–18, citing *Buckley v. Valeo*, 424 U.S. 1 (1976) and *Regan v. Taxation With Representation*. But in none of those cases did the practical consequences flow from the anticompetitive acts of government-created

---

25. Indeed, the new imbalance is reministcent of the situation in the *Associated Press* case—before the antitrust relief—where one group of competitors controlled a bottleneck facility and denied access to their competitors. *Associated Press v. United States*, 326 U.S. 1 (1945).

26. There is, however, no doubt as to the suppressive purpose of the NAB, which vigorously lobbied against must carry status for LPTV stations. Kompas Affidavit at 12. The demise of LPTV stations would doubtless facilitate full-power broadcasters conversion to high definition television. NAB Memorandum at 8, 11.

monopolies, as is true here. Cable operators have until recently enjoyed de facto exclusive franchises awarded by local governments and sanctioned by Federal law. 47 U.S.C. 541(A)(1)(franchising authority may award "one or more" cable franchises).

Uhe NAB further argues that there is no First Amendment Violation here because LPTV stations lack "distinct points of view." NAB Memorandum at 20. The Supreme Court, however, did not consider whether the disadvantaged newspapers in *Minneapolis Star and Tribune Co. v. Minnesota Comm'r of Revenue* held specific editorial positions before declaring the special use tax at issue there unconstitutional. Similarly, in *Arkansas Writers' Project v. Ragland* the Court did not identify any distinct points of view held by the non-exempt general interest magazines before declaring the state sales tax scheme at issue there unconstitutional. In each case it sufficed that the tax law at issue threatened to suppress particular viewpoints, i.e., particular speakers. That same principle should apply here.

B. Strict Scrutiny Is Also Appropriate Because the Must Carry Channels Are Designated Public Fora.

In urging minimal scrutiny, the NAB also relies on various cases in which the Supreme Court has upheld selective access to nonpublic fora. NAB Memorandum at 12, 14-15, citing *United States Postal Service v. Council of Greenburgh Civic Ass'n*, 453 U.S. 114 (1981) ("Greenburgh"); *Cornelius v. NAACP Legal Def. & Educ. Fund*, 473 U.S. 788 (1985) ("Cornelius"); *Perry Education Ass'n v. Perry Local Educators' Ass'n*, 460 U.S. 37 (1983) ("Perry"); and *Lehman v. Shaker Heights*, 418 U.S. 298 (1974) ('Lehman"). Reliance on these cases however, is misplaced because the must carry channels allocated under Section 4 of the Cable Act are designated public fora.

Such public fora "consist of public property which the State has opened for use by the public for expressive activity." *Perry*, 460 U.S. at 45. They "may be created for a limited purpose such as use by certain groups." *Id.* at 45 n 7, citing *Widmar v. Vincent* 454 U.S. 263 (1981) (university meeting facilities made available to student groups).

In allocating cable channels for must carry purposes, Congress has effectively designated new public fora in each community where there exists a cable system. It does not matter that cable channels may be private property, so long as they are *"controlled* by the government." *Missouri Knights of the Ku Klux Klan v. Kansas City, Missouri,* 723 F.Supp 1347, 1351 (W.D. Mo. 1989) (emphasis in original)(public access channel either traditional or designated public forum), citing *Greenburgh,* 453 U.S. at (privately owned mailboxes part of the United States Postal Service's nationwide system for the delivery and receipt of mail); *Southeastern Promotions. Ltd v. Conrad,* 420 U.S. 546, 555 (1975) (privately owned theater under long-term lease to city became designated public forum).

The cases on which the NAB rely are factually inapposite. The must carry channels bear no resemblance to the nonpublic fora at issue in *Cornelius* (charitable fund-raising campaign in federal offices), *Perry* (public school district's internal mail system), *Lehman* (advertising space on public buses), or *Greenburgh* (letter mailboxes). These channels do not implicate "the efficient operation of quintessential government functions . . . so clearly at stake as in the federal workplace *(Cornelius),* . . . in public schools *(Perry).* . . , in the operation of public transportation *(Lehman)* or postal systems ([Greenburgh])." *Stewart v. District of Columbia Armory Board,* 863 F.2d 1013, 1019 (D.C. Cir. 1988). Unlike those nonpublic fora, must carry channels are completely " 'compatibl[e] with expressive activity.' " *Id.* at 1018, quoting Cornelius, 473 U.S. at 802.

Moreover, local broadcasters are permitted to use must carry channels "as a matter of course." *Perry,* 460 U.S. at 47. By contrast, access to the nonpublic fora in the Supreme Court cases on which the NAB relies was only granted on an individualized basis. *See, e.g. id.* (permission to use public school district's internal mail system to communicate with teachers had to be secured from each school principal); "Where, as here, 'the granting of the requisite permit is merely ministerial,' and not attended by 'extensive admission criteria to limit access . . . to those organizations considered appropriate,' " the claim that a forum is nonpublic must fail. *Community for Creative Non-Violence v. Turner,* 893 F.2d 1387,1391 (D.C. Cir. 1990), quoting *Cornelius,* 473 U.S. at 804-05.

In designated public fora—even ones created for a limited public purpose—government "must demonstrate compelling reasons for restricting access to a single class of speakers. . . . When speakers are similarly situated, the State may not pick and choose." *Perry,* 460 U.S. at 55. Thus, a university that had made its meeting facilities generally available for use by registered student groups could not selectively exclude certain student groups unless the exclusion was "necessary to serve a compelling state interest and . . . narrowly drawn to achieve that end." *Widmar v. Vincent,* 454 U.S. at 270.

Likewise here, full-power and low-power television stations are similarly situated. Both are integral components of the nation's network of broadcast television stations. Both contribute to the diversity and localism in broadcast television service. Both are necessary to a fair, equitable and efficient distribution of such service in the United States. 47 U.S.C. 307(b). The differential grant of must carry status to full-power and low-power television stations therefore may only be justified by a showing that such differential treatment is necessary to serve a compelling state interest and narrowly drawn to achieve that end. *Perry*, 460 U.S. at *55; Widmar v. Vincent*, 454 U.S. at 270. Neither Defendants nor the NAB have made such a showing.[27]

II. THE DIFFERENTIAL GRANT OF MUST CARRY STATUS TO Full-power AND Low-power TELEVISION STATIONS FAILS EVEN MINIMAL SCRUTINY

Assuming *arguendo* that minimal scrutiny is appropriate, the differential grant of must carry status to full-power and low-power television stations is *not* "reasonable in light of the purpose" of the legislation. *Perry*, 460 U.S. at 49. The NAB's assertions to the contrary are patently absurd. They rest in large measure on mischaracterization of low-power television service's role in the nation's network of broadcast television stations. See [["Preliminary Statement, A" *supra*.

The NAB also attempts to narrowly read the Cable Act's declaration of findings and purposes as if they only referred to full-power television stations. NAB Memorandum at 21, 23. The most relevant of these findings expressly refer to "broadcast television" or "television broadcasters," without distinguishing between full-power and low-power television stations. See e.g., Cable Act 2(a)(14) ("broadcast television stations"); *id.* 2(a)(15) ("local television broadcasters"); *id.* 2(a)(16) ("local broadcast television"). When Congress intended a finding or purpose to apply only to one class of broadcasters, it expressly stated so. *Id.* 2(a)(7) ("noncommercial educational stations"); 2(a)(21) ("low-power television stations"). The only possible inference is that Congress intended the great majority of findings and purposes to refer both to full-power and low-power television stations. That statutory construction is buttressed by the Cable Act's legislative history. The declaration of finding and purposes derives almost verbatim from the Senate version of the legislation (S.12), which conferred broad must carry eligibility on LPTV stations. H.R Conf. Rep. No. 102-862, 102d Cong., 2d

---

27. Even assuming *arguendo* that full-power television stations have "special responsibilities" in the nation's network of broadcast television stations, that nevertheless does not justify denial of equal access to cable channels for LPTV stations. *Perry*, 460 U.S. at 50.

Sess. 49-51 (1992); S. Rep. No. 102-92, 102d Cong., 2d Sess. 103, 108 (1991) ("1991 Senate Report").

The nonpublic forum cases on which the NAB relies are again factually inapposite. In *Perry,* for example, exclusion of the rival union from access to the public school's district's internal mail system was deemed reasonable because "substantial alternative channels . . . remain open for union-teacher communications to take place." 460 U.S. at 53. By contrast, cable systems have become "bottleneck" facilities needed by other speakers to reach their audiences. 1991 Senate Report at 51.

Conclusion

The differential grant of must carry status to full-power and low-power television stations does not pass muster under either strict or minimal scrutiny. Simply put, denial of must carry eligibility to all but a very few LPTV stations is not justified by any governmental interest, let alone one which is compelling. The complete absence of any explanation in the legislative history for denial of must carry eligibility to most LPTV stations coupled with the Defendants' limited defense of that denial, makes patently clear that the public interest is not served by denying must carry eligibility to LPTV stations. For the foregoing reasons, the Court should grant summary judgment for the Local Community Broadcasters on their cross- claim.

—8—

The Alaska LPTV Network

Michael Havice

Broadcast and Electronic Communication, Marquette University

Signals in the Northern Lights

LPTV in Alaska demonstrates a unique concept in delivering network programming to the population of the state. The State of Alaska delivers network programming (ABC, CBS, NBC, and PBS) to Alaska's citizens using a separate network distribution system that utilizes satellite and LPTV technology. An investigation into the operation of the Alaska television network allows observers to see the impact of new technology, especially satellite technology and LPTV network technology, on the distribution of programming to the sparsely scattered and diverse populations of Alaska. This chapter investigates the history and development of networked television in Alaska, which uses low power transmission technology as part of its distribution system. It also describes the current status of LPTV in Alaska and comments on the future possibilities for telecommunication services there. Telecommunication services in Alaska depend upon the infrastructure established by the LPTV network.

The Alaska Division of Communication handled two-way communications in 1975. At that time the primary means of electronic communication in Alaska were telephone (where one could get it) and two-way radio. Technology improved communication opportunities when high frequency telephones and side-band radio were developed. At the same time satellite

The author wishes to acknowledge the help of research assistant Sara Halpin.

service expanded to include telephone service. These telecommunication advances threw open the door for Alaska's citizens by improving their communication with each other and the world. Alaska became a little less isolated.

Delivery of television by satellite throughout the State of Alaska became possible in 1975. Advances had made it easier to deliver telephone service to rural areas, and the state appropriated $5 million for the purchase and installation of 100 earth stations. The purpose of the appropriation was to provide telecommunication service to every community with twenty-five or more residents. By rural Alaska standards, a community of twenty-five citizens is a significant grouping. The feasibility of delivering of television signals to rural Alaskans was considered because there were enough satellite circuits to handle television and provide telephone service. In 1976, the legislature appropriated an additional $1.2 million for the Television Demonstration Project (TVDP). This project demonstrated the feasibility of delivering television by satellite through the newly installed small earth stations. The state benefited from the undertaking. The technical experience gained allowed for the planning of a permanent and statewide television distribution system. This state-financed television distribution system, based on satellites, earth stations, and 10-watt transmitters, occurred well before the establishment of LPTV in the lower forty-eight states.

There were 10-watt transmitters in operation throughout the state before satellites delivered television to earth stations. The first 10-watt transmission facilities broadcast programming schedules that consisted of locally originated programs and "bicycled" tapes. Though the programming was unreliable, programming practices were appreciated by community members. The advent of satellite delivery of program content changed program delivery forever. The problem of user choice during the early years of television in Alaska, addressed by Michael Porcaro,[1] arose over what was to be broadcast over the transmitters. Porcaro suggested solving the problem by combining licensee-selected programming via satellite with use of mini-TV cassettes for programming substitutions. A community member could make substitutions to satellite programming to serve local needs; that is, programming would be decided by the "locals." What later became Rural Alaska Television Network (RATNet) Council resembled Porcaro's suggested plan.

The distribution of television in Alaska became feasible when the governor's Office of Telecommunications provided for the lease of a full-time satellite television channel and downlink (receive) facilities at twenty-four communities. Each community had a mini (10-watt) television transmitter. A tape delay and program origination center in Anchorage serviced the twenty-four sites. The project became known as the Television

Demonstration Project (TVDP), and it assumed its current title of Television Project (TVP) after the demonstration period. In 1977, an additional $600,000 was appropriated to extend the operation of the TVP through June 30, 1978. The Alaska legislature had, in fact, put itself in the television network business by establishing, maintaining, and running a television distribution system.

Although not on the scale or with the purpose of commercial networks, the Alaska network carried out three of the four basic functions (general administrative, technical, programming, and sales) of a network. In the case of Alaska, the sales function did not exist outside of the context of providing programming that an audience wished to view. Like any network, the Alaska television network specialized in arranging relay facilities to deliver programs to stations. Concurrently, the Alaska network representatives, State of Alaska Satellite Television Project (TVP) and Rural Alaska Television Network (RATNet) Council, worked to maintain good relations with affiliates.[2]

Leonard Lewin has described controls that affect broadcast networks, which included "terrain, government, economic, audience influence, pressure groups, psychological/sociological, technical opportunities to increase media channels and other industry mediating controls."[3] The interactions of these elements and responses to the changing economic and technological climate in Alaska demonstrate a pattern of LPTV development, crisis, and rebirth.

Financing the Alaska Network

Three important trends surface when the background of television development in Alaska is examined. The first and most important is technological innovation in and the delivery of telecommunication services to remote areas; that is, the continual movement towards improving the availability and quality of communication by telephone and through television for Alaska's citizens.

The second trend concerns the TVP's strong reliance on diminishing state financial support for the growth and maintenance of television service in Alaska. The Television Demonstration Project (TVP) initiated the state's involvement in telecommunication delivery using satellites, earth stations, duplication facilities, and 10-watt transmission facilities. Although operated through relatively modest budgets, the TVP required additional state appropriations to handle maintenance and expenses for the acquisition of equipment and expansion of services to additional communities. New technologies, especially satellite technology, virtually eliminated terrain problems while enticing government to participate in communication services.

The third trend concerns an obvious characteristic of telecommunication transmission and reception: its cost insensitivity to distance.[4] The cost of reaching the most remote community was virtually the same as reaching nearby communities. Communication services for remote communities did not have to grow from major population centers toward lesser populated areas. Telecommunication services could be cost effective and could be provided where needed.

A major corollary of cost insensitivity to distance encountered when upgrading communication capability via telecommunication is that installation can be made according to priority of need, independent of location. Distant locations that have great need and high travel costs can be given service first. This complete flexibility of location can be important in coordinating communication installation with the specific needs of rural development projects.[5]

In 1978, despite Governor Hammond's line-item reduction, the TVP project continued to receive funding and added eleven more community regional centers.[6] The following year, a supplemental appropriations bill provided funding for eighteen additional communities. In addition, appropriations to the Department of Transportation and Public Facilities provided for the continuation of the project as well as the addition of forty-four more communities.

The Alaska television network continued to grow. In 1980, three more appropriations bills were passed.[7] First, the state operating budget appropriated $2,500,000 to the Department of Transportation and Public Facilities for the continuation of TVP. These funds included an Alaska Public Broadcasting Commission (APBC) appropriation for the operation of the tape delay center. Second, the State capital budget included $750,000 for a microwave system to bring four channels of commercial television to communities on the Kenai Peninsula. Third, the budget appropriated $210,000 to the APBC to provide satellite television reception facilities at five additional communities. The Free Conference Committee planned to provide an additional $16,318,840 for television services, including an additional channel for instructional television and expansion of the TVP to include virtually every community in the state.

The expansion of entertainment and instructional television service to each community proved to be an ambitious undertaking, however. Alaska's governor vetoed the appropriations relating to commercial/entertainment television, and in its final form, the budget appropriated $5,030,000, for instructional television (ITV) services only. The 1981 appropriations expanded ITV and TVP services to 141 communities. The 1982 appropriation of $6,800,000 provided for the continued management and operation of the two statewide television services, RATNet and LEARN/Alaska. An additional appropriation of $75,000 expanded TV service to one additional community. The 1983 appropriation of $6,593,000 for management and operation allowed for an additional appropriation of $20,000 to expand service to another community. The 1984 appropriation for management and operation of the two statewide television services was $5,840,000. An additional $70,000 appropriation provided for the expansion of service to two more communities, and a further $35,000 appropriation upgraded transmitter power in still another community. The 1986 appropriation for management and operation was approximately $6,000,000.

Managers directed almost all of their efforts and the financing for Alaskan television toward distribution management, maintenance, and duplication of television produced outside of Alaska. The funding did not cover the cost of Alaska-oriented instructional television program production. The RATNet Council had maintained a provision for allowing the financing of individual projects. This council, however, did not see itself as nurturing unestablished producers and considered, for project funding and cooperation, only those producers who had a proven track record. The experiences of even seasoned producers like those of *Alaska Native Magazine,* for example, exemplified the difficulties encountered by those who attempted to create Alaska-oriented programming.[8]

Much of the diminished support for RATNet and LEARN/Alaska had little to do with the concept of delivering telephone and television service to rural areas of Alaska. Financial resources for statewide television funding diminished when oil prices fell during the 1980s. The decline in oil prices affected the Alaska economy and created a ripple effect, which limited financial support of education and entertainment television in Alaska. However, declining funding spurred cost-effective technical advances that helped programming to continue.

How the RATNet and Learn/Alaska System Worked[9]

By 1976 the stage had been set for LPTV in Alaska (although LPTV as it is known today did not exist). Citizens expressed great excitement about getting television signals into Alaska. With a satellite in place, Alascom's "Aurora" transponder 24 (now AT&T) was up-linked from Anchorage and down-linked from the satellite to 4.5–meter C-Band small aperture earth stations in rural communities throughout the state. The local distribution system consisted of low-power transmitters or translators located at or near the rural area earth stations. A tape-delayed transmission system worked effectively in Anchorage, and it facilitated entertainment program delivery to Alaska citizens. The Alaska network secured programming by working out an arrangement with the commercial television networks. The agreement required a tape delay for network programming.

The system's newly organized plan set procedures for basic operation. In the evening, the system broadcasted network programming. During the day, it transmitted educational programs via its "only-one-channel-allowed" transmission system. Although the entertainment and education needs of the people were top priorities, the Public Broadcasting Service (PBS) did not get included until later.[10] Very little direct off-air transmission occurred in the early days. A special licensing agreement worked out through network affiliates in Anchorage[11] allowed for the taped-delayed transmission of network programming, as long as the programming was first broadcast in the primary market (Anchorage). This arrangement worked effectively for Alaska's four time zones. Down-link sites taped the programs when they were transmitted, and at the designated time, played them back for their respective communities.

A community preference for network entertainment and sports material quickly took hold. Educational programming aired during the day, and entertainment programming aired in the evenings. The state had succeeded in delivering television service to the residents of Alaska.

Organization Structures

Three organizations managed the Alaskan television system. The Division of Telecommunications Operations and the Rural Alaska Television Network (RATNet) Council constituted the initial organizational elements of the television network system. Later, the LEARN/Alaska Instructional Television (ITV) organization added an educational component to the system.

The Division of Telecommunications Operations performed all operational and maintenance functions associated with the TVP. These included the operation of the tape delay centers, support and coordination for the RATNet Council, placement of orders for program services with broadcasters and carriers, creation and distribution of program schedules, installation of equipment not provided by carriers, and shop and field maintenance of state-owned equipment. The Division of Telecommunications Operations also coordinated the work of the maintenance section and the tape delay center personnel. Maintenance section personnel installed and maintained state-owned equipment associated with the TVP, working primarily with the mini-transmitters (10-watt transmitters) and television receive-only (TVRO) earth stations. Operations division personnel also maintained six regional service centers. In addition to their TVP project duties, operations personnel provided services for telephone and all other telecommunication services in the state. The six tape delay center employees managed the centers, performed technical operations, and coordinated liaison activities with the RATNet Council, broadcasters, and Alascom (the original satellite provider). Their regular duties also included scheduling as well as taping and delivery.

The Rural Alaska Television Network (RATNet) Council comprised twelve regional representatives.[12] Each of the ten regional non-profit Native Corporations appointed one member, and two at-large members appointed by the governor completed the group. This council met four to six times each year to establish programming selection, schedules, and policy for the rural distribution network. The committee also met between regular meetings when special programming decisions were required. RATNet Council members were not paid for their involvement in TVP. The regional representatives for RATNet collected viewer information regarding community member interests in programming. The RATNet Council representatives voted as the voice of community viewer interests regarding desired programming. The Council representatives frequently heard praise as well as complaints regarding the program schedule. Community viewers expressed the greatest interest in commercial programming.

One overriding policy dominated management of the TVP: that the state avoid any direct involvement in deciding what programs would or would not be carried on the satellite system. The RATNet Council representatives were responsible for negotiating the television program schedule that would be broadcast to their respective communities. The central task of most meetings was to finalize the entire RATNet program schedule for blocks of time.

In 1980, the state provided funding for the project. The TVP added LEARN/Alaska, an instructional television (ITV) system. Each earth station added a second transmitter using the same satellite and delivery system as for TVP. LEARN/Alaska managed its own operations center in Anchorage and a receive-only earth station in Eagle River. The operations center distributed instructional programming to the state. LEARN/Alaska, managed by the University of Alaska Instructional Telecommunications Services, became a University of Alaska and Department of Education joint effort. The university accepted responsibility for ITV program selection relevant to university-level and continuing-education courses, while the Department of Education selected programming for pre-school and kindergarten through twelfth grade. The university handled selection and distribution, while the state handled the technical operation of the network. Program producers and suppliers leased or sold most of the education programs to this system. Since programs produced by Alaskans for Alaska constituted a very small segment of television programming, the schedule remained void of a distinctive Alaskan flavor. The Department of Education did, however, provide some funding for the production of Alaska-related programs.

Henry Chasia notes that technology transfer requires the completion of three processes: the ability to use, to maintain, and to invent/make technology.[13] After initiating the first and second processes (use and maintenance), the Alaska TVP provided the framework for the newly established telecommunication network to be the benefactor of its own technological and managerial innovations in subsequent years. Chasia also notes that users of technology are constantly struggling to reinvent the technology. Economic and technological changes would necessitate the reinvention of the Alaska television network.

LEARN/Alaska and the TVP ran together for about five years. In 1986, new legislation officially combined the two projects. RATNet and LEARN/Alaska struggled onward despite budget constraints that threatened reduction of television service to Alaska's citizens. Further budgetary restrictions in the large distribution network also became a real threat to the television network system that provided service to a sparsely distributed statewide audience.

Current Status of LPTV in Alaska

RATNet died in 1996's fiscal year, when funding for the network failed to meet the expense of leasing the transponder. Due to a drop in oil revenue during the mid-1980s, the State of Alaska eliminated funding for LEARN/Alaska. LEARN/Alaska's development process had left much to be desired with relation to its constituency, and the community's greater desire for entertainment programming left educational television poorly supported when the economic crunch came. When LEARN/Alaska disappeared, the public demonstrated, at best, a muted response.

The continued need for communication, education, and entertainment in Alaska did not go entirely without a government or commercial response. In the space of a few years, Alaska's public broadcasting completely restructured its operations. The Alaska Rural Communications Service (ARCS) reinvented the concept of RATNet. KYUK, PBS Channel 4, Bethel, took responsibility for the services formerly provided by RATNet. A regional system of cooperation, improved program networking, and reductions in overhead led to significant cost reductions. Public broadcasters created a satellite distribution system that improved service to Alaskan citizens and accommodated the sharp funding reductions of recent years.

Technological advancement through the move to digital technology solved many of the problems concerning funding and needed improvements in service. The Satellite Interconnection Project won an award of nearly $1 million in federal grants. Project managers in the Division of Information Services also received $700,000 in matching state funds. Digital conversion of the state's satellite, completed in November of 1996, made the original amount of transponder "space" available for additional channels. Once occupied by only one video channel (RATNet), the satellite now had the capacity for several additional video and radio channels.

Digital technology also helped meet increasing consumer demand for more diverse communication services in Alaska. William Hoynes wrote, "A ... continuing intrusion of the market is the single most important constraint on public television."[14] At the same time, the technological advances of digital technology brought cost-benefits to ARCS, distance education, public television, and public radio in Alaska. Digital technology replaced analog technology almost overnight. Chasia notes: "Users of technology are frequently participants in the technology too."[15] Local users of LPTV signals pitched in to install and maintain digital technology in the analog sites. The reinvented Alaska distribution telecommunication system still utilizes the backbone of the LPTV distribution concept first developed for the state, however.

New Organization Structure

The RATNet project had remained very centralized. While the RATNet Council made programming decisions, the state operated the facilities so that citizens could have television service. Although that service was better than nothing, it did little to enhance the self-image of Alaskans.

Despite the intent of the Ogfice of Telecommunications to ensure relevance and authenticity and supplement educational programming via *Alaska Native Magazine,* RATNet Council representatives worked within a system that made attempts for real community participation frustrating and inefficient. The council's ability to promote Alaskan television programming and represent "native" interests received criticism because the council members appeared to be leaders who moved comfortably in the white person's world.[16] Council members, saddled with creating program schedules for transmission and tape delay schedules, became frustrated while trying to create original television programming that would be supported by the divergent rural and city populations of Alaska. Despite their efforts, little room remained for decisions regarding original program planning and production.

Developers or those utilizing an LPTV network should consider the evolution of RATNet Council and LEARN/Alaska as important case studies. In any network, the technological aspects of delivery precede content issues. Once the delivery system is stable and system participation becomes decentralized, participation at the community level becomes enhanced.[17] The Alaska LPTV experience in particular and the American LPTV experience in general demonstrate how government and citizens can work together to provide a telecommunication vehicle, program and operate the telecommunication entity, and at the same time continually reinvent it. Beverly James and Patrick Daley[18] note from Rogers[19] the relationship between technological development, programming, and the need to reinvent technology (innovation) as delivery systems become established. The hope is that reinvention of technology delivery and its utilization will lead to more community involvement in telecommunication activities, including program development.

Moving Toward a New Paradigm

The transition from RATNet to the new communication paradigm began in 1995.[20] After the legislature cut funding below its operating budget, RATNet eliminated its six full-time staff and closed the network's center of operations in Anchorage. RATNet viewers faced the prospect of the channel disappearing. Funding at that time also failed to cover the satellite transponder lease. The legislature had already eliminated funding for maintenance and repair of earth stations and distribution centers. For years before the dissolution of RATNet, public broadcasters in Alaska had been dealing with significant reductions for their operations, especially after the insertion of public broadcast programming into the RATNet schedule; at best, the public broadcasting portion of that schedule was thin. Having already cut production staff and reduced their national and international programming, many public television stations faced the prospect of "going dark."

Opportunities followed with the economic and restructuring dilemma of providing television service to Alaska. These opportunities evolved into actions that directly affected the future of Alaska television service:

- The public television station in Bethel volunteered to originate the rural channel
- KUAC, Fairbanks, volunteered to originate a statewide public television service
- KTOO, Juneau, readied operations for daily coverage of the government.
- Public radio began start-up of regional networks and statewide programming streams

- The Division of Information Services negotiated with AT&T Alascom for a dependable, low rate for transponder leasing
- Alaska, Lieutenant Governor Fran Ulmer secured matching funds for a federal grant
- Dialogue began with other potential channels in need of finding cost-effective methods due to reduced funding

New Way of Working

The Alaska Rural Communications Service (ARCS) replaced RATNet in a new, rural location and took on the commitment to provide a mix of meaningful, substantive, and entertaining programming to 248 rural communities. ARCS, with the cooperation and support of the Anchorage television broadcasters, continued the practice of utilizing programming from the Anchorage stations. The television signals were relayed from Prime Cable to the up-link in Anchorage, which then sent the signal to the 248 ARCS communities across the state. Most daytime programming came from Bethel Broadcasting, which delivered educational, cultural, and children's programs that were handed off from public television. Overnight programming, courtesy of KAKM, Anchorage, and the University of Alaska–Anchorage, provided course work for the completion of an Associate of Arts degree.

ARCS has also produced specials on life in the rural communities, the problems they face, and possible ways to resolve them. For example, one program linked Barrow and Bethel for a discussion of alcohol problems and community-based prevention and treatment.

Although such a system was impossible within the RATNet model, ARCS has contributed to the sales function of the network. Viewers help to pay for the services they receive. Seeing the importance of their support for the television service system, Alaska's rural viewers have made significant financial contributions during on-air fund raisers.

Alaska One, the statewide public television channel, originates a complete schedule of educational, cultural, children's, and news and information programming from KUAC in Fairbanks. Resulting from cooperation among the state's four public television stations, Alaska One has led to better programming and improvement in the overall efficiency of station operation.

Three years of strategic planning and realignment contributed to the cooperation among the four stations. The cooperative arrangement, known as the Alaska Public Broadcasting Service, became functional in 1994. This service worked towards developing a common program stream, acting as an advocate for improved rate schedules from the national program providers, and planning Alaskan productions for the statewide network. Alaska One started distribution through the Satellite Interconnection Project in the fall of 1995.

By January 1996, three television channels, ARCS, Alaska One, and Alaska Two, utilized the satellite and paid jointly for the transponder lease. In subsequent months, the Satellite Interconnection Project supervised scores of volunteers in hundreds of ARCS communities, who installed the digital satellite receivers that would carry the channel to the local transmitters. Volunteers installed the ARCS equipment at no cost to the state in more than 220 communities. Chasia's concept of technology transfer again became operational.[21] The state government and the public again benefited from the ability to use, maintain, and (re)invent or make technology work.

In November of 1996, the conversion to a completely digital broadcast distribution system became complete. The analog LPTV system originally established by RATNet now functioned with new digital technology. By the fall of 1997, a fourth video channel featuring K-to-12 and university classes was originating from the University of Alaska–Southeast and the Distance Delivery Consortium in Bethel. These additions contributed greater cost effectiveness to the distribution system, especially in the area of distance education. In addition, audio channels, available alongside the video signals, carried consolidated public radio programming to the Alaskan countryside, so that citizens were able to choose from a variety of available video and audio channels to meet their entertainment, informational, and instructional needs.

Alaska One reached one-third of the state's population. Combining Alaska One's programming effort with that of KAKM in Anchorage made public television programming available to 80 percent of the population.

Alaska Two provided uninterrupted coverage of the legislature and other government activity through its "Gavel to Gavel" programming. The channel originated from KTOO in Juneau, with live and tape-delayed coverage of floor sessions of the House and Senate, committee and subcommittee hearings, speeches, and public forums. Alaska Two began broadcasting in 1996 when two cable television system managers worked out an agreement with cable television companies across Alaska to carry the channel in more than twenty locales, and it brought state government closer to Alaskan citizens. Alaska Two operated through the Satellite Interconnection Project, which had expanded the bandwidth capacity of the satellite. KTOO provided the channel as a public service, supported entirely by local and private funds; Alaska Two used no state dollars.

Alaska Three now has brought adult education, training, and college and

K to 12 courses to scores of villages and rural campuses. The involvement of education organizations with the Satellite Interconnection Project expanded the times available for course delivery, improved the variety of courses offered, reduced educational delivery expense, and protected courses from pre-emption due to scheduling conflicts.

Praised as a critical step toward meeting the distance learning needs of the Alaskan population, Alaska Three currently provides much-needed educational opportunities for rural Alaskans. The University of Alaska and the Distance Delivery Consortium share a commitment to meeting educational needs through a cost-effective Alaskan network of educational telecommunications. At first, Alaska Three delivered live and tape-delayed video programming to twenty-seven rural receive sites. Now, Alaska Three programming is distributed to fifty-three K-to-12 sites in the state. Interactivity will continue to develop, with concurrent two-way audio, complementary audio conferencing sessions, e-mail, list serves, World Wide Web resources, and multimedia instructional techniques.

The new telecommunication structure in Alaska, the Satellite Interconnection Project, expanded the initial LPTV network structure to include digital services that provide a variety of channels, audio and video, to the residents of Alaska. Since the original purpose of the distribution system was to provide emergency communication, the Satellite Interconnection Project also supports technology required for the selective or statewide distribution of an emergency alert signal. Currently, the original concept has expanded to the point that additional channel capacity has become available to Alaskan residents at a reasonable cost. This telecommunication technology can provide programming for Alaskan residents from the lower forty-eight states as well as original programming for and about Alaskans.

Lewin suggests that funding from diverse sources for public service programming will "occur only if the technologies are adequately managed. In that sense, the quality of the people drawn to and sustained in public broadcasting is as crucial a consideration as any. They must have a vision of public service telecommunications that is strong enough to guide them through the thicket of rapid technological and marketplace change, to help them make appropriate program service (marketing) choices, and to convey to policy makers and the public at large that this is an enterprise that is not only worth keeping, but one very important to the future of American public discourse and social, political and cultural development."[22] The private sector and the government of Alaska have responded to the challenges described by Lewin and the opportunity to mediate technology transfer as described by Chasia.

In the spring of 1996, the Association of America's Public Television

Stations (a private, non-profit membership organization representing the nation's 203 local public television licensees) presented the managers of three of Alaska's public television stations with a 21st Century Award, praising them before members of Congress, the FCC, other federal agencies, and the broadcasting, cable, and telecommunications industry. The three station managers from KUAC, Fairbanks, KYUK, Bethel, and KTOO, Juneau were recognized for their outstanding contributions to the public television system. The managers were lauded for their experimentation with new technologies and management techniques, creation of new services for underserved audiences, cooperation and collaboration with other public telecommunications institutions and private organizations, and their active role in contributing toward long-range planning for public television. The station managers were cited for their creative responses to a one-third cut in funding from the state legislature, consolidating their operations while increasing public television services to Alaskans. To preserve television delivery to the citizens of Alaska they laid off staff, negotiated new program deals, created a joint program guide, and offered new program services including Alaska One, Alaska Two, and Alaska Rural Communications Service.[23]

Local Programming on ARCS

The present telecommunication project in Alaska is decentralized. Numerous rural locations are scheduled for up-link completion and participation with Anchorage, Bethel, Fairbanks, and Juneau, together with public-radio up-links. The system's inherent capacity for rural origination and management ensures that programming of educational course material and news and information will continue to reflect Alaska's diversity. A variety of sources—representing in this case a wide array of voices and a genuine ongoing articulation of vision by Alaska's many cultures—can thrive when technology fosters, rather than limits, access to origination and production.

ARCS carries locally produced programs, such as a daily news program focused on rural issues, and occasional special public affairs programs. Alaska One, the Alaska public television channel from KUAC in Fairbanks, carries *Rain Country*, from KTOO in Juneau, a magazine series about the people and places of Southeast Alaska, and a weekly fishing program out of KUAC in Fairbanks. One program of note was *Make Prayers to the Raven*, a special series on the Athabaskan peoples of interior Alaska. The award-winning documentary was later carried by PBS and the BBC. KAKM in Anchorage produces specials on gold mining, the Alaska Highway, and other historical documentaries, along with many other programs and series. Each ARCS participant also produces public affairs call-in programs on a variety of politics, law, and general interest topics. Regularly scheduled television fare includes weather programming and interview shows.

There is also an abundant supply of locally originated radio programming available for statewide distribution. Most is news and information programming. The Alaska Public Radio Network produces three daily state news programs. Radio programming is distributed alongside the television signals.

Most local television program funding comes from local citizens, businesses, and organization underwriting. There is some foundation support. Money from the National Endowment of the Arts or the National Endowment for Humanities is sparse, and the state continues to reduce financial support for the network.

Sydney Head commented on LPTV station organization: "An LPTV station's role determines its organization. If it competes with other stations in its market, or if it functions as a mother station, providing services for its retransmitting stations, its structure usually follows traditional lines. If it operates simply as a rebroadcaster, however, its entire staff might consist of a single, outside contract engineer who maintains the retransmitter's technical facilities."[24] The new Alaskan system, like the old one, is part of an evolving information infrastructure. The system actively integrates state-supported broadcast services for Alaskans within the state's broad communications development strategy. Not an isolated phenomenon, public broadcasting's restructuring in Alaska is central to the state's social and economic development.

Future of LPTV Programming to Rural Alaska

The Lieutenant Governor's Telecommunications and Information Technology Plan of 1996[25] addressed the necessity for continued funding for the telecommunication and information technology infrastructure within Alaska. The plan recognized the requirement for a substantial capital investment and an ongoing operational and equipment replacement budget. The plan also encouraged community and private sector investment in modern telecommunication technology. It recognized that modern telecommunication technology is critical to the development of Alaska. It is incumbent on the state government to develop a plan that recognizes the necessity for development of a telecommunications infrastructure, which is vital to the well-being of the state, and a plan to fund the basic costs of the infrastructure. The Telecommunication Information Council recommended that the following eight goals be achieved by 1998:[26]

1. The Alaska Rural Communications Service, or ARCS, system should develop a way for communities and individuals to contribute their support for the system.
2. The State should propose a legislative endowment similar to Alaska Science Technology or recurring legislative appropriations for the creation and upkeep of the state's telecommunications infrastructure in Alaska.
3. The state should pursue partnerships with private, community consortiums. The consortiums could contribute matching funds on community based programs.
4. The state should pursue financial options such as revenue bonds for the acquisition of information technology.
5. The state should provide incentives for a provision or building of new services to providers, communities or companies for hardware and software requirements. Incentives should not be ongoing or provided if the service was going to be provided anyway as part of their business plan.
6. The state should consider a telephone surcharge for funding basic 911 systems and education technologies.
7. The TIC should investigate funding options, and its role and responsibilities for meeting information technology needs.
8. The state should develop a funding strategy to deploy new technology which will advance the state's investment in wide scale, cost-beneficial distribution of audio and video services, including public broadcasting signals.

The Lieutenant Governor's Telecommunications and Information Technology Plan identified the importance of continued growth of telecommunication services to Alaska residents. It also continued the reliance on an infrastructure established based on LPTV technology. Although the goal statements emphasized legislative interest in system expenses, continuing emphasis must be placed on the creation of content meaningful to Alaska's residents.

Appendix 8A: FCC Fact Sheet on LPTV

FEDERAL COMMUNICATIONS COMMISSION

March 1995

LOW POWER TELEVISION (LPTV)

The Low Power Television Service (LPTV) was established by the Federal Communications Commission (FCC) in 1982 to provide opportunities for locally-created and community-oriented programming television service in both rural locations and individual communities within larger urban areas.

LPTV service presents a less expensive and flexible means of delivering programming tailored to the interests and self-expression of viewers. LPTV has created opportunities for entry into television broadcasting and it has permitted fuller use of the broadcast spectrum. The FCC imposed few regulatory barriers to obtaining and operating LPTV stations. LPTV station operators are free to buy or create program material, subject only to copyright protection and other statutory requirements.

The principle LPTV regulations are the limits on transmitter output power (10-watts for VHF channels and 1000 watts for UHF channels) and the interference protection standards. LPTV stations MUST NOT cause interference to the reception of existing or future full-service television stations and must accept interference generated by such full-service stations.

There are more than 1,500 licensed and operational LPTV stations, 250 of which are part of a state-wide network in Alaska. In the lower 48 states, approximately 1,300 stations are operate by 700 licensees in nearly 750 towns and cities, ranging in population size from a few hundred to communities of hundreds of thousands. About two-thirds of the stations serve rural communities. An additional 5,500 "TV translator stations" rebroadcast the signals of the full-service stations, mostly in the western mountainous states.

LPTV stations are operated by diverse groups -- high school and colleges, churches and religious groups, local governments, large and small businesses and individual citizens. More than 10 percent of the stations are licensed to minority groups or individuals. LPTV stations also include those that primarily provide a translator rebroadcast function, but also desire the flexibility to originate programming. LPTV modes of operation and programming vary widely. These generally include satellite-delivered programming services, syndicated programs,movies and a wide range of locally-produced programs. Stations sometimes tailor program segments or entire schedules to specific viewer groups: for example, on the basis of age, language or particular interest.

On the technical side, LPTV stations transmit on one of the standard VHF or UHF television channels. The distance at which a station can be viewed depends on a variety of factors -- antenna height, transmitter power, transmitting antenna and the nature of the signal environment (rural or urban, hilly or flat terrain). Some stations have been received at distances of more than 20 miles by viewers with outdoor receiving antennas. Most LPTV stations use one or more satellite receiving antennas ("dishes") and may operators either own or lease studio facilities.

This Fact sheet is designed to answer the most frequently asked questions about LPTV and to provide information about other resources that are available. The Office of Public Affairs, Public Service Division Consumer Assistance Office can provide additional information. This information can be obtained by writing:

The Public Service Division
Federal Communications Commission
1919 M Street, N.W., Room 254,
Washington, D.C. 20554
Phone: 202-418-0200/TT202-418-2555.

Q. WHEN CAN I APPLY FOR AN LPTV STATION?

A. Applicants for new LPTV and TV translator station in construction permits and for major changes to existing facilities may be filed only during designated periods know as "filing windows." Widows are held periodically and are announced by Commission Public Notices at let 30-days beforehand. The announcements give the specific dated of the window (typically 5 days in duration), the exact locations to send or deliver applications and all other necessary information about window filing. Window announcements are published in the Federal Register.

Q. WHAT RESTRICTIONS APPLY TO FILING WINDOWS?

A. The filing of applications during a window is now subject to certain geographic restrictions. The Commission no longer accepts applications for new LPTV or TV translator stations at locations within 161 kilometers (100 miles) of 36 of the largest U.S cities. These cities are identified in the FCC Public Notice of March 3, 1994, which announced the most recent filing window (April 11 - April 15,1994). Applications for major changes to existing facilities are unaffected by the geographic restrictions on applications for new stations. It was necessary for the Commission to impose the geographic limitations in order to preserve broadcast spectrum for future advanced television systems and to minimize the extent to which LPTV and TV translator stations may be displaced, if and when advanced systems become operational. No more than five applications for new stations may be filed during a window by any individual or entity having an interest of one percent or greater in any applicant filing in that window. This limit does not apply to the filing of major changes applications.

Q. IS THERE A FILING FEE?

A. A filing fee of $490 must accompany each application. There is no fee for "minor change" applications, including those for extension of permit and channel for displacement relief.

Q. WHO IS EXEMPT FROM THE FILING FEE?

A. Governmental entities are exempt from the fee. As defined by the Commission's Rules, governmental entities include "any possession, state, city county, town, village, municipal corporation or similar political organization or subpart thereof controlled by publicly elected and/or dolt appointed public officials exercising sovereign direction and control over their respective communities or programs". Also exempted from filing fees are noncommercial education FM and full-service television broadcast station licensees seeking to make major changes in the facilities of their existing low power television translator stations or to construct new low power television or television translator stations, provided those new low power television or television translator stations, provided those stations operate or will be operated on noncommercial educational basis.

Q. WHAT FORM DO I USE?

A. Application must be made on FCC Form 346 February 1988 edition, and you must submit an original and 2 copies. Applicants required to pay and submit a fee with their applications must complete attach to their applications the Fee Processing Form (FCC Form 159). Applications are filed at the place indicated in the Public Notice announcing the filing window. All other types of feeble applications should be sent or delivered to the Pittsburgh, PA location identified in the FCC, FEE Filing Guides. Nonfeeable applications must be sent to the FCC, Office of the Secretary, Washington, D.C. 20554. Copies of Form 346 and other FCC forms may be obtained by calling the FCC's Forms Distribution Center at 1-800-418--FORM and leaving your request on the answering machine provided for this purpose. Forms may also be obtained from the Office of Public Affairs, Public Service Division Consumer Affairs Office, 1919 M Street N.W., Washington, D.C., 20554, Room 254, Phone (202) 418-0200/TT418-2555.

Q. DO I GIVE PUBLIC NOTICE OF THE APPLICATION?

A. Applicant must comply with the public notice requirements of Section 73.3580(g) of the Rules. Local notice must be published once in a newspaper in the community to be served within 30 days before or after filing the application.

Q. WILL MY LPTV APPLICATION BE INVOLVED IN A LOTTERY?

A. Yes, if your application is mutually exclusive with another application. Although many applications for LPTV or TV translator stations are grantable as filed, some other pending proposals would create objectionable interference to other nearby proposals if all were granted. Such applications to competition are considered mutually exclusive because only one can be granted. The winner from among mutually exclusive applicants is selected by a lottery.

Q. ARE ANY PREFERENCES AWARDED IN THE LOTTERY PROCESS?

A. Yes, the law requires that certain preferences be awarded to encourage:

1. MINORITY OWNERSHIP and
2. DIVERSITY IN THE OWNERSHIP OF MASS COMMUNICATIONS
MEDIA.

Preferences are computed by the Commission in the manner described in Section 1.1623 of the FCC Rules.

Q. WHO QUALIFIES FOR THE MINORITY OWNERSHIP PREFERENCE?

A. Here are examples:

1. "Minority" means a person who is a member of one of the following groups: Blacks, Hispanics, American Indians, Alaska Natives, Asians and Pacific Islanders. No other groups are recognized for the purposes of the lottery.

2. If the applicant is a sole proprietor, a preference will be awarded if the applicant is a minority.

3. Other entities will be entitled to a minority preference as follows:

a. Partnerships: If a majority of the partnership (computed on the basis of profits) is in the hands of minority, the applicant is entitled to a preference. Note that limited or "silent' partners are to be included in determining whether a preference may be claimed. Thus, in a five-person limited partnership in which each partner is entitled to 20 per cent of the profits, the partnership is eligible for a minor preference if any three partners (including three limited partners) are minorities.

b. Trusts: If a majority of the beneficial interests are held by minorities, the trust is entitled to a minority preference. The characteristics of the trustee are not considered.

c. Unincorporated associations or nonstock corporations with members: if a majority of the members are minorities, the entity is entitled to a minority preference.

d. Unincorporated associations or nonstock cooperations with members: If a majority of the governing board (including executive boards, boards of regents, commissions and similar governmental bodies where each board member has one vote) are minorities, the entity is entitled to a minority preference.

e. Stock corporations: If a majority of the voting shares are held by minorities, the corporation is entitled to a minority preference.

f. Where one form of entity owns an interest in a different form (e.g., a corporation owns 20 per cent of a partnership, the interest owned, in its entirety, follows the characteristics of the owner. Thus, in the example, if 51 per cent of the corporation's stock is voted in minorities, its entire 20 per cent interest in the partnership would be considered as minority controlled when determining whether the partnership is eligible for a minority preference.

Q. HOW DOES APPLICANT QUALIFY FOR A DIVERSITY PREFERENCE?

A. Here are guidelines:

1. In general terms, a preference will be given to an applicant if it and/or its owners have no recognizable interest (more than 50 per cent), in the aggregate, in any other media of mass communications. A smaller preference will be given to an applicant if it and/or its owners, in the aggregate, have a recognizable interest in no more than three mass media facilities. No preference is given, however, if any one of the commonly-owned mass media outlets serves the same area as the proposed low power television or television translator station, or if the applicant and/or its owners have more than three mass media facilities. The material that follows will set out in more detail the meaning of "own," "owner," "media of mass communications," and "serves the same area."

2. If an applicant and/or its owners, in the aggregate, do not own any other media of mass communications, the applicant is entitled to a preference. "Own" in this context means more than 50 per cent ownership.

3. "Owner" means: the applicant, in the case of a sole proprietor; partner, including limited or "silent" partners, in the case of a partnership; the beneficiaries, in the case of a trust; any member, in the case of a nonstock cooperation or unincorporated association with members: any member of the governing board (including executive boards, boards of regents, commissions, or similar governmental bodies when each member has one vote), in the case of a nonstock corporation or unincorporated association without members, and owners of voting shares, in the case of stock corporations. For the purpose of the diversity preference, holders of less than one per cent of any of the above interests will not be considered.

4. A medium of mass communications means:

   (a) a daily newspaper; or a license or construction permit for:

   (b) a television station, including low power and television translator station;

   (c) an AM or FM radio broadcast station;

   (d) a direct broadcast satellite transponder;

   (e) a cable television system;

   (f) a Multipont Distribution Service station.

5. The diversity preference is not available to applicants that control, or whose owners control, in the aggregate, more than 50 per cent of other media of mass communications in the same area. The facilities will be considered in the "same area" if the following defined areas wholly encompass or are encompassed the protected, predicted contour of the proposed low power television or television translator station (see Section 74.707 (a)).

a. AM broadcast station - predicted or measured 2mV/m groundwave contour (see Sections 73.183 or 73.186);

b. FM broadcast station - predicted 1.0 mV/m contour (see Section 73.313);

c. Television broadcast station - Grade A contour (see Section 73.684): and

d. Low power television or television translator station the predicted, protected contour (See Section 74.707 (a)).

e. Cable television system - the franchised community of a cable system.

f. Daily newspaper - community of publication.

6. No diversity preference is available to an applicant whose proposed transmitter site is located within the franchise area of a cable system controlled (owned more than 50 per cent) by the applicant and/or its owners. No diversity preference is available to an applicant whose proposed transmitter site is located within the community of publication of a daily newspaper controlled (owned more than 50 per cent) by the applicant and/or its owners

7. If a low power television or television translator applicant and/or the owners of the applicant, control no more than three other mass media facilities, none of which serve the same area as the proposed station, the applicant will be entitled to a smaller preference than an applicant with no other media facilities.

Q. I HAVE HEARD THAT LPTV STATIONS HAVE SECONDARY SPECTRUM PRIORITY TO FULL-SERVICE STATIONS. WHAT DOES THIS MEAN?

A. It means that LPTV stations:

(1) May not cause interference to the off-air reception of existing full-service TV stations (LPTV stations must correct any interference caused),

(2) Must accept interference from full-service stations,

(3) Must yield to increase in facilities of existing full-service stations and

(4) Must yield to new full-service stations, where interference occurs.

Q. DO SIMILAR RULES APPLY WHEN CABLE/LPTV INTERFERENCE IS INVOLVED?

A. Between cable systems and LPTV or TV translator stations, a "first in time, first in right"policy applies when there is interference at the cable headend the output channel of a cable system using a converter. In other instances of cable/low power interference, the cable operator is responsible for correcting the interference.

Q. WHAT ABOUT LAND MOBILE/LPTV INTERFERENCE?

A. LPTV stations are being authorized on a secondary basis to land mobile stations sharing UHF channels 14 through 20 with broadcast uses. LPTV stations must correct whatever interference they cause to these land mobile stations or cease operation.

Q. WHAT IS CHANNEL "DISPLACEMENT RELIEF"?

A. In 1987, the Commission adopted a procedure known as "displacement relief," to help LPTV and TV translator stations facing electromagnetic interference conflicts. This procedure allows an affected station licensee or permittee to file an application to modify its license or permit to a different channel in order to avoid interference with full-service TV stations, primary land mobile radio operations, and other protected video services. Displacement relief applications are considered a special type of "minor" change application that can be filed whenever necessary. Applicants for this relief submit Form 346 to the FCC at its Washington, D.C. location. A filing fee is not required. In order to be acceptable for filing "displacement" applications proposals, these proposals must not be predicted to cause interference to authorized facilities or those proposed in already pending LPTV and TV translator applications. Once found acceptable, displacement applications are granted without competition for use of the channel requested. In addition to channel replacement, applicants may move their station sites up to 16 kilometers (10 miles) in an effort to avoid interference conflicts.

Q. ON WHAT CHANNEL COULD I OPERATE AN LPTV STATION?

A. Low power stations may operate on any available VHF (channels 2-13) or UHF (channels 14-69), provided that they do not cause objectionable interference to full-service stations, earlier-authorized TV translators or low power stations or to land mobile stations that share frequencies with broadcast uses. Low power channels are to be allocated on a demand basis. There is no table of allotments and no channel are reserved solely for noncommercial use. Applicants select a channel and provide engineering information as required on the application.

Q. WHAT POWER AND ANTENNA HEIGHT LIMITS ARE AUTHORIZED?

A. Low power TV stations and TV translators are limited to transmitter output power of 10 watts (VHF) and 1,000 watts (UHF). VHF LPTV stations operating on channels in the TV table of assignments may use 100 watts. There are no limits on effective radiated power or antenna height.

Q. HOW MUCH TIME DO I HAVE TO CONSTRUCT MY LPTV STATION ONCE MY CONSTRUCTION PERMIT (CP) IS GRANTED?

A. Construction must be completed and the station must be ready for regular operation and the permittee must apply for a station license (FCC Form 347) within eighteen (18) months of issuance of the authorization, or the CP must be turned back to the FCC. Extensions of time will only be granted in cases where substantial progress has been made in construction, or no progress has been made for reasons clearly beyond the control of the permittee and the permittee has taken all possible steps to resolve the problem.

Q WHAT HAPPENS IF I WANT TO SELL MY LPTV CONSTRUCTION PERMIT?

A. An LPTV construction permit may not be sold for any amount in excess of the actual expenses incurred in obtaining the low Power CP. Further, if the permittee requests to sell the CP after the first nine months, the permittee must show that substantial progress was made in construction or no progress was made for reasons clearly beyond the control of the permittee. In such cases, the buyer must certify that construction will be completed expeditiously.

Q. WHAT HAPPENS IF I WANT TO SELL MY STATION AFTER I RECEIVE MY LICENSE?

A. The Commission has imposed a one-year "trafficking" rule on LPTV stations won through a lottery with a preference claim. This means that an LPTV licensee cannot sell his/her station at a profit until one year from the date the license is issued.

Q. DO I HAVE TO ORIGINATE PROGRAMMING ON MY LPTV STATION? IF SO, TO WHAT EXTENT?

A. While LPTV stations are permitted to originate programming to an unlimited extent, there is no requirement for them to do so. Program origination includes any transmission other than simultaneous rebroadcast from a full-service television station.

Q. MUST AN LPTV STATION HAVE A LICENSED OPERATOR ON DUTY?

A. If an LPTV station originates programming, it would be required to have a licensed operator on duty. That is, an operator must be in continuous attendance during all local origination. The statutory exemption from the operator-in-attendance requirement for translator whose primary function is rebroadcast remains in effect.

Q. MUST AN LPTV STATION MAINTAIN A PUBLIC INSPECTION FILE?

A. No. However, licensees must maintain station records for inspection by FCC personnel. These should include station authorization and office correspondence with the FCC, contracts, rebroadcast permission and required entries concerning improper functioning of tower lighting.

Q. DO THE COMMISSION'S RULES AND POLICIES GOVERNING EEO APPLY TO LPTV STATIONS?

A. The FCC's EEO rules and policies apply to all LPTV stations. Section 73.2080 of the FCC Rules imposes and EEO reporting requirement on all stations with five or more full-time employees.

Q. WHAT ARE THE LPTV RULES RELATING TO PROGRAMMING AND PROGRAM CONTENT?

A. LPTV stations are subject to a minimum of program-related regulations:
(1) There in no community ascertainment requirement.
(2) There are no prescribed amounts of non-entertainment programming or local programming.
(3) There are no limits on commercialization.
(4) There are no minimum hours of operation required.

But the statutory prohibiting on the broadcast of obscene material, lotteries, plugola and payola and the obligation to run licensee-conducted contests fairly, do apply to the LPTV service. Rules mandating access for contests fairly, do apply to the LPTV service. Rules mandating access for political candidates and victims of personal attacks apply in a sliding scale, to the extent that the LPTV station's origination capability permits. The copyright and rebroadcast consent laws apply to a LPTV stations. This means that consent from the copyright holder or full-service TV station must be obtained for program rebroadcast and commercial substitution.

Q. MAY MY LPTV STATION CONDUCT ITS OWN STV OPERATION?

A. LPTV stations may provide STV (pay) programming. There are no minimum hours of free programming required.

Q. MUST A CABLE TV SYSTEM CARRY THE SIGNAL OF MY LPTV STATION?

A. Under certain conditions a cable TV system is required to carry the signal of an LPTV station. Further information to what qualifies an LPTV station to be carried can be obtained in the Report and Order adopted March 11, 1993 and released March 29, 1993, Paragraph 62, under the tile of Low Power Television.

Q. MAY I OWN MORE THAN ON LPTV STATION?

A. The LPTV rules do not impose any limit on the number of low power stations that may be owned by any one entity.

Q. WHAT IF I ALREADY OWN A RADIO STATION, TV STATION, CABLE TV SYSTEM, OR NEWSPAPER?

A. Current broadcast licensees, cable operators and newspapers may own LPTV stations.

Q. ARE THE COMMERCIAL NETWORKS ALLOWED TO OWN LPTV STATIONS?

A. The national commercial networks may own LPTV stations.

Q. DOES THE FCC'S "ONE-TO-A-MARKET" RULE APPLY TO THE LPTV SERVICE?

A. The one-to-a-market rule, which prohibits commonly-owned stations in different services with overlapping contours, does not apply to the LPTV service. This means:

(1) An entity may own both an AM radio station and an LPTV station in the same market;

(2) An entity may own both an FM radio station and an LPTV station in the same market;

(3) An entity may own both a full-service TV station and an LPTV station in the same market.

Q. DOES THE FCC'S "DUOPOLY" RULE APPLY TO THE LPTV SERVICE?

A. The duoply rule, which prohibits commonly-owned station in the same service with overlapping contours, does not apply to the LPTV service. This means that an entity may own more than on LPTV station in the same community.

BACKGROUND MATERIAL ABOUT THE LPTV RULES

(1) LPTV Report and Order -- Federal Register, Volume 47 page 2148, May 18, 1982.

(2) FCC Rules

The Order discusses the rules for the low power television service, which became effective June 17, 1982. (You may find the Federal Register in most public or law libraries.)

FCC Rules

Most of the rules for low power and translator stations are found in Part 74, Subpart G, Volume III of the Commission's Rules. The FCC rules for broadcast stations are found in Part 73, Subpart E, Volume III. The FCC rules for painting and lighting of antenna structures are found in Part 17, Volume 1. The Commission's Rules (Title 47, Code of the Federal Regulations) may be found in law libraries or may be purchased from the Superintendent of Documents, U.S. Government Printing Office, Washington, D.C. 20402; Phone (202) 512-1800. The FCC Rules cannot be obtained from the FCC.

(3) Notice of Proposed Rulemaking (NPRM) adopted September 9, 1980.

The NPRM discusses the proposed rule for the LPTV service. It can be found in the Federal Register, Volume 45, page 69178, October 17, 1980.

(4) Further Notice of Proposed Rulemaking (Further NPRM)

The Further NPRM discusses the technical standards for the LPTV service. It can be found in the Federal Register, Volume 46, page 42478, August 21, 1981.

(5) "Channel Displacement Relief"-- Report and Order. The Order discusses special rules for filing applications to change channel in order to prevent or eliminate an interference conflict with a subsequently authorized primary service. It can be found in the Federal Register, Volume 52, page 7420, March 11, 1987.

(6) "Review of the Commission's Rules Governing the Low Power Television Service." Report and Order. Adapted, May 19, 1994 MM Docket No. 93-114. The Commission expanded the circumstances where terrain shielding can be used to show the absence of objectionable interference and to permit LPTV operators to request to use of standard broadcast call signs.

HOW TO FIND A COMMUNICATIONS ATTORNEY AND ENGINEER

(1) Attorneys and consulting engineers specializing in broadcasting are listed in both the

Television Factbook and Broadcasting/ Cablecasting Yearbook, available in public libraries from:

Television Factbook, Warren Publishing, 2115 Ward Court, N.W., Washington, D.C. 20037; Phone (202) 872-9200.

Broadcasting/ Cablecasting Yearbook, R.R. Bowker. Attn/ Dean Hollister, 121 Chanlon Road, N-2, New Providence, NJ 07974; 1-800-521-8110.

(2) Broadcast trade publications often contain advertisements by consulting engineer and attorneys, or the following associations may be contacted:

o Association of Federal Communications Consulting Engineers, P.O. Box 19333, 20th Street Station, Washington D.C. 20036; Phone (202) 898-0112. A directory of consulting engineers may be purchased from the AFCCE.

o Federal Communications Bar Association (FCBA), 1722 I St., NW, Washington, D.C. 20006. A directory of communications attorneys may be purchased from the FCBA by writing to this address.

---FCC---

Appendix 8B: CBA Petition for Rulemaking to FCC

Before the
FEDERAL COMMUNICATIONS COMMISSION
Washington, DC 20554

In the Matter of

Advanced Television Systems and)
Their Impact upon the Existing)
Television Broadcast Service)

RM -9260

PETITION FOR RULE MAKING

1. The Community Broadcasters Association ("CBA") hereby petitions the Commission to adopt rules promptly to create a new "Class A" television station class, under Part 73 of the Commission's Rules and Regulations. Class A status would be made available to qualified low power television ("LPTV") stations providing substantial local programming service and would avoid the unnecessary displacement of such stations and loss of their local programming by affording them primary spectrum user status as against all but full power television stations authorized as of the date of this petition.

2. Throughout the proceedings in MM Docket No. 87-268 [*Note: Advanced Television Stations and Their Effect on the Existing Television Broadcast Service*], CBA has urged the Commission to establish a primary class of license for certain low power television (LPTV) stations that originate programming and provide unique programming sources to their communities. In the *Sixth Report and Order* in this proceeding, the Commission stated its intention to address

this issue [*Note: Id*., 7 CR 994, 1033-34 (1996)]. CBA respectfully submits that the need to adopt primary licensing rules is immediate, as full power television stations are rapidly making plans to implement digital broadcasting, and the threat of displacement and silencing of LPTV stations is becoming increasingly real and imminent. It is important to define now what the rules will be, as well as to find out how many stations will actually apply and qualify for primary status.

3. To that end, CBA requests the Commission to fulfill its commitment and to initiate a rule making proceeding at an early date to address the LPTV issue. Attached hereto (Appendix A) is a draft of suggested rule amendments to provide for Class A television stations. These amendments provide for Class A television stations to be regulated under Part 73 rather than Part 74 of the Commission's Rules [*Note*: LPTV stations are currently regulated under Part 74. The only sections of Part 73 that apply to LPTV stations are those specified in Sec. 74.780.] and to be subject to all sections of Part 73 except those that

(continued)

Appendix 8B (continued)

clearly cannot apply because of the way in which channels have been assigned to LPTV in the past [Note: Those rule sections are 73.606, 73.607, 73.609, 73.610, 73.614, 73.622, and 73.623 (except subsection (c)), involving the NTSC and digital tables of allotments, mileage separations, and minimum power and height requirements. CBA also proposes different principal city coverage requirements for Class A stations and believes that the multiple ownership restrictions of Section 73.3555 should not apply to Class A stations. The coverage area of Class A stations will be substantially less than full power stations, so cross-ownership and multiple ownership raise far fewer adverse implications for the diversity of ideas.] A substantial filing fee is provided for to discourage applications by those who are not seriously prepared to meet the obligations imposed on the new class of station [Note: The filing fee for conversion by an LPTV station to Class A status would be the same as the filing fee for an application for construction permit for a new full power television station.]

4. CBA urges the Commission to adopt the rules proposed herein at the earliest possible date. The threat of losing local community programming service that is not otherwise available is too near in time, given the short digital conversion and spectrum auction timetables announced in MM Docket No. 87-268. If remedial action is not taken soon, dozens, if not hundreds, of communities will lose unique and irreplaceable local programming services they now receive from LPTV stations whose operators have invested significant amounts of toil and money in providing the kind of local service that is the bedrock of American broadcasting.

Respectfully submitted,

Sherwin Grossman, President
Michael Sullivan, Executive Director
Community Broadcasters Assn.

Peter Tannenwald
Elizabeth A. Sims

Irwin, Campbell & Tannenwald, P.C.
Counsel for the Community
Broadcasters Association

September 30, 1997

Before the
FEDERAL COMMUNICATIONS COMMISSION
Washington, DC 20554

In the Matter of)
)
Advanced Television Systems and)
Their Impact upon the Existing)
Television Broadcast Service)

RM -9260

AMENDMENT TO PETITION FOR RULE MAKING

On September 30, 1997, the Community Broadcasters Association ("CBA") hereby petitions the Commission to adopt rules promptly to create a new "Class A" television station class, under Part 73 of the Commission's Rules and making to assure the long-term future of qualifying low power television stations is becoming critically urgent. CBA urges the Commission to invite comment on its proposals at the earliest possible date.

Appendix 8B *(continued)*

Regulations. Class A status would be made available to qualified low power television ("LPTV") stations providing substantial local programming service and would avoid the unnecessary displacement of such stations and loss of their local programming by affording them primary spectrum user status as against all but full power television stations authorized as of the date of this petition.

CBA's petition included an Appendix with the text of its proposed rules. Since the filing of the petition, CBA has discussed its proposal with interested parties and now wishes to offer the attached substitute Appendix A in place of the Appendix A submitted with the original petition.

The process of construction of digital facilities by full power stations has begun, and one low power station has already been displaced. [*Note*: W35BA, Cincinnati, Ohio, has been displaced from Channel 35 by WLWT-DT, Cincinnati, and is being forced to move to Channel 39.] Thus the need for rule

Respectfully submitted,

Sherwin Grossman, President
Michael Sullivan, Executive Director
Community Broadcasters Assn.
1600 Aspen Lane
St. Cloud, MN 56303
Tel. 320-656-5942
Fax 320-255-5276

March 18, 1998

Peter Tannenwald
Elizabeth A. Sims

Irwin, Campbell & Tannenwald, P.C.
1730 Rhode Island Ave., NW, Suite 200
Washington, DC 20036-3101
Tel. 202-728-0400
Fax 202-728-0354
Counsel for the Community
Broadcasters Association

REVISED APPENDIX A

A new Section 73.627 is added to read as follows:

73.627. Class A Television Stations

(a) Licensees of low power television and television translator stations under subpart G of part 74 of this chapter may apply to convert their licenses to Class A television station licenses under this section. Applications for Class A television licenses must be filed by [*one year after effective date of rules*].

(b) A separate application must be filed for each channel on which Class A operation is proposed. Each application must contain a showing of the following for a continuous period of 3 months immediately preceding submission of the application:

(i) Compliance with the minimum operating schedule required for television broadcast stations under section 73.1740.

(ii) The broadcast of not less than 3 hours in each calendar week of programming produced within the principal city contour (as defined in section 73.683(a) for NTSC service and section 73.625(a)(1) for digital service) of the station, or produced within the principal city contour of any of a group of commonly controlled stations that carry common local or specialized programming not otherwise available to their communities.

(c) An Application for a Class A Television license must be filed on Form 301, including all information and exhibits required by that form, except for Section III (financial qualifications), and must include the following supplemental material.

(i) A statement of the file number and date of issuance of the station's initial license under part 74.

(continued)

Appendix 8B *(continued)*

(ii) A certification that from and after the date of the application, the station is operating and will continue to operate in compliance with all requirements of subparts E and H of part 73, except for sections 73.606(b), 73.607, 73.609, 73.610, 73.614, 73.622, 73.623 (except subsection (c)), and 73.3555, which sections shall not apply to Class A television stations, and compliance with subsection (d) of this section.

(iii) All Class A stations shall request and be assigned call signs pursuant to section 73.3550 of this part.

(iv) A showing that the Class A station will not cause interference within the Grade B contour of any television station that is operating on a channel specified in sections 73.606(b) or 73.622(b) as of the date of filing of the Class A application, or within the protected contour of any low power television or television translator station authorized by construction permit or license prior to the date of filing of the Class A application.

(d) An application for a Class A television may not propose a change in channel or an extension of the station's principal city coverage area as defined in section 73.685(a) of this part. However, separate applications for Class A status and for facilities changes will not be considered inconsistent and may be pursued at the same time. Applications proposing no change in channel or increase in coverage area will not be subject to mutually exclusive applications.

(e) A Class A television station licensee may apply for a construction permit to modify its facilities to operate with any combination of effective radiated power and antenna height that will not cause interference within the Grade B contour of any television station that is operating on a channel specified in sections 73.606(b) or 73.622(b) as of the date of filing of the Class A application, or within the protected contour of any low power television or television translator station authorized by construction permit or license prior to the date of filing of the Class A application, under the interference standards applicable to full power television stations under this part. Class A stations shall be limited to the following maximums:

(i) NTSC effective radiated power:

Channels 2–6:	10 kW
Channels 7–13:	31.6 kW
Channels 14 and above:	500 kW
Digital effective radiated power:	Limits in sections 73.622(e)(4), (5), and (6)

(ii) The effective radiated power in any horizontal or vertical direction may not exceed the maximum values permitted by this section.

(iii) The effective radiated power at any angle above the horizontal shall be as low as the state of the art permits, and in the same vertical plane may not exceed the effective radiated power in either the horizontal direction or below the horizontal, whichever is greater.

(iv) If antenna height above average terrain exceeds 2,300 meters, effective radiated power shall be reduced to produce predicted coverage no greater than the equivalent of the maximum effective radiated power at 2,300 meters height above average terrain.

(f) An ownership report, as required by section 73.3615, and copies of contracts, as required by section 73.3613, shall be filed within 30 days after grant of a Class A license.

Appendix 8B *(continued)*

(g) A Class A television station shall be protected from interference within its principal city grade contour, except from stations (including low power television and television translator stations) with facilities that were authorized on or prior to the date of filing of the Class A application and stations authorized in conformance with section 73.622(f). If a station authorized on or prior to the date of the filing of a Class A application will receive interference from the Class A television station, the Class A television licensee may apply for a change of channel. Such applications may be filed at any time and will be processed on a first-come, first-served basis, not subject to mutually exclusive applications. An application for a change of channel filed by a Class A television station to avoid interference that would be caused to or received from a full power digital television station based on the Class A station's authorized facilities shall be given priority over an application for a change of channel by a low power television or television translator station.

A new Section 73.622(i) is added to read as follows:

(i) Class A television licensees may apply for digital facilities as follows:

(1) A Class A television licensee may apply for an additional channel for digital operation, without regard to section 73.622(b), provided that the proposal would comply with Section 73.623© and (f) with respect to stations authorized prior to the date of the application. Such applications will be processed on a first-come, first-served basis.

(ii) A Class A television licensee may apply at any time to convert from NTSC to digital operation on its existing channel, provided that such conversion complies with interference standards applicable to full power digital stations or would not cause any more interference to any other station authorized under part 73 prior to the date of the conversion application than was caused by NTSC operation.

(iii) Class A television licensees may apply for any digital channel listed in section 73.622(b) at any time if the television licensee eligible for such channel under section 73.622© has not filed an application for construction permit by the deadline specified in section 73.624(e).

A new Section 73.624(g) is added to read as follows:

(g) Any application for digital operation by a Class A television station filed pursuant to section 73.622(l)(1) will require completion of construction and commencement of operation within 18 months. Class A television stations that provide digital service on a separate channel from NTSC service will also be subject to the deadlines specified in sections 73.624(d)(1)(iii) and 73.624(f).

Section 73.625(a)(1) is amended to read as follows:

(a) Transmitter location.
(1) The DTV transmitter shall be chosen so that, on the basis of the effective radiated power and antenna height above average terrain employed, the following minimum F(50,90) field strength in dB above one uV/m will be provided over the entire principal community to be served:

(continued)

Appendix 8B *(continued)*

Channels 2–6	28 dBu
Channels 7–13	36 dBu
Channels 14–69	41 dBu

For Class A television stations, the required minimum values shall be as follows and shall be placed over 75% of the community of license:

Channels 2–6	22 dBu
Channels 7–13	31 dBu
Channels 14–69	36 dBu

Section 73.683(a) is amended to read as follows:

(a) The transmitter location shall be chosen so that, on the basis of the effective radiated power and antenna height above average terrain employed, the following minimum field strength in decibels above one microvolt per meter (dBu) will be provided over the entire principal community to be served:

| Channels 2–6 | Channels 7–13 | Channels 14–69 |
| 74 dBu | 77 dBu | 80 dBu |

The following minimum field strength must be provided over at least 75%, of the community of license of a Class A television station:

| Channels 2–6 | Channels 7–13 | Channels 14–69 |
| 62 dBu | 68 dBu | 74 dBu |

Section 1.1104 is amended to read as follows:

1. Commercial TV Stations:
   a. New and Major Change Construction Permits and
      Applications for Class A Licenses . . . . .

Notes

Chapter 1. A New Medium: The Nature and Purpose of Low Power Television

1. Telephone interview, May 22, 1998.
2. Lydia Kleiner, "Mini-Stations for Mini-Audiences," *American Film,* May 1981, p. 2.
3. "Low Power TV Gains Strength," *New York Times,* May 14, 1990, p. 8.
4. "Outlets for Forgotten Viewers," *Los Angeles Times,* April 19, 1990, p.1.
5. "The New Order Passeth," *Broadcasting,* December 10, 1984, p. 43.
6. "Low-Power TV: The 'Local Newspaper' of Broadcasting," *Business Week,* October 22, 1984, p. 45.
7. "Low Power TV Gains Strength," p. 8.
8. "LPTV West: An Industry Wanting to Happen," *Broadcasting,* April 2, 1984, p. 52.
9. "The New Order Passeth," p. 43.
10. Ibid.
11. "Freeze Gets Warm Reception," *LPTV,* November 1983, p. 6.
12. "The New Order Passeth," p. 43.
13. "LPTV Complaints," *Broadcasting,* March 21, 1983, p. 60.
14. "LPTV West," p. 52.
15. "FCC May Revise Methods of Processing LPTV Applications," *Broadcasting,* December 19, 1983, p. 87.

Chapter 2. The Screen Over the Fence: The Evolution of Neighborhood Television in America

1. "CBA Asks FCC for LPTV Name Change," *Broadcasting,* June 17, 1991, p. 62.
2. Ibid.
3. Ellen S. Mandell, "LPTV Eligibility for Four-Letter Call Signs," com-man.com/pepper/memos/LPTV/LPTV.HTM, April 20, 1998.

4. *Broadcasting and Cable,* March 31, 1997, p. 96.

5. "Outlets for Forgotten Viewers," *Los Angeles Times,* April 19, 1990, p. 1.

6. Ibid.

7. Ibid.

8. Correspondence, May 18, 1998.

9. Correspondence, May 19, 1998.

10. "Schools Get License to Air TV Lessons," *St. Petersburg Times,* December 6, 1988, p. 1.

11. "UPI Owners Launch LPTV Venture," *Broadcasting,* July 16, 1984, p. 34.

12. "New Low-Power Lobby Formed," *Broadcasting,* August 6, 1984, p. 71.

13. Telephone interview, June 16, 1998.

14. Ibid.

15. "Low-Power TV," *Business Week,* October 22, 1984, p. 45.

16. "LPTV Outlets Fight for—and Win—Cable Carriage," *Multichannel News,* March 9, 1992, p. 32.

17. Ibid.

18. Ibid.

19. Amos Brown, III, "Low-Power TV Station's Cable Dilemma," *Indianapolis Star,* July 23, 1995, p. D03.

20. "LPTV Says Cable Overprotected," *Broadcasting,* March 16, 1998, p. 22.

Chapter 3. See LPTV Run: Its Organization and Structure

1. WCEA public information release.

Chapter 4. And Now the News: Programming for the 'Hood

1. John K. Waters, "Low Power TV: Narrowcasting Finds its Niche," www.videomaker.com.edit/leased/lowpower.htm

2. Ibid.

3. "Plotting the Future of LPTV," *Broadcasting,* January 31, 1983, p. 69.

4. "Nader Brings 'Community TV' to Buffalo," *New York Times,* July 30, 1990, p. 2.

5. "Ashland to Get New TV Station," *Courier-Journal,* July 17, 1996, p. 01B.

6. Ibid.

7. "Low-Power TV Makes Its Local Debut," *San Francisco Chronicle,* March 23, 1994, p. E1.

8. "Outlets for Forgotten Viewers," *Los Angeles Times,* April 19, 1990, p. A1.

9. Lynne Gross, *The New Television Technologies.* Dubuque, IA: William C. Brown, 1990, p. 111.

10. Interview with Katie Siska, April 20, 1998.

11. "Network TV's New (Low) Powers That Be," *Broadcasting and Cable,* September 11, 1995, pp. 24–28.

12. Rich Brown, "TCI Plans to Grow America One . . . ," *Broadcasting and Cable,* August 21, 1995, p. 32.

13. WCEA public information sheet.

14. Interview with Raphaela Loguillo, 1996.

15. John K. Waters, "Low Power TV: Narrow Casting Finds Its Niche," http://www.videomaker.com.edit/leased/lowpower.htm

Chapter 5. The Bottoming Line: Subsidizing the Hidden Screen

1. Verne Green, "Low Power TV: A Rough Birth," *Marketing and Media Decisions,* January 1983, p. 68.

2. "TV7: An Investment in the Community," *LPTV,* January/February 1984, p. 24.

3. "A Low-Power Challenge," *Orlando Sentinal,* January 17, 1994, p. 1.

4. "High Hopes for Low-Power TV," *Philadelphia Inquirer,* April 12, 1992, p. D1.

5. "Low-Power TV Here Has Low Level of Local Input," *St. Louis Post-Dispatch,* December 26, 1993, p. 1E.

6. Adam Shell, "Low-Power TV: High Power Placement Opportunities?" *Public Relations Journal,* May 1990, 9.

7. Phil Porter, "Low-Power TV Signs on to New Orleans," *Columbus Dispatch,* March 27, 1992, p. 1E.

8. Thomas J. Murry, "LPTV: A Hot New Investment," *Dun's Business Month,* June 1984, p. 13.

9. "Outlets for Forgotten Viewers," *Los Angeles Times,* April 19, 1990, p. 1A.

10. Edmond Rosenthal, "Low Power Stations Opening New Doors in Advertising Sales," *Television-Radio Age,* December 28, 1987, p. 83.

11. Adam Shell, "Low-Power TV: High Power Placement Opportunities?" *Broadcasting and Cable,* April 12, 1989, p. 9.

12. Steve Coe, "Nielsen to Measure LPTVs," *Broadcasting and Cable,* November 13, 1995, p. 55.

13. Ibid., p. 56.

14. Steve McClellan, "Downey Plans to Resurface LPTV Deal," *Broadcasting and Cable,* March 31, 1997, p. 37.

15. cyberplex.com.cyberplex/usw/owning.html

16. "The Case for STV," *LPTV,* January/February 1984, p. 42.

17. Jacqueline Biel, *Low Power Television Development and Current Status of the LPTV Industry.* Washington, DC: National Association of Broadcasters, 1985, p. 38.

18. Chris McConnel, "LPTV Says Cable Over Protected," *Broadcasting and Cable,* March 16, 1998, p. 22.

19. *Television Digest,* October 13, 1997, p. 13.

20. Ibid.

21. Interview with Katie Siska, April 20, 1998.

22. Interview with Raphaela Loguillo, 1996.

23. WCEA information sheet for advertisers.

Chapter 6. Maintaining the Image: Technical Considerations, Other Micros, and the Future

1. Written statement, August 15, 1998.

2. Ibid.

3. Ibid.

4. Ibid.

5. Ibid.

6. Ibid.

7. Telephone interview, May 22, 1998.

8. Correspondence, May 15, 1998.

9. Correspondence, May 19, 1998.

10. Correspondence, June, 12, 1998.

11. Telephone interview, May 22, 1998.

12. Correspondence, May 19, 1998.

13. Telephone interview, May 22, 1998.

14. "LPTV Manufacturer Chalks Up Another Year of Losses," *Broadcasting and Cable,* January 6, 1986, p. 166.

15. Correspondence, May 18, 1998.

16. Correspondence, May 19, 1998.

17. Correspondence, June 9, 1998.

18. "TV Giveaway Is Take Away," *Arizona Republic,* March 9, 1997, p. H4.

19. "Louisiana Republican Questions FCC," *Broadcasting and Cable,* March 31, 1997, p. 96.

20. "FCC Acts on Class A Petition," *Community Television Business,* May 6, 1998, p. 1.

21. Ibid.

22. Telephone interview, May 22, 1998.

23. Jackie Biel, "Kennard Promises Action on Class A LPTV," *Community Television Business,* April 22, 1998, p. 1.

24. "Rebel Radio," *Village Voice,* May 19, 1998, p. 64.

25. "Low-Power Radio Brings High-Intensity Response," *Broadcasting and Cable,* May 4, 1998, p. 22.

26. Telephone interview, May 19, 1998.

Chapter 8. The Alaska LPTV Network

1. Michael Porcaro, "A Mini-TV: The Case for Cassettes," *Journal of Communication* 27 (1977), pp. 188–90.

2. Sydney W. Head, Christopher H. Sterling, and Lemuel B. Schofield, *Broadcasting in America,* 7th ed. Boston: Houghton Mifflin, 1994.

3. Leonard Lewin, ed. *Telecommunications: An Interdisciplinary Text.* Dedham, MA: Artech House, 1984, pp. 133–71.

4. ———, ed., *Telecommunications in the United States: Trends and Policies.* Dedham, MA: Artech House, 1981).

5. Ibid., pp. 434–35.

6. James R. Shea, "History and Current Management of State-Provided Television Service," prepared by Division of Telecommunications Services, Ted McIntire, Director, State of Alaska Department of Administration, December 1985.

7. Mark Badger, Director of the Division of Information Services, State of Alaska, e-mail, March 1997.

8. Beverly James and Patrick Daley, "Origination of State-Supported Entertainment Television in Rural Alaska," *Journal of Broadcasting and Electronic Media* 11, no. 2 (Spring 1987), p. 174.

9. This section based on an interview with John Morrane, Deputy Director, State of Alaska Division of Telecommunication, May 1996.

10. "Policy Guidelines" regarding the use of the State of Alaska satellite television project adopted by the Rural Alaska Television Network council, December 3, 1981.

11. Augie Hiebert was the person who coordinated the agreement that allowed the tape-delayed transmission of all three network signals and educational material.

12. Department of Administration, State of Alaska, "How Are Programming Decisions Made for RATNet?" date unknown.

13. Henry Chasia, "Choice of Technology for Rural Telecommunications in Devel-

oping Countries," *IEEE Transactions on Communications* 24, no. 7 (July 1976).

14. William Hoynes, *Public Television for Sale: Media, the Market, and the Public Sphere.* Boulder, CO: Westview Press, 1994, p. 19.

15. Henry Chasia, "Choice of Technology for Rural Telecommunications."

16. Beverly James and Patrick Daley, "Origination of State-Supported Entertainment Television in Rural Alaska," pp. 169–80.

17. Henry Chasia, "Choice of Technology for Rural Telecommunications."

18. Beverly James and Patrick Daley, "Origination of State-Supported Entertainment Television in Rural Alaska."

19. E.M. Rogers, *Diffusion of Innovations,* 3rd ed. New York: Free Press, 1983.

20. Douglas Samimi-Moore, Project Coordinator, Satellite Interconnection Project, State of Alaska, e-mail descriptions of Interconnection project, March 1997.

21. Henry Chasia, "Choice of Technology for Rural Telecommunications."

22. Leonard Lewin, ed., *Telecommunications: An Interdisciplinary Text,* p. 218.

23. KTOO news release, Juneau, Alaska, March 29, 1996.

24. Sydney Head, Christopher H. Sterling, and Lemuel B. Schofield, *Broadcasting in America,* p. 189.

25. Fran Ulmer, State of Alaska Telecommunications and Information Technology Plan, passed by Telecommunications Information Council, December 18, 1996.

26. ———, "An Open Letter on the State of Alaska Telecommunications Planning Process," June 17, 1996.

Further Reading

Abramson, Albert. *The History of Television.* Jefferson, NC: McFarland, 1987.

Adler, Richard P., ed. *Understanding Television: Essays on Television as a Social and Cultural Force.* Westport, CT: Praeger, 1981.

Albarran, Alan B. *Management of Electronic Media.* Belmont, CA: Wadsworth, 1997.

Barnouw, Erik. *Tube of Plenty,* 2d ed. New York: Oxford University Press, 1991.

Benson, K.B. *HDTV: Advanced Television for the 1990s.* New York: McGraw-Hill, 1991.

Blum, Richard A. and Richard D. Lindheim. *Network Television Programming.* Boston: Focal Press, 1987.

Buzzard, Karen. *Electronic Media Ratings.* Boston: Focal Press, 1992.

Carroll, Raymond L. and Donald M. Davis. *Electronic Media Programming.* New York: McGraw-Hill, 1993.

Carter, T. Barton, *et al. The First Amendment and the Fifth Estate.* 3rd ed. Westbury, NY: Foundation Press, 1993.

Creech, Kenneth C. *Electronic Media Law and Regulation.* Boston: Focal Press, 1993.

DeSonne, Marcia L. *Advanced Broadcast/Media Technologies.* Washington, DC: NAB, 1992.

Dominick, Joseph R., et al. *Broadcasting/Cable and Beyond.* New York: McGraw-Hill, 1993.

Eastman, Susan Tyler, et. al. *Broadcast/Cable Programming: Strategies and Practices,* 4th ed. Belmont, CA: Wadsworth, 1993.

Erikson, Hal. *Syndicated Television: The First Forty Years.* Jefferson, NC: McFarland, 1989.

Fang, Irving. *A History of Mass Communication.* Boston: Focal Press, 1997.

Hanson, Jarice. *Understanding Video: Applications, Impact, and Theory.* Newbury Park, CA: Sage, 1987.

Head, Sydney W., et al. *Broadcasting In America,* 7th ed. Boston: Houghton Mifflin, 1995.

Hilliard, Robert L. and Michael C. Keith. *The Broadcast Century: A Biography of American Broadcasting,* 2nd ed. Boston: Focal Press, 1997.

Hilliard, Robert L. *The Federal Communications Commission: A Primer.* Boston: Focal Press, 1991.

————. *Television Stations, Operations and Management.* Boston: Focal Press, 1989.

Howard, Herbert H. et al. *Radio, Television, and Cable Programing,* 2nd ed. Ames: Iowa State University Press, 1994.

Inglis, Andrew F. *Behind the Tube: A History of Broadcasting Technology and Business.* Boston: Focal Press, 1990.

Krasnow, Erwin and G. Geoffrey Bentley. *Buying or Building a Broadcast Station,* 2d ed. Washington, DC: NAB, 1988.

Lacy, Stephen, et al. *Media Management.* Hillsdale, NJ: Lawrence Erlbaum, 1993.

Limburg, Val E. *Electronic Media Ethics.* Boston: Focal Press, 1994.

Mirabito, Michael and Barbara Morgenstern. *The New Communications Technologies,* 2nd ed. Boston: Focal Press, 1994.

Orlik, Peter B. *The Electronic Media.* Boston: Allyn and Bacon, 1992.

Parson, Patrick R. and Robert M. Frieden. *The Cable and Satellite Television Industries.* Boston: Allyn and Bacon, 1998.

Pringle, Peter K. et al. *Electronic Media Management,* 3rd ed. Boston: Focal Press, 1995.

Sterling, Christopher. H., ed. *Focal Encyclopedia of Electronic Media* (CD-ROM). Boston: Focal Press, 1998.

Walker, James and Douglas Ferguson. *The Broadcast Television Industry.* Boston: Allyn and Bacon, 1998.

Index

About the Authors

Robert L. Hilliard is professor of media arts at Emerson College. He is the author or coauthor of over a dozen books, including *Surviving the Americans: The Continued Struggle of the Jews After Liberation* (1997) and *Writing for Television and Radio,* the longest-in-print mass communication book by a single author and the most widely used text on that subject; it is in its seventh edition in 1999. Hilliard served in Washington, D.C., as chief of the educational/public broadcasting branch of the Federal Communications Commission and as chair of the Federal Interagency Media Committee, reporting to the White House, among other positions. He has worked in commercial and educational television, radio, and theater as a writer, producer, director, and performer. Hilliard holds a Ph.D. from Columbia University.

Michael C. Keith is senior lecturer in communications at Boston College. He is the author or coauthor of over a dozen acclaimed books on the electronic media. Of special note are *Signals in the Air: Native Broadcasting in America* (1995), *Voices in the Purple Haze: Underground Radio and the Sixties* (1997), and *Talking Radio: An Oral History of American Radio in the Television Age,* to be published by M.E. Sharpe. Keith is also the author of the most widely adopted textbook on radio in America, *The Radio Station,* soon to be in its fifth edition. Prior to joining Boston College, Keith served as chair of education at the Museum of Broadcast Communications in Chicago, taught at George Washington University and Marquette University, and worked as a professional broadcaster for over a dozen years. He holds a Ph.D. from the University of Rhode Island.

Hilliard and Keith have coauthored three other books in addition to *The Hidden Screen.* They are *The Broadcast Century: A Biography of American Broadcasting* (second edition, 1997), *Global Broadcasting Systems* (1996), and *Waves of Rancor: Tuning in the Radical Right,* published by M.E. Sharpe in 1999.

www.ingramcontent.com/pod-product-compliance
Ingram Content Group UK Ltd.
Pitfield, Milton Keynes, MK11 3LW, UK
UKHW020431010325
455677UK00029B/1104